The Americanization
of the Synagogue,
1820–1870

THE BRANDEIS SERIES
IN AMERICAN JEWISH HISTORY,
CULTURE, AND LIFE
Jonathan D. Sarna, Editor

The Americanization of the Synagogue, 1820–1870
LEON A. JICK, 1992

Follow My Footprints:
Changing Images of Women in American Jewish Fiction
SYLVIA BARACK FISHMAN, 1992

The Americanization of the Synagogue, 1820–1870

Leon A. Jick

BRANDEIS UNIVERSITY PRESS
Published by University Press of New England
Hanover and London

BRANDEIS UNIVERSITY PRESS
Published by University Press of New England, Hanover, NH 03755
© 1976 by Trustees of Brandeis University
Foreword © 1992 by Trustees of Brandeis University
First paperback edition 1992
Printed in the United States of America 5 4 3 2 1
CIP data appear at the end of the book

Contents

Foreword

WHEN first published in 1976, Leon Jick's *The Americanization of the Synagogue* diverged markedly from the standard themes of American Jewish historiography. While most scholars of American Jewry, at that time, focused on the East European period in American Jewish life, emphasized the study of immigrants or their children, and wrote social history, Jick focused on the German (Central European) period in American Jewish life, emphasized the study of American Judaism, and wrote religious history. Other scholars tended to interpret religious reforms as cultural importations, if not evidence of assimilation, and pointed to statements of religious ideology to clinch their point. Jick, examining these same reforms from the perspective of immigrant worshippers, found them to be pragmatic responses to new socioeconomic conditions, evidence of Americanization rather than of ideological influences from abroad. Whereas many of his colleagues in the field gave short shrift to synagogues, preferring, if they investigated religious life at all, to talk about religious leaders, Jick made the synagogue his prime subject of inquiry. He understood that it, more than any other Jewish institution, reflected the changing currents of American Jewish religious life as a whole.

In the years since *The Americanization of the Synagogue* first appeared, scholarly fashions have shifted. New volumes on the "German" period of American Jewish history have been published, the history of American Judaism has come into its own, and the American synagogue itself has become a recognized subject for historical research. As a result, some of Jick's questions no longer seem as novel as they did when he first asked them, and in a few cases his answers have gone on to be disputed. What cannot be disputed, however, is the overall significance of this book. It offers not only a synthetic overview of religious developments from 1820 to 1870, but also a first step in what one hopes will someday be a full-scale reinterpretation of how Judaism developed on America's shores.

The Americanization of the Synagogue was the first book in American Jewish history to appear under the imprint of the University Press of New England. It is, therefore, a special pleasure to welcome it back into print in this new, more accessible format, and as part of an exciting new series of volumes to be published by UPNE, entitled "The Brandeis Series in American Jewish History, Culture, and Life."

Jonathan D. Sarna

Acknowledgments

O F the many teachers and colleagues to whom I owe a debt of gratitude, I wish to single out three for special thanks. Professor Ellis Rivkin of the Hebrew Union College, Jewish Institute of Religion, first enabled me to appreciate the integral relationship between the history of the Jewish group and the larger context within which this history unfolded. Professor Robert Cross, formerly professor of American History at Columbia University and now a member of the faculty of the University of Virginia, guided me to an understanding of the history of American immigration and was teacher, mentor, and model for me. His patient critique and continuous encouragement made it possible for me to complete this manuscript despite countless distractions. Professor Joseph Blau of Columbia University was extremely helpful in supervising the preparation of the manuscript. His insights and suggestions saved me from numerous errors of commission and omission. Those which remain are solely my own responsibility.

Finally I affirm my gratitude to my wife, whose forbearance and encouragement were essential to the assumption of the task and to its completion.

Waltham, Massachusetts   *L.A.J.*
June 1975

Introduction

IN the first decades of its independence the United States received relatively few immigrants. European governments imposed restrictions on emigration, and in the turbulent aftermath of the French Revolution few travelers were inclined to risk the substantial hazards of a transatlantic journey. Although the absence of official records makes it impossible to determine exactly how many newcomers arrived in the United States prior to 1820, contemporary scholars judge the total immigration between 1783 and 1815 to have been about 250,000. During the Napoleonic Wars, annual immigration declined to about "3,000 or so" and after the outbreak of the War of 1812, "the stream dried up altogether."[1]

With the return of peace, a tide of immigration began which has been aptly described as "one of the wonders of the age." After 1820 the federal government required masters of ships to submit lists of passengers to the Customs, and available statistics thereafter document the extraordinary influx. Between 1826 and 1828 the number of registered passengers rose from 15,000 to 30,000.[2] In all, 151,000 immigrants reached the United States during the 1820's. The 1830's brought a fourfold increase to 599,000. By the 1840's the number had grown to 1,713,000. Even this figure seemed modest compared to the 2,314,000 who arrived in the 1850's. Between 1815 and 1860 the number of immigrants exceeded the entire population of the United States at the time of the first census in 1790.

One and one-half million of the immigrants during these years originated in the provinces that were to become part of the German Empire. A significant proportion of that group—perhaps as many as 200,000—were Jews, for whom the contrast between the society they entered and the one they left behind was even greater than for Protestant or Catholic Germans. In Europe, German Jews continued to hold a position of statutory inferiority; severe discrimination was a legal as well as a social reality. Moreover, a semi-autonomous, self-governing Jewish communal structure exercised controls over individuals and groups within the community. In the New World both external and internal restraints fell away. The experience of German-Jewish immigrants as they sought to reorient themselves and to reestablish their religious and communal life in the American environment is the subject of this study.

For a variety of reasons the economic advance and acculturation of these immigrants proceeded at an astonishing pace. Precisely because of the rapidity of their advancement, the process through which the adjustment took place was obscured. Most observers came to believe that the achievements of the German Jews resulted from the fact that—unlike later East European Jewish immigrants—they had been substantially secularized and westernized by their exposure to German culture prior to their arrival in America and that in fact they had brought their radically reformed version of Judaism with them. According to this view the emergence of Reform Judaism in America could more accurately be described as a transplantation rather than a transformation.

Source materials dealing with the height of this immigration (1830–1860) indicate, however, that the prevailing view distorts the actual experience of religious adjustment. Most accounts have failed to recognize the relationship between upward mobility and acculturation, and to identify the dynamics through which the German-Jewish immigrants—initially similar to the Eastern Europeans who followed them—developed a pattern of Jewish life in America. In this book I analyze contemporary documents in an attempt to reassess the process through which the new reformist synthesis emerged.

I have attempted to avoid preconceived notions or theoretical models of acculturation or social change. If, in fact, the evidence adduced tends to confirm some of the insights of sociologists who have developed general explanations for the process of acculturation, that testifies to the validity of the models and not my bias.

The material that follows is an examination of the social, economic, and cultural experiences of the immigrants as well as their religious attitudes and practices at the time of their arrival in America. It is concerned with their relationship to the Jewish settlers who preceded them as well as to the total society, and documents their struggle to achieve economic security and social identity. It reviews their attempts to redefine their religious and cultural ideas in the new setting, and to restructure a communal apparatus that would enable them to enter fully into American society while preserving links with the Jewish tradition of which they continued to feel themselves a part.

Confronted by radical economic, social, and intellectual challenges, German-Jewish immigrants in the mid-nineteenth century sought in the New World to maintain a balance between assimilation and distinctiveness, change and continuity. Their experience constitutes a unique chapter in the annals of American-Jewish history and provides significant insights into the ongoing processes of social adaptation.

The Americanization
of the Synagogue,
1820–1870

1 The Earliest American Jewry, 1654–1820

"OF all the Jews who had emigrated to these shores between 1620 and 1829, there were not 200 families left that belonged to congregations, while the great majority had disappeared among the masses." Thus did Isaac Mayer Wise summarize the state of early American Jewry at the time of his arrival here in 1846.[1] Wise was hardly a dispassionate observer; he was hostile to descendants of the early settlers and inclined to minimize their achievements. In this instance the evidence supports his estimate, however, and indicates that by 1820 American Jewry appeared to be in a state of precipitous decline. "Certainly a synagogue, as it exists under the present organization, will not be found in the U.S. fifty years hence," wrote Joseph Lyons of Savannah, Georgia.[2] There were few who disputed that gloomy prognosis.

An identifiable Jewish group had existed in North America since the arrival in New Amsterdam in 1654 of twenty-three refugees from Brazil.[3] The earliest immigrants were Sephardic Jews (of Spanish and Portuguese extraction) associated with the thriving mercantile Jewish community of Amsterdam. In 1664 English conquerors renamed the city New York, and increasingly London replaced Amsterdam as the mother city. During the century that followed, a small but steady trickle of immigration led to the establishment of Jewish congregations along the eastern seaboard in Newport, Philadelphia, Charleston, and Savannah, as well as in New

York. All of these followed the Sephardic rite in their worship.

After the beginning of the eighteenth century an increasing percentage of the immigrants were Ashkenazim (Jews of central European origin). Almost without exception, their arrival in America was preceded by a period of residence in London, where they established connections with overseas trading establishments. In America they frequently served as representatives of European firms. Their prior acculturation and their involvement in trade enabled them to find acceptance in the established Sephardic congregations. Colonial American Jewry remained Sephardic in its religious practice and mercantile in its economy.

There is virtually no reliable information concerning the number of Jews who settled in North America during the Colonial and early national period. Studies based on the names recorded in the census of 1790 estimate that American Jewry at that time numbered 2,000-2,500. Hannah Adams, who compiled a dictionary of American religions in 1817, estimated the Jewish population in the United States at 3,000.[4] Since she corresponded with Jews in a number of cities who had information concerning existing congregations, it is likely that hers is a reasonably accurate guess.

Because of the small size and loose organizational pattern of the community, little information is available concerning the details of institutional existence. During the Colonial and early national era no ordained rabbi served in America. With the exception of one short-lived effort between 1823 and 1825, not a single journal of any kind was established, nor was there any other instrument for the exchange of ideas or information. American Jewry prior to the 1840's was too weak in intellectual resources to have any significant literary achievements to its credit, and it left only the sparsest documentary record. Repeated attempts to establish schools all ended in failure. The handful of seaboard congregations functioned under the leadership of well-meaning laymen whose efforts to preserve the old patterns and ritual practices met with diminishing success.

From the time of their first settlement, Jews in America had enjoyed a degree of religious freedom unknown since the ancient Roman Empire. As early as 1656 American Jews had demanded and were accorded a large measure of equality. Occasional references in legal and business documents and in the accounts of non-Jewish observers suggest a pattern of tolerance and acceptance. In 1682 a Dutch cleric recorded that the Jews "hold their separate meetings in New York." In 1695 an English clergyman, writing his memoirs while held prisoner by the French, stated that among the approximately 855 families in New York were 20 Jewish families. On a map of the city which he drew, he marked a site as "The Jews Synagogue." These comments testify to the existence of a small congregation but offer no information concerning its character.

In 1728 the Jewish citizens of New York undertook the erection of the first building intended for use as a synagogue. In the absence of records, there are no known circumstances which might explain the relationship of this event to the internal developments within the congregation. It is interesting to note, however, that in 1727 the Dutch Church obtained permission to build a new edifice; in the same year the Lutheran Church resumed work on a new house of worship; in 1728 the Baptist congregation constructed its first church. It seems likely that the construction of a synagogue at this time is as much an evidence of acculturation and response to *Zeitgeist* as it is an intensification of particularist religious fervor.

The earliest records left by American Jews reveal that at a very early date many of them were highly integrated into their general environment socially as well as intellectually. Letters written in the 1730's and '40's by Abigail Franks, wife of a leading New York merchant, show that she was sufficiently far removed from traditional Judaism to be characterized as "representative of the Eighteenth Century Enlightenment [with] an abiding and deep interest in literature, perhaps to be expected of one who read the then contemporary novels of Fielding and Smollett and the essays of Dryden, Montesquieu, Addison and her favorite, Pope." In 1739 (more than forty years before Moses Mendelssohn translated the Bible into German to encourage German Jews to learn German; more than sixty years before the earliest talk of "reforming" Judaism in Germany), Abigail wrote to her son as follows: "I must own I can't help condemning the many superstitions we are clog'd with and heartily wish a Calvin or Luther would rise amongst us. I answer for my Self, I would be the first of there followers."[5] It may be argued that Abigail represented an extreme position, which would have been disavowed by many of her contemporaries. The evidence we possess indicates that she may have differed in the degree of her outspokeness but not in the essence of her life style and point of view. Assimilated, outspoken Abigail was more a trend setter than a deviant.

In the American milieu no Calvin or Luther—not even a Moses Mendelssohn—was required. Without so much as the suggestion of a reformation or the consciousness of ideological revision, the natural process of institutional and intellectual adaptation made it possible for Judaism to be recast so completely that it could be regarded by its spokesmen as "the religion of nature—the religion of reason and philosophy." Thus was "the religion of the Jews" described by Mordecai M. Noah at the dedication of the new synagogue edifice for Congregation Shearith Israel in 1818.[6] Between the era of Abigail Franks's letter and Mordecai Noah's address neither the formal structure nor the theology of Judaism in America was openly challenged. In fact, however, both structure and ideology were profoundly altered, and a new relationship emerged between the community and the individual.

In their personal lives Americanized Jews rapidly abandoned the pattern of social separation that had characterized their existence for centuries. While business and family contacts continued to foster a measure of self-segregation, individuals entered into the general communal life to a degree that would have been inconceivable in Europe. They spoke, read, and wrote English and prided themselves on their friendship with Christian neighbors. Moses Michael Hays of postrevolutionary Boston was described by a Christian clergyman as a man whose "family moved in what were then the first circles of society."[7] Conrad Doehla, a German officer who fought in the American Revolution, recorded the following comment in his diary in 1777: "The Jews [in America] cannot . . . be told, like those in our country, by their beards and costume, but are dressed like all other citizens, shave regularly, and also eat pork . . . moreover do not hesitate to intermarry. The Jewish women have their hair dressed and wear French finery like the women of other faiths. They are very much enamored of and attached to Germans."[8] Clearly, Jewish knowledge and practice and, indeed, general involvement in Jewish concerns were becoming more and more marginal. In the traditional community an all-pervasive pattern of Jewish thought, action, outlook, and association had been punctuated by occasional excursions into the general society primarily in pursuit of economic ends. In the newly developing American-Jewish mode, a distinctively American style of thought, action, outlook, and association was punctuated by occasional excursions to the synagogue for the performance of increasingly attenuated ceremonial functions.

Most authors who have dealt with American Jewry in this early period have chosen to emphasize its orthodoxy and its adherence to traditional Judaism. Jacob Marcus, for example, is surprised that "a whole community could receive enfranchisement, could live in a monolithic political world of strong Christian overtones, could participate intimately in it, and yet remain Jewish in a traditional sense."[9] Moshe Davis concludes that although Jews "came in close contact with their Christian neighbors, this open contact did not substantially change the basis of religious life and observance which the Jews had inherited from their fathers."[10]

No revision of historical viewpoints can minimize the achievement of this small and isolated Jewish group in retaining its identity at all. At the same time it is clear that the American Jewry which emerged in the early decades of the nineteenth century was highly acculturated and substantially transformed. Its life patterns, religious institutions, and general outlook were so completely Americanized—so far from the traditional sense or the life style inherited from their fathers—as to be an entirely new phenomenon in the Jewish experience.

The low level of Jewish education on the American continent—before and after the Revolution—was both an effect and a cause of the changed value system. As early as 1761 the lack of familiarity with the Hebrew language moved Isaac Pinto, the chazan (cantor) of Shearith Israel in New York, to translate the prayer book into English. In his introduction he asserted that Hebrew was "imperfectly understood by many, by some not at all" and expressed the hope that an English translation would "tend to the improvement of many of my Brethren in their Devotion."[11] The propriety of publishing such translations was the subject of violent controversy in Central Europe more than half a century later. In America not a word of opposition was sounded.

Contemporary comments indicate a continuing atrophy of Judaic knowledge in general and knowledge of the Hebrew language in particular. In 1783 Haym Solomon wrote to an overseas relative that there was *venig yidishkayt* (very little Jewishness) in America. A letter from Philadelphia to Amsterdam in 1785 reports that "most of the sons of this province [North America] are not devoted to Torah and do not understand our holy tongue (Hebrew)." A survey of documents of the period which contain Hebrew references has led one historian to conclude that with one or two exceptions "men trained in New York [the same held true for the other settlements] were grossly ignorant even of the pronunciation of Hebrew. Corruption of terms in common use in the community were frequent. Often one meets the grossest misspellings in the sources."[12] In the American setting it was precisely these Jewishly "ignorant" laymen who presided over the affairs of synagogues. Increasingly the institutions that evolved reflected American social customs and Protestant patterns of religious expression.

The one individual who provided leadership in Jewish religious life during this period was Gershom Mendes Seixas, born in New York in 1745, who served as "minister" of Shearith Israel in New York from 1768 to 1776, and again from 1784 to 1816. During the British occupation of New York, Seixas, a patriot, moved to Philadelphia, where he served as minister of Mikveh Israel congregation from 1780 to 1784. Seixas can hardly be described as a scholar. Though he mastered the elements of Jewish ritual practice, he was unable to write Hebrew without making numerous grammatical errors.[13]

Seixas' official position was chazan of the congregation. When he assumed his office, his prescribed duties were limited to the conduct of public worship under the strict supervision of the Adjunta (Synagogue Board). It was understood that he would supplement his income by performing circumcisions and tutoring the young in elements of Hebrew. Within the framework of eighteenth century American Jewish life, Seixas, lacking ordination or even formal Jewish education, became a Jewish "minister," the prototype of the American rabbi.[15] As such he took on the functions required of the ecclesiastical leader of an American denomination.

In the traditional Jewish pattern rabbis almost never conducted religious services, and delivered sermons only on rare occasions. The chazan in the Sephardic tradition was even less likely to act as preacher. Nevertheless, Seixas began delivering sermons early in his career, and this aspect of his work became even more important. When he complained of frequent interruptions which made it difficult to prepare sermons, he was voicing a complaint often repeated since his time but probably never previously uttered by a Jewish clergyman. Seixas was the first Jewish example of a type of religious leadership characteristic of Protestantism in the American setting but new to the Jewish tradition.

One of the most revolutionary aspects of Seixas' ministry was his involvement in ecumenical endeavors. He is reported to have been one of the clergymen present at the inauguration of George Washington as President. He served as a Trustee of Columbia University, a Christian denominational institution, from 1784 to 1814. In August 1800 he preached a sermon from the pulpit of St. Paul's Episcopal Church in New York. This was probably the first address by a Jewish clergyman to a Christian congregation since the medieval disputations at Barcelona and Tortosa. Such incidents demonstrate the emergence of a peculiarly American Judaism, which took its place as one among a variety of compatible denominations. As George Washington had indicated, the government of the United States "requires only that they who live under its protection should demean themselves as

good citizens."[16] This requirement was enthusiastically fulfilled by America's Jewish inhabitants, whose eagerness to
participate in an open society led them to reshape their religious ideas and institutions with hardly any awareness of the
transformation they had wrought.

The new American version of Judaism was viable, but it
never succeeded in becoming vital. In postrevolutionary
America all religious institutions were suffering from the
chilling effects of religious indifference. American Jewry,
small in numbers and weak in intellectual resources, entered
a phase of steady attrition. When in April 1804 Congregation Shearith Israel called a meeting of parents to discuss its
newly opened school, not a single parent responded. A letter
from the Board of Trustees of the school lamented that
"few, very few indeed, are concerned about it."[17] In the
years that followed, the school experienced a checkered history, closed at times for lack of students, at other times for
lack of a teacher. Despite the financial support provided by a
private bequest and by the State of New York, the community never succeeded in establishing a school on a firm
basis.

When Gershon Mendes Seixas died in 1816, his place was
assumed by a merchant who continued his own business
activities and served as chazan on a part-time basis. In 1822
only 102 of the 167 men's seats in New York's single congregation, Shearith Israel, were spoken for, and attendance by
seat holders was increasingly infrequent. "Alas," Rebecca
Gratz later complained, "it is thought among our degenerate
sons and daughters of Israel that only its women and priests
acknowledge the force of patriotism and zeal for Judaism."[18]

The publication in New York in 1823–25 of a periodical
called *The Jew* suggests that some elements in the community still possessed sufficient energy to undertake such an
enterprise. The content of the journal during the short span

of its lifetime, however, gives evidence of defensiveness and anxiety rather than confidence. In the two years of its existence the monthly limited itself to an uninterrupted polemic against Christian missionaries and the missionary magazine *Israel's Advocate*. No article or comment dealing with any other concern of the Jewish community or reporting on the activities of individuals or groups was ever published. The appearance and rapid disappearance of this journal reflect the anxiety of a community concerned with threats to its survival but unable to master sufficient resources to initiate a positive program of response.

Only one attempt was made to respond vigorously to the generally acknowledged deterioration of the quality of Jewish life. In Charleston, South Carolina, in 1824, a group led by native-born Isaac Harby, a teacher, playwright, and journalist, attempted to introduce reforms into the ritual of Congregation Beth Elohim. Charleston, which contained the largest Jewish community in America during the first three decades of the nineteenth century, had attracted few recent immigrants. Harby reported that the Jewish population of Charleston had remained stationary for at least twenty years prior to 1826. The Charleston reformers were aware of similar efforts to modify the form of Jewish worship then being made in Germany but—as far as is known—never established contact with like-minded groups overseas. Their initial statement and subsequent activities indicate that neither the initiative nor the model for their activities was derived from abroad.

Their primary goals were stated: to combat the "apathy and neglect which have been manifest toward our holy religion" and "the gradual decay of that system of worship which for ages past peculiarly distinguished us from among all nations of the earth," to restore "a more respectable state of discipline [in order to] elicit that regard from Jew and

Gentile which its great character deserves," and to present to "the rising generation the more rational means of worshipping the true God." Noting that "a number of Israelites . . . are now wandering gradually from the true God and daily losing those strong ties which bind every pious man to the faith of his fathers," the reformers specifically "disclaim any idea of wishing to abolish such ceremonies as are considered landmarks to distinguish the Jew from Gentile; they are wholly influenced by a warm zeal to preserve and perpetuate the principles of Judaism in their utmost purity and vigour."[19]

The specific reforms proposed were modest and related to intelligibility and decorum rather than ideology: portions of the prayers were to be read in English as well as Hebrew; a discourse was to be delivered in English explaining the Biblical portions read on each Sabbath; the length of the service was to be somewhat abridged, so that it might be conducted "with due solemnity and in a slow, distinct, impressive tone"; and the public solicitation of "offerings" was to be replaced by annual subscriptions. These were to be the same changes proposed by subsequent waves of immigrants who sought to harmonize the practice of the old faith with the style of the new world.

The congregation founded by the Charleston reformers flourished for a brief period, during which Isaac Harby declared that its "principles are rapidly pervading the whole mass of Hebrews throughout the United States." Its decline after 1828 and its demise in 1833 cannot be explained as a triumph of traditionalism. Rather it is related to the general decline of Charleston after 1828 and to the increasing apathy of the native Jewish community toward Jewish concerns. Harby himself left for New York in 1828. Charleston and its Jewry went downhill together, sustained and embittered by memories of vanished preeminence.

It seems clear that by the late 1820's the first American

Jewry, generally prosperous and acculturated, had reached a degree of integration into the general society where its survival as a distinct entity seemed to be highly precarious.

Precisely at this time the new immigration began. It provided a new constituency and new concerns to stimulate the old institutions and to establish the basis for new ones. The immigrants, originating in Central Europe, confronted a relatively homogeneous population of Americans and American Jews with the necessity of absorbing newcomers of diverse social, economic, and cultural backgrounds. Out of this confrontation between old settlers and new immigrants the pattern of a culturally and religiously pluralistic America emerged.

2 Blazing a Trail, 1820–1830

IN 1784 Congregation Shearith Israel of New York was formally incorporated under a newly adopted state law governing religious corporations. Its bylaws stipulated that every Jew residing in the city who attended services for one year, contributed financial support in an unspecified amount, was twenty-one years of age, and signed the constitution of the congregation was eligible for membership.[1] Undoubtedly, this formulation merely confirmed the practice that had been followed throughout the preceding century of the congregation's existence. In 1820 a new element was added to these requirements: an applicant had to be approved by a vote of the entire membership. The new provision does not seem to have been invoked until 1825, when the names of sixteen candidates who had applied were submitted to the members for consideration. In a secret ballot only two of the sixteen were accepted. In view of the fact that in 1822 only 102 of the 167 men's seats and only 108 of the 133 women's seats were spoken for, this action clearly constituted a negative response on the part of Americanized Jews to the incursion of what were seen as disturbing immigrants. In the absence of reliable statistics on Jewish population, this action provides the clearest possible evidence of the increase in the number of immigrants and the widening gap between the generally affluent and acculturated old timers and the impoverished and alien newcomers. Indeed, the minutes of the Congregation are explicit in citing the unease aroused by

"the increased number of our brethren and also the proba-
bility of many more coming to reside in this city."[2]

Congregation Mikveh Israel in Philadelphia showed comparable signs of anxiety and ambivalence toward the brethren
who were arriving. As early as 1813 this congregation had
stipulated that an individual must have lived in the country
for six months before applying for membership. An admittance fee of five dollars was instituted. In 1823 the residence
requirement was increased to four years and the admittance
fee was raised to twenty dollars. Apparently the stringency
of these new demands created some controversy, and in 1824
the fee was lowered to ten dollars and the residence requirement to three years.[3] Even these reduced figures reflect a
desire to discourage the increasing number of immigrants
from joining the congregation, at least until they were somewhat Americanized.

The intruders in both New York and Philadelphia were
Central European Jews predominantly from the Rhineland,
Bavaria, and Posen, areas in which economic dislocation,
resulting from the inroads of developing commercial capitalism, had disrupted traditional feudal patterns and deprived
multitudes of Jews and non-Jews of their livelihoods. A series of disastrous harvests intensified the hardships; 1816 was
the climax of many bad years. In addition, Jews suffered
special abuses from the reactionary regimes that came to
power following the Congress of Vienna in 1815. In most
German provinces the rights of emancipation and citizen-
ship granted during the Napoleonic period were revoked.
In 1819 old-fashioned folk riots had broken out in many
German cities. The lot of Jews worsened in all German
states. Even Prussia, which did not rescind the newly acquired rights, reinterpreted them so as to exclude Jews from
civil appointments, the army, and most professions. Prussia

denied all the benefits of emancipation to the 80,000 Jews in the annexed Polish province of Posen.

Large-scale immigration to America had resumed in 1815, when the return of peace to both the New World and the Old restored normal transportation across the Atlantic. At the same time, the renewal of the westward flow of population in the United States created growing opportunities for absorption on this side of the Atlantic. An estimated 30,000 immigrants, of whom almost one-third came from the German provinces, reached these shores in 1817 and again in 1818.[4]

During the next decade the number of arrivals fluctuated considerably in response to changing economic conditions in America and abroad. Compared to the masses who came after 1830, this early migration was small. Nevertheless, its impact was palpable, particularly on a group as minute as American Jewry. In 1818 Mordecai Manuel Noah estimated the Jewish population of America at 3,000.[5] By 1826 Isaac Harby had put the number at 6,000.[6] The presence of immigrants and the prospect of further immigration stirred signs of life in the near moribund American Jewish community.

Grandiose schemes for encouraging immigration proliferated in America during these years. In 1817 and 1818 English, German, and Swiss groups attempted to establish national settlements in what was then the West (Indiana and Illinois), as well as in Brazil. In 1817 Congress sold four townships in Alabama on extended credit to a French organization known as the Society for the Olive and the Vine. Despite the lack of success of these experiments, the colony idea died hard.

A proposal for a Jewish settlement in the "Upper Mississippi and Missouri territory" was published in London in 1819 by W. D. Robinson, a Christian from Philadelphia. At the same time, a more substantive initiative was undertaken by Mordecai M. Noah, an American-born Jew of predominantly Sephardic background. In 1819 Noah attempted without success to gain authorization from the New York legislature for a Jewish settlement on Grand Island in the Niagara River near Buffalo. He subsequently cited the prospect of attracting Jewish immigration, and especially Jewish capital, in soliciting an appointment from John Quincy Adams as "Chargé des Affaires at Vienna, at the Hague, at Denmark, or any other court in Europe," adding that the "Consul General at Algiers . . . is, or will be, vacant and . . . with some privileges would answer the purpose."[7] Adams did not respond to Noah's letter but noted the request in his diary, stating his opinion that Noah was an "incorrect and very ignorant writer and as a partisan editor of a newspaper had considerable power."[8]

In 1822 Noah published the text of a letter from Edward Gans and Leopold Zunz, two leaders of the Berlin society for Wissenschaft des Judentums (science of Judaism), expressing an interest in the possibility of emigrating to the United States. Although there is no record of ongoing communication and none of the members of the society actually came to America, the letter indicates the growing interest in emigration as an option for German Jews.

Three years later Noah persuaded friends to buy land on Grand Island and revived his scheme of establishing a Jewish colony there. The somewhat bizarre episode—including Noah's proclamation of himself as "Judge and Governor of Israel" and the "cornerstone ceremony" conducted in August 1825 in Buffalo—is described in a number of works.[9] In view of Noah's shifting interests and occupations before and after this event, there is little reason to stress his proto-Zionist aspirations. His proposition was similar to many other colonization schemes that abounded in America in the period. Noah himself can best be understood as a Jacksonian entrepreneur and Tammany Hall adventurer, the prototype of the American politician who enhances his political career and, if possible, his financial standing by exploiting his associations with his immigrant "brethren." After a flurry of publicity, he dropped his proposal without ever having set foot on Grand Island.[10] The significance of his scheme lies in its testimony to the consciousness of the Jewish immigration in process and the expectation of an increased flow in the near future. Unlike his comfortable and conservative fellow Sephardim who were alarmed by the threat of disruption, Noah was intrigued by the potential for expansion.

In the meantime, a more important institutional response developed to deal with the real problems of Jews who had already arrived in the promised land. In 1822 a group of acculturated Ashkenazim, immigrants of an earlier time and members of Shearith Israel in New York, formed a Hebrew Benevolent Society. The congregation itself had from time to time sponsored a variety of charitable Hevrot (associations) to perform mutual aid functions in the traditional Jewish mode. The new society, created outside of the congregational framework, was designed to serve the growing number of destitute newcomers who were not affiliated with the congregation and whose needs were not being met by the existing committees.

The organizers of the society attempted to maintain their links with the congregation; they apprised its leaders of the formation of the new society, sending them a copy of their constitution and requesting permission to have offerings to its funds made in the synagogue.[11] At the same time, they were willing to bypass the old establishment and create a new instrument outside the synagogue to cope with unmet needs. Without ideological formulation or revolutionary intent, the foundation for a new communal pattern was laid.

We have previously noted the appearance in New York in 1823 of the first American Jewish periodical, a monthly called *The Jew* and devoted to counteracting the work of missionary societies, especially the so-called Society for Ameliorating the Condition of the Jews. In its two years of publication, *The Jew* did not include a single reference to the events in the Jewish community of its time. It is nonetheless worthy of mention that the editor, Solomon Jackson, was an Ashkenazi immigrant from England who participated in the emerging endeavors on behalf of new immigrants. Although the circumscribed content of his paper reflects the meagerness of Jewish life, the very existence of such a paper is a token of slowly awakening enterprise and growing awareness of need and opportunity. In 1825 Jackson was one of those who seceded from Shearith Israel and founded a second congregation in New York following the Ashkenazi ritual.

The first American synagogue to follow the German rite had been established in Philadelphia possibly as early as 1795. Initially it called itself the German Hebrew Society, and later Rodeph Shalom (Pursuer of Peace).[12] The congregation never gained sufficient strength to establish itself on a sound footing. In 1811 only twenty-one of the twenty-six seats in the congregation were assigned. By 1825 it was near extinction as most of its founders, no longer deterred by residence requirements or financial demands, defected to the Sephardic, Americanized, and socially prestigious Mikveh Israel. "It was only as new, foreign language immigrants, not entirely at home with the by-then Americanized Germans of a generation before, arrived that Rodeph Shalom received the infusion of new blood which enabled it to survive and grow." An interesting insight into the changing character of the congregation and its constituency is to be found in the variety of languages in which its records were kept: the earliest records were in Yiddish; in 1820 English was introduced; in 1830 German replaced English.[13]

The influx that revived Rodeph Shalom in Philadelphia led to the formation of two new Ashkenazi congregations, one in New York and the second in Cincinnati. The establishment of these, the first new congregations in thirty years, marked the end of the period of attrition in American Jewish life. A new era of growth in numbers, in diversity, and in vitality was under way.

In New York in 1825 the same group of members of Shearith Israel who, three years earlier, had formed the Hebrew Benevolent Society announced the formation of a new congregation. A sense of dissatisfaction with the old community and its attitude toward newcomers was growing; a sense of urgency to accommodate the increasing number of immigrants was manifesting itself in a variety of ways.

The stated reason for the schism was the conduct of ritual, but the events preceding the break reveal deeper conflicts. The incident that seems to have precipitated the break was on the surface relatively minor. In April 1825, one Baruch A. Cohen, an immigrant from England, was brought to trial before the Board of Trustees for refusing to offer the required two shillings when called to the reading of the Torah. Cohen contested the right of the Trustees to hold such a trial and protested that others had acted similarly without reproof. In addition, he claimed that he was unaware that the offering was compulsory. On the grounds of "ignorance of the Law" Cohen was excused with the warning that, in the future, he would have to comply with all synagogue regulations. Cohen's rejection of the Trustee's letter with an expression of contempt and the resignation of a Trustee (of Ashkenazi origin) reflect the depth of feeling aroused by this episode and the overtones of social and economic discrimination implicit in the congregational practices.

Apparently the Cohen trial served to focus and consolidate the disaffection of the less affluent, immigrant Ashkenazi members of Shearith Israel. In the following month a group of "about fifteen members" formed an organization and petitioned the trustees for the right to conduct separate services according to the Ashkenazi mode. They called themselves "Hebra Hinuch Nearim," The Committee for the Education of Youth.

Although the ostensible reason for their request was related to the use of the Ashkenazi as opposed to the Sephardic rite, the constitution and bylaws of the proposed hebra go much further in limning dissatisfactions.[14] They require that "no person can be a member of this society unless he strictly adheres to our religion as regards the observance of our holy Sabbaths and Holidays." Moreover, synagogal honors are to be "distributed in such a manner that every member shall have an equal portion," and all meetings of the officers of the society shall "be open to every member to see and hear proceedings." The offering to be made at the reading of the Torah is not fixed but may be as low as six and a quarter cents. The minister or reader is not to "assume or perform any function or service other than that of a private individual."[15]

The proposals of the dissidents constitute a far-reaching critique of the religious and social atmosphere of Shearith Israel. Their stress on the importance of personal piety, on equality in sharing honors and in decisionmaking, and on the elimination of financial requirements as a prerequisite for participation in Torah reading, all indicate dissatisfaction with ritual laxness outside the synagogue and oligarchic privilege inside. The stricture against any special function for the minister is a repudiation of what was viewed as un-

Jewish ecclesiastical professionalism, which grew as the Jewish knowledge and interest of the membership declined.

The Board of Trustees of Shearith Israel lost no time in unanimously rejecting the proposal. Their action was confirmed by a "large and respectable majority" of members at a congregational meeting who saw this decision as "promoting the welfare and dignity of the congregation."[16] The Board now required that the membership vote on the admission of new applicants. As indicated above, at a meeting held in September 1825 only two of sixteen applicants were deemed acceptable. The Ashkenazim were left with no choice but to organize a synagogue of their own.

On October 1 a meeting was held, at which $4,000 was pledged toward the erection of a new synagogue. Five days later a letter was addressed to the trustees of Shearith Israel informing them of the formation of a new congregation and declaring that the action "is urged by motives of necessity." Reasons stated include the desire to worship in the "German and Polish minhag," "the increase of our brethren [which] is so great and in all probability will be much greater in a few years," and the "distant situation of the 'Shul'." The letter ends with a request for aid to "ensure success and give respectability and character to our project," and concludes with good wishes for "peace to Israel and prosperity and life to you gentlemen." No acknowledgment or reply was received from the trustees of Shearith Israel. On October 18 a resolution formally announcing the formation of Congregation Bene Jeshurun was adopted, and on November 15 the charter of incorporation was framed. Fifteen years later a foreign observer writing from New York spoke of "the poor Jews of Elm Street [Bene Jeshurun] and the rich Jews of Crosby Street [Shearith Israel]."[17]

In the light of the increase in numbers and diversity of the Jewish population, the development was not only necessary but inevitable. Although the stated reason for the schism was a preference for the Ashkenazic manner of conducting the ritual, the grievances were in fact far more complex. Acculturated native Americans found the newcomers alien, abrasive, and uncouth, while immigrants found their Americanized fellow Jews lax in religious observance. The old settlers tended to be affluent and comfortable; the newcomers poor and struggling. The natives were assertive in their Americanism; the aliens, though eager to adapt, still yearned for reminders of the old home. The language of the established synagogue was English; the language of newcomers was Yiddish or German or a homespun mixture of both. Established burghers wanted an orderly and undemanding Jewish church that would affirm their respectability without interfering with their life style. Insecure strangers sought an environment of involvement and interaction that was accepting and supportive, a setting in which they were not foreign, not inferior, not merely tolerated. In their own "shul," reminiscent of the intimate village gathering place they had known, they could pray in their accustomed way among sympathetic peers and find acceptance by God and men. Here they could make the rules, assert leadership, speak freely, quarrel without inhibition, and bolster their shaken self-esteem as they strove to move from alienation to adjustment.

In nineteenth-century America few obstacles were placed in the way of establishing such institutions. The society was open and permissive; in the words of the founders of Bene Jeshurun, "the wise and republican laws of this country are based upon universal toleration giving to every citizen and sojourner the right to worship according to the dictate of his own conscience."[18] Moreover, the lack of a well-developed Jewish communal structure and the total absence of religious or intellectual leadership created a vacuum in which no internal restraint could be exercised to inhibit the development of ideas or institutions. Neither wealth nor learning was a prerequisite for the assumption of responsibility; the only credentials required were initiative and drive.

Each succeeding wave of immigration brought a repetition of the pattern. The bewildered newcomers of one decade became the solid and settled gentry of the next. The pace of growth and change led to the establishment of a variety of institutions, each reflecting a stage in the process of adjustment. Soon each nuance of difference in European background or American experience was providing a reason to form a new organization. Once separate institutional entities had emerged, they usually survived, even as rapid acculturation eroded the special circumstances that had called them into being. Bene Jeshurun came into existence in 1825 in protest against the elitist and discriminatory membership policy of its predecessor. By the 1850's "members [of Bene Jeshurun] were selected with discrimination. It was customary to post a list of applicants in the vestibule of the synagogue for a period of thirty days."[19]

Meanwhile, Shearith Israel, ever determined to maintain the distinction between the parvenus and the real elite, had made its membership requirements still more rigid. In 1835 a committee on membership rights declared that "situated as our Congregation at present is and with prospects under the blessing of Providence of future wealth and a respectability and standing of which its members may well feel proud, it becomes its imperious duty to cherish and protect its resources by the introduction of laws rendering the admission of improper persons as members more difficult than it has heretofore been." As a result of an "elaborate report," the congregation added further requirements, including a contribution of "not less than ten dollars," a written request to the electors, and the approval of two-thirds of membership in a "ballot of white or black balls."[20] It is not surprising that the congregation found it necessary to make admission procedure even more stringent in 1893 and again in 1895, when the flood of East European Jews inundated New York.

Some scholars have described the schism between Shearith Israel and Bene Jeshurun as an unfortunate end of "the united Jewish community of New York" which "both sought to save."[21] This view is not supported by the evidence and projects the European experience onto the American scene. No such united community ever existed in this country. What had existed was a small, relatively homogeneous group that for a long time was able to absorb the occasional newcomer who shared its aspirations and outlook and readily assumed its life style. As the old community became more acculturated, more affluent, and predominantly native born, the process of integration became increasingly difficult. Once significant numbers of newcomers with meager preparation and dim prospects had arrived, the development of a pluralistic and diversified community was inevitable. In 1828 a third synagogue was established in New York; by 1839, before the largest wave of immigration had begun or a single rabbi had yet arrived, the number of congregations had risen to six. This early development was but a preview of the proliferation to come.

At the same time that American Jewry was becoming more heterogeneous, it was expanding in geographic distribution. The early Jews had concentrated along the Atlantic seaboard, establishing congregations in Newport, Richmond, and Savannah as well as New York, Philadelphia, and Charleston. A study of the census of 1820 identified Jewish residents in Baltimore, New Orleans, Cincinnati, St. Louis, Vincennes and Fort Wayne, Indiana.[22] As the move westward accelerated, immigrants—Jews among them—settled in the newly opening territories. In 1824 the first congregation west of the Alleghenies was established in Cincinnati. At the time of its formation the Jewish population numbered "about twenty," most of whom were English Jews of Central European descent. In 1829, when the community numbered "thirty-two male and twenty female adults," the congregation applied to the Ohio legislature for formal incorporation as "Kal a Kodish Beneh Israel according to the form and mode of worship of the Polish and German Jews."[23]

The late 1820's and early 1830's brought a new spurt of immigration from abroad. In 1828 thirty-thousand registered passengers entered "the United States, twice the number of two years before." In 1832 over fifty thousand arrived, and "a new movement was underway which was to culminate in the tidal wave of the 1850's."[24] The year 1830 marked an increase in the proportion of immigrants from Germany. Economic distress and unsettled political conditions in Europe, combined with an increasingly favorable view of America, served to provide the stimuli. The presence of fellow countrymen in the new world helped to dispel the fear of strangeness; their example proved to be both incentive and model for those to come. For Central European Jews, a trail had been blazed.

3 The Rising Tide, 1830–1840

IN 1830 and 1831 there were anti-Semitic outbreaks in numerous areas in Germany. Although such episodes are frequently cited as the primary or even the sole explanation for a rise in Jewish emigration to America, a number of circumstances refute this view. In the first place, there is a long history of anti-Semitism in Germany and elsewhere which did not result in emigration. Moreover, during the 1830's and '40's some Jews migrated and others did not; while Jews in Southern Germany were on the move, those in North Germany did not leave in significant numbers, because, as Reissner points out, "expected economic improvement caused the Jewish lower middle class and the poor in North Germany to put up with the degree of religious discrimination decreed by reactionary sovereigns."[1] Much Jewish movement during this era was directed to cities in Germany where economic opportunity existed; the Jewish population of Berlin grew from 6,456 in 1840 to 36,015 in 1871. Most significantly, non-Jews who were not affected by anti-Semitism also emigrated from the same areas at the same time in ever-increasing numbers.

Both anti-Semitism and emigration are symptoms of increasing stress in society, of shrinking economic opportunity and rising social dislocation which deprives large numbers of the population of the basis for existence. Both are responses to growing frustration and despair. Anti-Semitism is a complex phenomenon. Whatever its causes and consequences, it frequently represents an attempt by some segments of the majority group to place the blame for disintegration on the shoulders of a scapegoat minority and to alleviate economic distress by expropriating one competing element in the society. Emigration represents the determination of all affected groups to recover in a new setting the opportunity that has been undermined in the old. For Central European Jews in the 1830's and '40's anti-Semitism merely added to the pressures created by the disruption of the semifeudal agrarian society in the areas in which they lived. With Marcus Hansen we must conclude that Jewish emigration was caused "not so much by persecution as by the prevailing depression which weighed upon Jew and Gentile alike."[2]

The element of the Jewish population which migrated to the United States was remarkably like the migrant element of the general German population. Both groups have been described as lower middle class who were "squeezed out by interacting social and economic forces." Many of the non-Jews were small farmers who had cultivated their own lands. Others—Jews and non-Jews—were petty village shopkeepers and artisans displaced by the development of transportation, the consolidation of tariff regions, and the introduction of manufactured goods. All were harassed by marriage restrictions which were imposed and made more stringent "with the aim of preventing the establishment of households without adequate economic bases." The "surplus population" in Germany was on the land and in the villages; most of this surplus was absorbed in growing cities, and the rest emigrated to America. "Next to no one [came] from the larger towns and cities."[3]

The emigrants themselves left little in the way of documentation. As Walker says, "The Auswanderer themselves do not tell us much. They were not much concerned with communication, with introspection, or with orderliness of thought and decision." This description applies to both Jews and non-Jews. Despite the paucity of direct testimony, a study of available materials reveals a striking similarity and helps explain the patterns of development which emerged in the American setting.

The Jewish immigrants were universally poor and usually minimally educated in either Jewish or secular learning. Almost all of them came from hamlets and villages in Bavaria, Southeast Germany, or Posen. (The Poseners are always referred to as Polish even though their native province was under Prussian rule.) Their previous occupational experience was either in petty trade or a craft—most commonly tailoring or shoemaking. In 1849–1850 over one quarter of the German-Jewish immigrants were tailors or shoemakers. Most arrived without specific vocational training. With few exceptions they had little or no involvement in political, cultural, or religious ferment prior to their arrival in America. As late as 1849, after the arrival of the so-called "48ers," an attempt to found a German-Jewish weekly failed after three months. Its editor, Isidore Busch, wrote: "A Jewish literary periodical is a complete impossibility here. There are hardly ten people who would have any interest in it."[4]

Arriving in America in the 1830's and '40's, the immigrants went where opportunity beckoned. This was the era of rapid expansion in the mid-continent—the area between the Alleghenies and the Rocky Mountains. Between 1820 and 1860 the population of what was then known as the Northwest increased from 790,000 to 7,600,000; the Southwest grew from 1,345,000 in 1820 to 4,730,000 in 1860.[5] To some degree these increases resulted from internal migration, the resettlement of native Americans from the East in search of richer lands or more promising prospects in business, but a significant part was attributable to the growing stream of immigrants. The number of newcomers to the United States numbered 599,000 in the 1830's, 1,713,000 in the 1840's, and 2,314,000 in the 1850's. More than one and a half million came from the German provinces. Of these, one half settled in Ohio, Illinois, Wisconsin, and Missouri.[6] The phenomenal rise in population and in agricultural production and the growth of towns and cities created a booming market for goods and services in these areas.

Among all immigrant groups, economic pursuits and geographic distribution were largely determined by the application of the occupational skills brought from Europe to the opportunities provided by the burgeoning American economy. German Jews whose prior experience prepared them to become merchants and traders moved into the newly developing areas where their skills were most needed. The economic integration and the dispersal of German Jews in the United States, as Jones notes, was "directly traceable to their having been predominantly petty tradesmen."

From time to time proposals were made to settle Jewish immigrants on the soil. In 1837 a New York group calling itself "Zeire Hazon" (The Young of the Flock) announced that its members "have organized for the purpose of removing West and setting on some part of the Public lands, suitable for agricultural purposes." While the declaration states that "the members of the Association are mostly from Germany and have arrived here within the last three years," both the president, S. H. Jackson, and the secretary, T. W. Donovan, were earlier immigrants. Jackson had been the editor of *The Jew*; both men were among the founders in the 1820's of the Hebrew Benevolent Society, the Hebra Hinuch Nearim, and Congregation Bene Jeshurun. The association appealed for financial assistance, stating that its members had no funds and were forced to spend all of their meager earnings "in obtaining the bare necessities of life." The by-laws of the Association stipulated that its proceedings were to be kept in German-Jewish (Yiddish) as well as in English, thereby providing additional evidence of the absence of general cultural background and secular education among the early German immigrants.[7] The only congregation to show interest in the appeal was the newest and poorest in New York, Anshe Chesed, established in 1828. Bene Jeshurun agreed to participate in a meeting and to discuss the project, but failed to send representatives. Shearith Israel never replied. The "Zeire Hazon" disappeared with no record of further activity.

The following year a group of individuals associated with Anshe Chesed actually purchased land in New York's Ulster County and attempted to found a settlement with the Hebrew name of Sholem (German-Jewish pronunciation of "Shalom," meaning peace). Prior to settlement, the group requested the loan of a "sefer torah" (torah scroll) from Anshe Chesed. Apparently a village was actually established, existed for a short time, then vanished without a trace. From fragmentary evidence, Grinstein concluded that "Sholem lasted from 1839 to 1841, and possibly somewhat longer."[8]

These two abortive attempts are illustrative of the failure of significant numbers of Jewish immigrants to settle on the land. Subsequent proposals in the 1840's proved equally futile. Like the Irish immigrants of that period Jews lacked both the necessary capital and the skills required to succeed in agriculture in America. Only in a few isolated instances did individual immigrants become farmers. The masses took advantage of more realistic opportunities.[9]

With the expansion of population into new areas of settlement, an urgent need developed for a means of distributing manufactured wares. This need was intensified by the growing profitability of agricultural production for market and the consequent decline of home industry. Venturesome and hard-working peddlers who were willing to make the tedious trek into the countryside in order to bring supplies to isolated farmers found a ready market. As Glanz observed: "It is the merit of the peddlers to have emancipated the early settler from his economic isolation and forced self-sufficiency."[10]

The life was difficult and occasionally dangerous, and the status was low, but it required no investment of capital and yielded speedy though scanty reward to the diligent and the thrifty. Jewish immigrants, many of whom had similar occupations in German villages, found in peddling the means of earning a livelihood. Even those who were trained as craftsmen frequently chose this route to economic advancement.[11] In Easton, Pennsylvania, 46 percent of the Jews were engaged in peddling in 1840, 70 percent in 1845, 55 percent in 1850, 59 percent in 1855, 39 percent in 1860, and 12 percent in 1870.[12] The number of peddlers in the United States has been estimated at 10,669 in 1850, and 16,594 in 1860. In these decades most were German-Jewish immigrants. In view of the rapid rise of peddlers to other more exalted occupations, the number of individuals who served an apprenticeship in this pursuit may be even greater than these figures indicate.

The roster of notable business careers that grew out of peddling is impressive. It includes virtually all of the investment bankers who came to be known as "our crowd": the Seligman brothers of Baiersdorf, Bavaria; the Lehmans of Rimpar, Bavaria; Marcus Goldman (of Goldman, Sachs) from Burgbrebac, Bavaria; Solomon Loeb (of Kuhn, Loeb) from the Rhineland City of Worms; Meyer Guggenheim from across the river in German Switzerland.[13] To this list may be added the names of the department store magnates Lazarus Straus, Benjamin Bloomingdale, Adam Gimbel, Samuel Rosenwald, and many others.[14] The vast majority of immigrants were far less successful and achieved neither wealth nor fame. For them, peddling simply provided a way to obtain a foothold in the new land. In the 1840's all of the newcomers, even the tycoons-to-be, were still struggling to establish themselves. Some had already become proprietors of small retail stores; others were traveling with their wares in the back country. The great leap forward did not come until after the Civil War.

The spectacular success of the few and the ultimate adjustment of the multitudes cannot obscure the difficulties encountered by the immigrants in their early days in America. Memoirs written years later by long-since affluent burghers tend to gloss over or romanticize the hardships and the initial struggles. One of the few contemporary accounts is found in the diary of Abraham Kohn, a native of the Bavarian Village of Mönchsroth who arrived in New York in 1842. The city bewildered him: "As I proceeded through the crowded streets . . . I felt somewhat uncomfortable. The frantic hurry of the people, the hundreds of cabs, wagons, and carts —the noise is indescribable. Even one who has seen Germany's largest cities can hardly believe his eyes and ears."[15] Kohn described his dismay at being unable to find a job in New York and being forced "to do as all the others; with a bundle on my back . . . to go out into the country peddling various articles." In moments of despair, he regretted his decision to come to America, and longed for the old home: "This then is the vaunted luck of the immigrants from Bavaria! O misguided fools, led astray by avarice and cupidity! You have left your friends and acquaintances, your relatives and your parents, your home and your land, your language and your customs, your faith and your religion—only to sell your wares in the wild places of America, in isolated farm houses and tiny hamlets."

As Kohn plodded from town to town in Western Massachusetts and Southern New Hampshire, he met numerous fellow countrymen similarly engaged, and he described the difficulties they suffered. "In Gill I met Bendel from Furth carrying ninety pounds on his back and mere skin and bones." Some weeks later he encountered another "landsman." "Alas how the poor devil looked." Family men fared the worst and "bring suffering to their women. . . . On how many nights must a woman sit forlornly with her children at the fireplace, like a widow, wondering where this night finds the head of her family, which homestead in the forest of Ohio will offer him a poor night's shelter."

The impact of this way of life on Jewish religious observance was devastating. Like most of his fellow immigrants, Kohn came to America from a simple but firm traditional background. His fidelity to Jewish religious practices was assaulted from the moment he left home en route to the port of embarkation and faced the necessity of travelling on the Sabbath. "For the first time in my life I have desecrated the Sabbath in such a manner," he wrote. "But circumstances give me no choice. May God forgive me!"

Kohn's wish to remain an observant Jew and his inability to fulfill this aspiration are recurrent themes. After his arrival in America, he spent his first two days in a synagogue in New York observing the Jewish New Year. His diary is interspersed with pious sentiments and Biblical citations. Remorsefully his account details the obstacles encountered by an observant Jew and the inevitable compromises that had to be made: "To follow God sincerely we must observe his holy Scriptures, the sacred law given from Mount Sinai. But leading such a life none of us is able to observe the smallest commandment. Thousands of peddlers wander about America; young strong men they waste their strength by carrying heavy loads in summer's heat; they lose their health in the icy cold of winter. And thus they forget completely their Creator. They no longer put on the phylacteries; they pray

neither on working day nor on the Sabbath. In truth, they
have given up their religion for the pack which is on their
backs. . . . God in Heaven, Father of our ancestors, Thou
who hast protected the little band of Jews unto this day,
Thou knowest my thoughts. Thou alone knowest of my
grief when on the Sabbath's eve, I must retire to my lodging
and on Saturday morning carry my pack on my back, pro-
faning the holy day, God's gift to his people Israel." Despite
the difficulties, he continued to "pray twice each day," stating that "the open field is my temple where I pray. Our
Father in Heaven will hear me there." In a mood of depression on the festival of Shavuos (Pentecost), he vowed that "I
would not spend another sacred holiday in this manner."

Hardship, longing for home, "grief" over religious trans-
gressions—none of these prevented Kohn from rapidly becoming Americanized. He socialized with local people in
whose homes he lodged, appreciated attractive young women
("I met the most beautiful girl I had ever seen. Her name is
Helena Brown and she is from Boston. But despite this girl, I
do not yet like America as well as I might wish.") and visited
church services. Six months after his arrival he noted: "I
could write this journal entirely in English." Two years
later, he moved to Chicago and opened a small store. By
1860 he was a friend of Abraham Lincoln and a respected
citizen whose activity in the Republican party was rewarded
by election to the post of City Clerk of Chicago.

Other accounts confirm the impression that Kohn's was a
typical experience. In 1939 Guido Kisch discovered a voyage
diary of S. E. Rosenbaum, a Bohemian Jewish immigrant. At
the time it was the first such Jewish document dating from
the first half of the nineteenth century to have been published.[16] Rosenbaum, who emigrated in 1847, was somewhat
better educated than the earlier immigrants. He had lived in
Hamburg for a time after leaving his native village, and

wrote German well. Nevertheless his attachment to traditional Judaism and his struggle to retain his Jewish practices
on board ship are poignantly portrayed: "Unshaved, in
weekday clothes, I must greet the 'Schabes.' The Waves
intone the Borchu" (the opening prayer of the Jewish service). On the festival of Shavuot, Rosenbaum omitted his
usual diary entry, explaining "I am not allowed to write
during Pentecost." During the holiday he acted as cantor for
a minyan (prayer quorum) held on board ship by Jewish
passengers.

Rosenbaum notes even the minor Jewish fast day of the
17th of Tammuz—which commemorates the breaching of
the walls of Jerusalem by the Babylonians in 586 B.C.: "Now
everyone in beloved Jenikau [his home town] is hurrying to
mincha [afternoon prayer]. . . . I doubt whether those who
have fasted look as exhausted and starved as we do here on
our ship, despite the fact that no one here has fasted." At first
Rosenbaum avoided eating bacon, writing "Bacon eating is
not my thing" (das Speckessen ist meine Sache nicht) and
subsisting on bread, butter, and cheese. With the passage of
time he began to eat nonkosher meat even though "the passengers say it must be horse meat." After five weary weeks
on board ship he is still consoled by the coming of the Sabbath: "Now will I go forth to greet the beloved Sabbath"
(dem lieben Schabes entgegengehen). When his ship is be-
calmed in a heat spell just outside New York, he reports,
"The Poles are reciting psalms" (De Polen sagen Tehillim)
as pious Jews were wont to do in the face of calamity.

When Rosenbaum arrived in America, he concluded his
voyage diary enthusiastically: "I have seen America, my wish
is fulfilled." Two undated postscripts follow. The first, probably written shortly after his arrival, echoes the familiar
plaints of the struggling newcomer: "How much I have sac-
rificed, how have I renounced everything that was dear to

me . . in order to suffer and go peddling in America. . . .
Here I am buried alive, required to peddle and to ask 'do you
want to buy' [the author mixes English and German—und do
you want to buy fragen] to sweat and carry my basket."
The second undated postscript reveals the changed situation
and mood of a later date: "I landed in New York on July 9,
1847 with my stomach and my pockets frightfully empty.
. . . For many, it goes very badly here in their early time,
but for me, it goes well. Very soon I found employment in
the vicinity of New York and I earn good money as a win-
dow shade painter."[17] Rosenbaum's diary ends abruptly at
this point. Little is known about his later life except that he
eventually settled in Allentown, Pennsylvania, where he
married, raised a family, and lived to a ripe old age.

The pattern of immigrant experience is summarized in
Isaac Mayer Wise's *Reminiscences*, first published serially in
German in 1874 and 1875. Wise recalled an encounter that
took place soon after his arrival in America in 1846: "One
afternoon I met on the street a man with a large old straw hat
drawn far over his face. He was clad in a perspired linen coat
and carried two large tin boxes on his shoulders . . . and
dragged himself along with painful effort. I looked at him
closely and recognized my friend Stein. Upon noticing my
astonishment he said smilingly: 'Most of the German and
Polish Jews in America look like this, and the rest of them
did till a very short time ago.' "[18]

Wise's friend proceeded to "describe graphically the mis-
ery and drudgery of the peddler's life" and the "class structure" of German Jewry at that time:

> Our people in this country, said he, may be divided into
> the following classes: (1) The basket peddler—he is as
> yet altogether dumb and homeless; (2) the trunk carrier,
> who stammers some little English and hopes for better

times; (3) the pack-carrier who carries from one hundred to one hundred and fifty pounds upon his back and indulges the thought that he will become a business man some day. In addition to these, there is the aristocracy which may be divided into three classes: (1) the wagon baron who peddles through the country with a one- or two-horse team; (2) the jewelry count, who carries a stock of watches and jewelry in a small trunk . . .; the store prince who has a shop. . . . At first one is the slave of a basket or a pack; then the lackey of the horse, in order to become finally the servant of the shop.[19]

During the decades of the 1830's and '40's the problems of social adjustment and economic advancement absorbed all of the energies of the immigrants. The task of rising from basket peddler to "store prince" was a fulltime job.

A group thus occupied could not be expected to have the time, the motivation, or the financial resources to create an extensive communal, religious, or cultural life. Their problem was intensified by the almost total lack in their midst of intellectuals or religious leaders. Even professionals such as physicians or lawyers were extremely rare. It has been estimated that the Jewish population of New York in 1838 reached 2,000; of these, only three physicians and three lawyers can be identified.[20] As late as 1858, the Jewish population of Cincinnati, numbering 15,000, included merely three physicians, four lawyers, and ten teachers.[21]

During the first half of the nineteenth century educated individuals simply did not emigrate. As Reissner observed: "The educated spokesmen of the [European Jewish] community persevered in hypersensitive opposition to the thought of emigration to America, even after it had reached the masses."[22] The leaders of the Wissenschaft des Judentums who had expressed an interest in the possibility of emigration turned their activities in other directions. Leopold Zunz, who was one of the signers of the 1822 memorandum to Mordecai M. Noah expressing interest in conditions in America, later returned to the sender a letter addressed to him inquiring about Noah's colonization proposals. Thereafter, only in fleeting moments of despair did the idea of emigration ever cross his mind again. Gabriel Riesser, liberal leader of the struggle for emancipation in Germany also rejected emigration. Heinrich Graetz, the noted historian, had virtually no contact with America.

Traditional rabbinic leadership in Europe generally opposed emigration because of the difficulties in maintaining Jewish observances in the New World. Even the more enlightened strongly opposed propaganda for emigration on religious grounds.[23] As for the reformers, they were concentrated in the larger cities, from which little emigration stemmed. Moreover, they regarded America as a cultural desert unfit for cultivated human beings. Shortly before his death in 1874, Abraham Geiger, intellectual leader of the Jewish reform movement in Germany, wrote: "My contact with America is very loose." His request of America was: "Send us new pupils from America. We could use them and they us."[24] In general, intellectual leadership, religious and secular, was preoccupied with issues of emancipation and assimilation and ignored the question of emigration. "The emigrant [problem] was drowned out by the loud clamor of the speeches delivered in the assemblies of the various states or in the rabbinical synods."[25] Not until the 1840's did a handful of rabbis reach America, and these were men without prior distinction and with credentials that were frequently questionable.

An article in *Die Deborah* in 1860 recalled the earlier bias against the immigration of the educated: "How wonderfully . . . conditions have changed since 1837! In those days, when a Europe-weary Jewish journeyman used to tie up his valise and say: 'I am emigrating to America,' it meant that he was a black sheep that was good for nothing at home. . . . If an educated Jew . . . expressed his determination to go to live in the land of freedom, the father used to bewail the money he had spent in vain on his education, and the 'aristocracy' could not comprehend at all how an educated man could so lower himself that he could prefer the distant America, the land of the uneducated, the land of the blacks and Indians, to beautiful Europe."[26]

As late as 1854, when the circumstances of the American Jewish community had improved and the degree of acculturation of German Jewry had risen considerably, the *Allgemeine Zeitung des Judentums* commented on the continuing reluctance of the educated to emigrate. Noting the "great movement among German Jews," an article in the *Zeitung* asked: "Jewish university trained men, physicians, jurists, philologists, mathematicians, natural scientists, architects, why do you languish in Europe or barter your religion? There is a stupid delusion that there is no place in America for university-trained men. To be sure, this may be true for those who are willing to be nourished with European dry rot for their barren researches . . . but learn to make your knowledge useful . . . and you will have bright careers for yourselves in America." In the judgment of this commentator, the "intellectuals, the scientifically trained . . . are seen not to be as bright as the people who let themselves be guided by their instinct."[27]

It was precisely these simple, untutored "people who let themselves be guided by their instinct" who were faced with the task of constructing Jewish life in America. As we have already observed, they were primarily villagers who came from poor but devout homes. Their educational background in both secular and Jewish learning was minimal, and even the Yiddish vernacular in which they frequently wrote was full of errors in grammar and spelling. Lacking authoritative leadership, definitive patterns, viable precedents, or ideology, they nonetheless undertook to reconstitute the fabric of Jewish life in America. Wherever a handful settled, they attempted to establish the rudiments of a community.

Because of the informal organization of many early synagogues and the paucity of professional officiants, it is difficult to determine the precise date of their establishment. A minyan (quorum of worshipers) might have assembled more or less regularly in private homes on Sabbaths and festivals for some time before the formal step of incorporation was actually taken. The problem is further complicated by the subsequent generations the result is uncertainty about details. absence of any record-keeping agency. Prior to 1843 not even a periodical existed which might have recorded developments in American Jewish life. For the settlers themselves these difficulties served to deepen the sense of isolation; for subsequent generations the result is uncertainty about details.[28]

During the 1830's congregations were formally organized in Baltimore (Nidhay Israel—the Dispersed of Israel, 1830), Louisville, Kentucky (Adath Israel—Congregation of Israel, 1836), St. Louis (established in 1838 as German Hebrew Congregation; name changed in 1841 to United Hebrew), Albany (Beth El—House of God, 1838), Easton, Pennsylvania (Brith Sholom—Covenant of Peace, 1839). In addition, new congregations were established by more recent immigrants in New York and Philadelphia. In 1840 a second synagogue was founded in Cincinnati.

The pace of institutional growth accelerated sharply in the 1840's. During this decade congregations were organized in Augusta (Georgia), Boston, Buffalo, Chicago, Cleveland, Columbia (South Carolina), Danville (Pennsylvania), Mobile, Montgomery, Newark (New Jersey), Norfolk (Virginia), Pittsburgh, Rochester and Syracuse, Wheeling, and Wilkes-Barre. An assembly for prayer was held in San Francisco in 1849, and within a few years three congregations had been established in that city. Before the end of the decade two or more congregations existed in cities where substantial Jewish population clustered, such as Albany, Baltimore, New Orleans, Philadelphia, Richmond, and St. Louis.[29] In 1850 New York boasted (or endured) the existence of fifteen congregations, with more in the process of formation.

Isaac Leeser, in 1843, established a monthly journal called *The Occident and American Jewish Advocate*. Five years later he commented on the remarkable fact that "synagogues |were| springing up as if by magic" despite the fact that "our people are poor and many of them [are] laboring hard for their daily bread." "We need not tell our readers," he wrote, "that the country is fast filling up with Jews; that from the newly gotten Santa Fe to the confines of New Brunswick, and from the Atlantic to the shores of the western sea, the wandering sons of Israel are seeking homes and freedom."[30] Indeed they were, seeking and finding.

4 The Pattern of Congregational Life, 1825–1840

WHEN George Washington was elected the first President of the United States, the six Jewish congregations in existence in 1790 corresponded with each other in an attempt to arrange for a joint letter of congratulation to be addressed to him. Misunderstandings arose, and no agreement was reached. As a result, three letters were dispatched: one from Newport, one from Savannah, and one on behalf of the congregations of New York, Philadelphia, Richmond, and Charleston.[1] American Jewry, though still a small and relatively homogeneous group, was incapable of achieving unity of action even on such a simple and noncontroversial matter. This early incident is illustrative of the endemic disunity that has characterized the American-Jewish experience. At no time has American Jewry been able to create a general structure for coordinating endeavors, much less for anticipating needs, for planning, or making a communal response to common problems.

In part this lack of cohesiveness stems from the characteristics of Judaism and the Jewish tradition. Since the disappearance of the ancient priesthood, Judaism has been a religion without a scripturally ordained hierarchical organization or a universally accepted pattern of authority. Specific Jewish communities succeeded in establishing governing institutions which functioned within given geographic and political entities for considerable periods of time. But hegemony over new and distant areas of settlement was always tenuous and subject to erosion as the power and influence of the central authority waned.[2]

On the European continent no central Jewish authority was ever able to take root firmly. Europe was far too fragmented culturally and politically to sustain such unity even before the onset of the modern era. Modernization with its attendant social, ideological, and political upheavals undermined even the authority structures that had existed on regional and local levels.[3] As a result, the pre-American experience offered no readily adaptable models, and the contemporary nineteenth-century European-Jewish community lacked an agency that could be expected to assume the responsibility for maintaining continuity and providing guidance to newly settled areas. American Jewry, deficient as it was in precedents or in religious and intellectual leadership, was on its own.

The centrifugal forces inherent in the Jewish tradition were intensified by geographical as well as social and political conditions in America. Distances were great and communication was difficult. The permissiveness and openness of the society hampered attempts to impose the binding authority of any tradition. In America of the mid-nineteenth century autonomy and diversity of religious thought and action led to repeated schisms within established denominations and the emergence of a host of new sects.[4] Daniel Rupp's *History of the Religious Denominations*, published in 1844, includes "authentic accounts" of no less than five distinct varieties of Baptists, Presbyterians, and Methodists. Mennonites and Reformed Mennonites are represented together with such new sects as Millenarians, New Jerusalem Church, Restorationists, Second Advent believers, and the Church of the Latter Day Saints.[5]

The 1830's and '40's in America were decades of accelerating religious fragmentation. Cleavages between the frontier country and areas of older settlement, between new immigrants and acculturated natives, between Southern proslavery elements and Northern antislavery advocates, between theological traditionalists and liberals racked every denomination. Even the Roman Catholic Church with its long-established hierarchical structure and its dogmatic theology was shaken by the conflict over "Trusteeism," in which laymen sought to usurp the powers of the episcopate by administering their own affairs and appointing pastors of their own choice. In view of the prevailing climate, what is remarkable about the Jews is that despite their lack of coordination and centralized direction, they maintained continuity and avoided major schisms or massive defections.

Between 1790 and 1840 no significant united effort was undertaken within the American-Jewish community. As we have already noted, an occasional request for general support of a specific project was directed to "our brethren"—as, for example, the announcement of Mordecai Noah's settlement scheme in 1825, or Bnai Jeshurun's request for assistance in acquiring a synagogue building, or the appeal issued by the "Zeire Hazon" in 1837 for support of an agricultural colony. But no serious attempt to mobilize a widespread response was ever made, nor was any such response forthcoming. Instead, groups of immigrants gathered wherever they were living and organized congregations, determining their own procedures and practices and governing their own affairs in matters of ritual and faith as well as in fiscal and organizational matters. Neither guidance nor advice was available.

Despite this complete autonomy, a relatively uniform pattern emerged in the religious institutions that were established. With one exception, discussed below, all of the thirteen congregations established between 1800 and 1840 followed the North European ritual, and all sought to recreate the traditional synagogues of their European villages. Because minor variants in ritual had existed in various European localities, they sometimes distinguished between German and Polish minhag (rite). The difference between the two is one of nuance, not essential substance or style, and frequently, as we shall see, they are used interchangeably. After 1840, when the Jewish population of many cities increased considerably, deviations in conduct of the ritual frequently became the focus for controversies that led to the establishment of separate congregations. Such disputes do not reflect differing degrees of piety or doctrinal distinctions. Rather, they reveal a desire for the meticulous emulation of practices in the old country. The prevailing function of the synagogue in the strange new land was that it should serve as the stronghold of the familiar and unchanging.

The earliest Ashkenazi congregation, Rodeph Shalom of Philadelphia, typifies this pattern. When it was formally incorporated in 1802 as the German Hebrew Society, its records were kept in Yiddish and included the following notation: "This day, the Eve of the Holy Sabbath, the 12th of Iyar in the year 5562, we have, in Mazal Tov, dedicated our new German Shul, and named it Rodeph Shalom. For this may we have a share in the World-to-come, and may we witness the coming of the Messiah, and may redemption come into Zion, Amen!"[6] This spirit of traditional piety characterized the life of the congregation for decades.

The influx of new immigrants which began after 1820 served to reinforce adherence to traditional norms. The competence of the shochet (ritual slaughterer who also served as chazan and operated a clothing store) was closely scrutinized. The attitude toward members who had married out of the faith stiffened (though not to the extent of requiring the expulsion of Aaron Dropsie, who was the synagogue's financial mainstay).[7] Despite such an exception to accommodate an acculturated benefactor, the new immigrants who joined the congregation in increasing numbers expected that it would adhere to the norms and tenets of traditional Judaism.

Bnai Jeshurun of New York, founded in 1825, was dedicated "to worship according to the rites, customs, and usages of the German and Polish Jews."[8] The bylaws of the congregation raised barriers against those who kept their businesses open on the Sabbath, and several applicants for membership were denied admission because of this transgression. The congregation was also much concerned with provision of kosher meat and with the qualifications of the shochet. A mikvah (ritual bath) was built for use by the women of the congregation. Marriages and burials were strictly supervised by the congregational officers. On rare occasions questions of ritual propriety deemed to be too intricate for lay leaders to resolve were referred to London for response.[9] When a split developed in the congregation in 1844, the reasons were apparently related to fiscal and personal matters rather than to doctrine. In the early years of its existence Bnai Jeshurun was a congregation in which fidelity to traditional practices was not challenged.

Bnai Israel in Cincinnati followed the same pattern. The original resolution calling for the establishment of a synagogue stipulated "a congregation for the purpose of glorifying our God and observing the fundamental principles of our faith as developed in the Laws of Moses. Its charter, obtained in 1828, provided that the service be conducted "according to the form and mode of worship of the Polish and German Jews of Cincinnati." The style of this congregation, strengthened by the continuing immigration from Europe, continued to be so firmly traditional that in 1842 a move to establish a Sunday school was rejected in favor of a day school in which Hebrew and German as well as English would be taught. Because of a lack of qualified teachers, attempts to fulfill this resolution were never entirely successful, although the congregation did maintain a day school until 1859. Even as polemical a reformer as David Philipson conceded that until 1855 the congregation remained "strictly orthodox." The "reforms" that were then introduced were minor changes designed to improve decorum rather than drastic revisions in ideology or practice.[10]

The Baltimore Hebrew Congregation, established in 1829, reveals a parallel history. Its constituents were primarily poor immigrants from Bavaria, and their charter provided for the "building of a synagogue wherein they may worship God according to the rites and customs of their Fathers." Further provision was made that the electors of the congregation were not permitted to make any bylaws or regulations that were "contrary to the rights [*sic*], usage and discipline of the said Synagogue." Once again the most urgent concerns in the early years involved the provision of kosher meat and of a mikvah for ritual purification. In 1851 a proposed change in procedure (for conducting the ceremony of Bar Mitzvah and not involving Jewish law at all) provoked the congregation to adopt an amendment to its bylaws prohibiting "alterations in the present mode of worship, and in the rites and ceremonies now used, except with the assent of two-thirds of the male members in attendance at the regular called meeting."[11] Not only did the bulk of the German Jewish immigrants reject Reform, but they resisted reforms.

Adath Israel of Louisville was founded in 1836. Its formal charter, adopted in 1842, called for the expulsion of members who married contrary to Jewish law. Here, too, there was "constant trouble [in the early years] as to the qualifications of the persons holding the position of shochet." As in all other instances, the problem reveals both the desire to maintain traditional standards and the difficulties encountered by small, struggling, new communities in fulfilling this desire. In

the late 1840's the congregation succeeded in obtaining a
teacher and opened a day school in which Hebrew and German were taught, as well as English and other secular subjects. The school remained in operation until 1866. Only
then did the congregation engage in the "supreme battle for
reform in mode of worship and observance."[12]

The first congregation to be established west of the Mississippi River was United Hebrew, founded in St. Louis in
1838. The earliest minutes of the congregation have not been
preserved, but a constitution drafted in 1841 notes a change
in the name of the congregation from "German Hebrew" to
"United Hebrew." The constitution stipulates that "the
prayers shall never be performed otherwise than among the
Polish Jews [the words Minhag Polin appear in Hebrew
script]. This section shall never be altered or amended under
any pretense whatsoever."[13] The time eventually came, in
this as in all other congregations, when strictures designed to
prevent changes proved futile. Nevertheless, the initial limita-
tion demonstrates the intent of the immigrants in their first
years in America. If they were at all aware of the reformist
tendencies then being debated in Germany (and they give no
indication that they were), their attitude was to ignore them.
A series of bylaws adopted by the congregation in 1843
emphasized the point: "We will be guided only by the laws
laid down in the Shulchan Aruch [the traditional code of
Jewish law. The name is written in the text in Hebrew
characters]."[14]

Although the members of this congregation were unwavering in their zeal, they were not particularly distinguished
in their learning. Thus in 1843 when they resolved to hire a
shochet, the word appears in transliteration in the minutes as
"shoukit." The author reveals his German accent (in which
o is pronounced *ow*) and was probably unfamiliar with the
Hebrew spelling of the word. Similarly in 1847, in the deci-

sion to elect a reader, the Hebrew Ba'al K'riya (literally "master of reading") is transliterated as "Balchrier." Minhag appears as "Minach," a distortion common in the colloquial usage of the uneducated to this day. Literate or not, the congregation discharged its shamas [sexton] in 1850 because he had been seen in a "barber shop" on the Sabbath. It was not known whether he had been shaven, but his mere presence in the shop cast doubt on his "character as a responsible Israelite."[15]

The record of Congregation Brith Sholom [Covenant of Peace] in Easton, Pennsylvania, offers evidence that the experience of immigrants in small communities was essentially the same as in larger cities. The earliest settlers arrived "without means and with only the most rudimentary education." Their knowledge of Hebrew was poor, "so poor as not even to enable them to write common Hebrew terms or even their own names correctly. . . . Their German literary baggage was even lighter."[16] When they established their synagogue in 1839, records were kept in an ungrammatical Yiddish that included "every peculiarity of German orthography." Their initial constitution is brief and fails to mention most of the items normally contained in such documents. What is included is a precise statement about the sale and distribution of honors during the service (for example, a bridegroom is entitled to take the Torah scroll from the ark on the Sabbath before his wedding and to roll the Torah scroll on the Sabbath following).[17] When the constitution was revised in 1842, the expanded provisions stated that "no person shall be elected to administer the affairs of this Congregation who shall publicly profane the Sabbath by attending at his place of business on that sacred day."[18] Moreover "any Israelite who shall marry or is already married to any other than a Jewess" was to be excluded from membership.

As in every other congregation, the religious "professional" in Easton was a chazan who also served as shochet. His duties are described in a contract drawn in 1848: "he must fulfill the duties of chazan and shochet; conduct school daily for six hours; supervise the mikvah and provide the necessary kettles of hot water; provide a substitute at his own expense during illness or absence; be at the slaughterhouse winters not earlier than seven o'clock and summers not before five A.M. to inspect the meat."[19] Compensation for performance of these myriad tasks was set at $10 per year in 1842. By 1846 the salary had been raised to $100 per annum. Small wonder that the caliber of men attracted to such work was low and that complaints about their behavior—personal as well as professional—were continuous. In Congregation Brith Sholom in Easton, as well as in other mid-nineteenth-century American Jewish religious institutions, aspirations were narrowly tradition bound, and leadership, such as it was, was provided by laymen. The concept of the religious leader as preacher and pastor awaited the waning of old ritual emphases and the awakening of new sociocultural needs.

The consistency of attitude and practice in German Jewish immigrant society is further illustrated by the experience of Anshe Chesed, the third congregation in New York. It was organized in 1829 by newcomers who found the existing Ashkenazi congregation, Bnai Jeshurun, too Americanized and probably too affluent. The surviving minute books of this congregation, which begin in 1835, reflect the intimate involvement of its members with the institution and with each other. In the early days the board of trustees met frequently, often more than once a week. Special committees seemed to be in almost continuous session dealing with such matters as inspection of the skins on which a Torah scroll was to be written (for fiscal and utilitarian as well as ritual surveillance), supervision of the individual appointed to write the scroll (the work was to be examined weekly as it progressed), purchase of various items needed (coal for heat, oil for light, etc.), sale of used items no longer needed (benches, lamps, etc.), and disbursement of small amounts of money to the needy. The synagogue seems to have served as a rudimentary community center, social club, extended family, welfare agency, and bridge between the world left behind and the world not yet entered.[20]

This congregation—like others of the era—was characterized by poverty as well as piety. When a room was rented above the New York Dispensary for use as a "shul," a request was addressed to Shearith Israel for "anything they may have by them that may be useful to us for the above purpose." In response, Anshe Chesed received "3 benches, 2 green doors, 2 colums, railing for the galleries and some ornaments being all the things they was willing to spare." Poor and preoccupied as they were, members of the congregation asked the Dispensary for permission to erect a "booth" in the yard for the celebration of the festival of Succoth. During the early years there was continuous concern with maintenance of ritual purity regarding the slaughter of meat, the provision of wine and unleavened bread for Passover, and the erection of a mikvah.[21]

Anshe Chesed also had problems with its chazan. The minutes record a complaint concerning his "being round in parter [parterre or porter, a house of prostitution?] houses at all times of the day and night playing at cards, billiards, dominoes, etc. and very often with persons unfit for him to be associated with." He was warned by the trustees to "alter his course of conduct." Despite their obvious dissatisfaction with his behavior, the congregation was not ready to avail itself of the services of a newly arrived rabbi who sought to become a "lecturer or teacher." For the performance of traditional and ritual functions a chazan sufficed.[22]

Not until 1844 was the congregation on a sound enough

footing to "inquire into the expense of having the synagogue floor and white walls painted."[23] Such a move indicates a modest increase in esthetic expectations as well as in fiscal resources. At the same time a proposal was made for the enactment of "rules for the purpose of elevating our divine services and avoiding the present confusion in our Synagogue during service." Apparently the attainment of a degree of affluence which made possible the painting of the walls and floor also stimulated the desire for orderliness.

The specific changes suggested were minimal. They prescribed no reform in the content or conduct of the ritual but merely provided that a fine of fifty cents be imposed on "everyone who reads prayers aloud or chaunts with the choir without being authorized to do so," and that "the mitzvot [honors] be sold in lashon hakodesh [the Holy Tongue, i.e., Hebrew] that is, that the word dinar be employed in place of pence, shillings and dollars and that the Hebrew alphabet or the Hebrew names of figures be used to express the number."[24] Precisely how this latter procedure would "elevate" the service was not made clear. We may assume that the use of Hebrew in selling honors (actually a return to a more traditional practice) seemed somewhat less offensive to a constituency that was beginning to be embarrassed by the presence of marketplace techniques in the synagogue. Hebrew terminology apparently added a degree of elegance (or at least of mystification) to a crass procedure. In this, as in previous instances, the modesty of the proposed change and its lack of ideological connotations serves to emphasize the essential conservatism of the immigrants.

Of all of the new congregations established prior to 1840, only Shaarei Chesed (Gates of Mercy) in New Orleans, founded in 1828, deviated slightly from the pattern described above. This exception resulted from the presence in New Orleans of a number of acculturated individuals who had been associated with the old Sephardic establishment. While the impetus for organizing the congregation was provided by the arrival of new immigrants from Germany, affluent resident Sephardim assumed leadership in the beginning. As a result, Shaarei Chesed became the only new congregation in which the liturgy was to follow "the custom of the Portuguese Israelites." It was also the only new congregation to deviate from traditional Jewish norms. In violation of Jewish law, Shaarei Chesed made provision for the burial of non-Jewish spouses of its members—women as well as men—in the congregational cemetery. Indeed, the first president of the congregation, a Sephardic Jew, was himself married to a Catholic. He was reported to have given a sermon in the congregation denouncing fasting on the Day of Atonement as "damned nonsense."[25]

The minutes of the congregation during the 1830's have not been preserved. By the time new bylaws were adopted in 1841, however, they stipulated that services should be conducted "in conformity with the rules and customs of German Israelites."[26] In addition, anyone who had intermarried was banned from membership. The influx of German immigrants, which had brought about a change in the mode of the ritual, had also led to the elimination of laxity in the rules of the congregation. Once the German element became predominant, this congregation conformed to the traditional standards of midnineteenth century American Jewish life.

The experience of New Orleans confirms the conclusion that the only reformist tendencies among American Jewry prior to the 1840's were to be found among the Americanized Sephardic community. We have already noted the attempt by native American Jews to establish a new reformed congregation in Charleston in 1825. Sixteen years later Beth Elohim, the original Sephardic congregation in that city, became the first in America to introduce an organ into its sanctuary.[27] By 1841 the reformist sentiment had become so dominant that the congregation declined to participate in a proposed union of American congregations on the ground that such an organization "must be hostile to the march of improvement or the progress of enlightened and rational reform."[28] During the intervening years, Charleston was the only center of Jewish settlement that was not significantly affected by the influx of German immigrants. As late as 1850 Isaac M. Wise reported that the congregation was composed of "American aristocrats . . . of Portuguese descent."[29] This congregation of "aristocrats" was the first to introduce reforms in traditional Jewish practice.

As in the Lutheran Church of that era it was primarily the native-born adherents who sought linguistic and ritual modifications of historic practices. As for the immigrants, the description of the non-Jewish German "auswanderer" provided by Mack Walker seems equally applicable to the Jews. They came to America "less to build something new than to regain or conserve something old . . . to till new fields and find new customers, true enough, but ultimately to keep the ways of life they were used to. . . . They were not characterized by the willingness to break with old traditions. . . . Something like that may have happened to them in America, but few intended it when they left [their homelands]."[30]

The record of the congregations organized by Central European Jewish immigrants prior to 1840 shows that consideration of "reform" was never even on their agenda. Struggling to gain an economic foothold and to overcome the psychological hardships of loneliness and alienation, they built synagogues in a quest for the comforts of fellowship and the reassurance of the familiar. The uniformity that emerged in the widely scattered institutions they founded did not derive from any preplanned design or deliberate intention. It resulted from the similarity of their previous experience, their present situation, and their aspirations for the future.

Conditions in America made it virtually impossible for them to maintain traditional Jewish practices in their daily lives, but these same conditions did not preclude their establishing synagogues, through which they attempted to salvage the way of life they had left behind but had not repudiated. In fact, the American milieu fostered the establishment of independent and self-governing "churches." In adding their own houses of worship to the existing mélange of religious institutions, they were becoming a part of the American mainstream even as they preserved their links to their Jewish identity. In 1840 there were eighteen formally organized Jewish congregations in America. A decade later the number had risen to at least seventy-six and, by 1877, to two hundred and seventy-seven.[32] The institution that had been intended to serve as a link with the Old World soon emerged as a bridge to the New.

5 The First Leaders, 1830–1845

TRANSPLANTATION from the European setting to America necessitated a substantial reorientation on the part of every religious and ethnic group. Seldom were the necessary adjustments made without stress and controversy, but in most instances leaders within the various immigrant communities were able to direct, or at least to influence, the development of strategies for survival. Within the Roman Catholic Church, with its centralized hierarchical leadership, the responsibility for reformulating the Church's role was left almost exclusively to the clergy. By way of contrast American Jewry, structureless and leaderless, experienced great difficulty even in designating an appropriate forum in which issues and problems could be raised. As for planning or reformulation, they were clearly beyond the capacity of the rapidly growing Jewish population. As Morais noted in 1894, since there was "no ecclesiastical authority existing in this country, matters were allowed to shape their own course —each congregation doing as it saw fit; without referring its action to any other but its own minister and even he at times was overruled by the laymen who composed the membership of the Board of Trustees."[1]

In the decades following the onset of large-scale immigration the situation was even more anarchic than Morais suggests. Frequently, congregations did not refer actions even to their own ministers. As we have noted, these ministers generally functioned as chazan and shochet. As a rule, they were not consulted about matters of policy but were instructed to perform their ritual duties under the close supervision of laymen. The resolution of Anshe Chesed Congregation forbidding its chazan "to make a public act without the approval of the trustees" was typical of the contemporary attitude of Jewish congregations.[2]

In part, this attitude may have resulted from the low caliber of the individuals who served as religious functionaries. Ministers who frequented barber shops and "parter houses" could not be expected to elicit respect from their constituents. The congregations made little or no effort to attract leaders with higher qualifications, however, and when the first few such men arrived in America uninvited, they were received with indifference and often hostility.

After the death of Gershom Mendes Seixas in 1816, the first to attempt a leadership role in American Jewish life was Isaac Leeser. Leeser immigrated to America from Westphalia in 1824 at the age of eighteen. Little is known of his early life except for scattered autobiographical references in the journal which he founded in 1843. Despite the fact that he was orphaned at an early age, he was able to attend a gymnasium at Muenster for two and a quarter years. His formal Jewish education concluded when he was still an adolescent. "I do not pretend to be a great talmudist," he wrote. "At fourteen years old I left the Hebrew school and learned worldly things."[3] Throughout his life Leeser was handicapped by the meagerness of his formal educational background, and his adversaries never lost an opportunity to remind him of his deficiencies.

On his arrival in America, Leeser went to Richmond, Virginia, to work as a clerk in the shop of his uncle, Zalma Rehine. Rehine had arrived in America in 1789 and had married a relative of the Seixas family.[4] These family connections made it possible for Leeser to develop close ties with prominent Jews in the community. He became an active participant in Richmond's Sephardic congregation and assisted the chazan in teaching children's classes. He apparently applied himself with great zeal to the task of learning English and by 1828 was able to publish two articles in the *Richmond Whig* intended "to rebut the calumnies which had been spread abroad through an English Review against the character of the Jewish faith and the people."[5] His grasp of English, the force of his argument, and his initiative in responding demonstrated his potential for leadership. He was described by the editor of *The Whig* as a "young gentleman of that community [the Jews] whose early and rare attainments give promise of great future reputation."[6]

The following year Leeser was elected to the post of chazan of the Sephardic Congregation of Philadelphia, Mikveh Israel. In view of his personal experience and given the conditions of American Jewish life at that time, the affiliation of a young German immigrant with this congregation is entirely plausible. He had been associated with a Sephardic congregation since his arrival in America and had acquired familiarity with the Sephardic practices. Moreover, even if he had desired a post in an Ashkenazic congregation, no suitable opportunity existed. In 1829 no Ashkenazic congregation was yet in a position to support a chazan even on a minimal level. Most important, Mikveh Israel was a prestigious congregation of Americans and not a struggling aggregation of greenhorns. It was an acceptable context for an energetic young man who spoke and wrote English and who had great ambitions for himself and for Jews in America. That Mikveh Israel was willing to choose an untrained twenty-three year-old testifies to the paucity of qualified candidates for such positions.[7]

Leeser at once introduced a controversial innovation. He

began to preach regular sermons, though the practice "was frowned upon with disdain."[8] Leeser later wrote: "At that period the duties of the minister were confined to the conducting of the public worship in the synagog and elsewhere, and it was not expected that he should be at the same time a preacher and exhorter."[9] Not until 1843 did the congregation give its official consent to the delivery of his exhortations.

In addition to delivering sermons, Leeser undertook an active program of publication. In 1830 his translation of a popular German school text, *Instruction in the Mosaic Religion*,[10] appeared. Three years later he published *The Jews and the Mosaic Law*, an enlargement of his articles in defense of Judaism in the *Richmond Whig*. A third volume of early sermons, entitled *Discourses, Argumentative and Devotional on the Subject of the Jewish Religion*, was printed in 1836. Although they are not distinguished either for erudition or for inspiration, their publication demonstrated Leeser's determination to educate and organize American Jewry and to assert his own role as teacher and leader. As he wrote in the preface: "Let me hope that the exertions I have made . . . may redound to diffuse knowledge of the commandments among our people, and to contribute to cement stronger the bond that unites us."[11] In pursuing these objectives, he issued *The Form of Prayer according to the Custom of Spanish and Portuguese Jews* (1837), *The Hebrew Reader* (1838), and *Catechism for Younger Children* (1839).

Leeser's association with the Sephardic community provided him with a relatively stable institutional base, but it created problems in establishing relations with the newly arriving immigrants. Not only did he officiate according to the Sephardic ritual, but, because he lectured and wrote only in English, his ideas were not immediately accessible to the newcomers who constituted a majority of the Jewish population. Moreover, his involvement with an Americanized congregation led him to support projects that often seemed inappropriate to the more traditional immigrants.

For example, Leeser was closely associated with Rebecca Gratz in establishing the first Jewish Sunday School in America, inspired by the Christian Sunday School movement which had its center in Philadelphia. Rebecca Gratz acknowledged the model for the program. On the eve of its opening, she wrote: "We have never yet had a Sunday school in our congregation and so I have induced our ladies to follow the example of other religious communities."[12] Leeser had earlier advocated the establishment of a day school in which Hebrew and English would be taught.[13] He now backed the more modest enterprise, which was a response to the desires of the Americanized segment of the community to provide minimal religious education in the American Protestant pattern.

Without exception German-Jewish congregations rejected the Sunday School. Leeser denounced the opposition, citing "prejudice" against this "blessed undertaking" emanating from "various persons who fancied that they discovered an objectionable imitation of Gentile practices." He praised the school for filling a void and for providing children with "at least an elementary and comprehensive idea of their duties . . . without interfering with the exercises of other [secular] schools and the avocations of the teachers."[14] The argument did not persuade the recent arrivals.

As we have seen, every immigrant congregation, however impoverished it was, aspired to organize a school in which Hebrew and German (and in at least one instance Yiddish)[15] would be taught as well as English. Not until the late 1860's were German Jews ready to settle for the Sunday School as a desirable or at least acceptable form of Jewish education. By that time they and their synagogues had undergone a radical transformation. In the early 1840's the Sunday School of Rebecca Gratz and Isaac Leeser appeared to them to be an unacceptable accommodation.

Leeser's concern for Jewish education led him to produce a steady stream of written materials for children—textbooks, "catechisms," and guides. Once again his exclusive use of English and his Christian approach to the Jewish religion (Judaism has no catechism) limited the initial acceptance of his work. Nevertheless, he was the first to address the problem of producing educational materials for American Jewish schools, and his pioneering work marked a significant breakthrough. The task was not easy, and he received little encouragement. Even his friend and supporter Rebecca Gratz advised him not to publish and commented that he "had taken too much upon himself and does not seem to get along as happily as if he had reserved his whole strength and attention to the duties of the reading desk."[16] He encountered serious financial reversals and had difficulties in raising funds for his publications. "As yet I have found no publisher for my works and I have therefore to undertake both the literary and mercantile part of the enterprise," he wrote. "The first work I issued brought no profit and the second caused a considerable pecuniary loss."[17] Only the fact that he was a bachelor who was able to pour all his fiscal and human resources into his projects made it possible for him to continue.

The opportunity for Leeser to become a recognized national leader was provided by a calamity that roused the entire Jewish community and moved it to the first concerted effort of its history. In 1840 the ancient blood libel was revived in Damascus, where a group of Jews were arrested and tortured on the charge of murdering a Catholic priest and using his blood for ritual purposes. The storm of indignation and anxiety reached even to the shores of the United States, where the specter of revived medieval bigotry shook native

American as well as immigrant Jews. Abraham Hart, president of Congregation Mikveh Israel of Philadelphia, articulated their anxiety: "If such calumny is not nipped in the bud, its effect will not be limited to any particular place, but will be extended to every part of the globe."[18]

Hart's concern cannot be dismissed as Jewish overreaction, for Jasper Chasseaud, American consular representative in Damascus, reported to John Forsyth, Secretary of State, that the accusation against the Jews had been proven: "The reverend Thomas had been beheaded in the house of David Arari, a rich Jew, by seven of his co-religioners of Damascus, and that, in order to take his Blood, it being ordered by their religion to make use of Christian Blood in the Unleavened Bread at Easter." He added the gratuitous comment that the Jewish practice "of serving themselves of Christian Blood in their Unleavened Bread at Easter . . . in these 1840 Years must have made many unfortunate victims."[19] Chasseaud, who was American consul for Beirut, Damascus, and Said, is reported to have been a Macedonian. Despite his scurrilous report, he was not dismissed, or as far as we know even reprimanded, and continued to serve as United States Consul until 1848. Some months later Secretary Forsyth wrote to the American Consul in Alexandria and the American Minister to Turkey repudiating the charges and urging them to use their "good offices in behalf of an oppressed and persecuted race." [20] It is understandable that Jews should have been aroused by the revival of canards which (to use Forsyth's words) "in less enlightened times were made the pretexts of fanatical persecution or mercenary extortion."

In England the Board of Deputies of British Jews had met on April 21, 1840, to consider the Damascus Affair and had appointed a delegation to meet with the Secretary of State for Foreign Affairs in London. A series of meetings and conferences was held, culminating in a public mass meeting called by the Lord Mayor of London. Sir Moses Montefiore and Baron Lionel de Rothschild acted as emissaries to the British government. On June 15 the Board of Deputies decided that Montefiore and Adolphe Cremieux, the influential French-Jewish leader, should go to Egypt to meet with the Viceroy in person to demand release of the Damascus victims.[21]

American Jewry, possessing neither a central body nor recognized leaders, was slower in responding to the crisis. Late in August and early in September 1840 meetings were held in New York (August 19), Philadelphia (August 27), Charleston (August 29), Cincinnati (August 31), Savannah (September 2), and Richmond (September 4).[22] These assemblies were held too late to influence matters in Damascus.[23] They did, however, mark the growing self-awareness and confidence of American Jews. For the first time Jewish communities addressed petitions to the President of the United States requesting him (in the words of the New York resolution) "to use every possible effort to induce the Pasha of Egypt to manifest more liberal treatment toward his Jewish Subjects."[24] Moreover, non-Jews, including public officials and Christian clergymen, were invited to participate in some of the public meetings that were held. In Charleston, Mayor Henry L. Pinckney spoke, as did the Right Reverend John England, the Roman Catholic Bishop there.

Most significant of all, disparate Jewish groups in all of the major urban centers joined together with each other, with Jews in other American cities, and with communities in Europe in an expression of mutual interest and concern. The action was belated and minimal, but it signified an awakening of group consciousness.

There was a notable abstention from the unanimous response. The Board of Trustees of aristocratic Congregation Shearith Israel of New York, ever aloof and isolationist, reto take a stand on the Damascus issue and denied use of its premises for the protest in New York. Nevertheless, individual members of the congregation participated prominently in the meeting that took place at Bnai Jeshurun. Elsewhere Sephardim and Ashkenazim joined together without incident. The protest meeting held at Congregation Mikveh Israel in Philadelphia was arranged by a committee that included the president of Rodeph Shalom.[25] The diminution of hostility between Ashkenazim and Sephardim in the wake of the threat to the entire Jewish community is evident in a letter of Rebecca Gratz dated October 4, 1840. In discussing the Damascus affair, she comments:

> In Phila we have now two Synagogues. It was at first thought that there was some pride and other unlawful passions engaged in the elements of which the new congregation was composed, but by the exercise of a little prudence and accommodation the evil was crushed, and now the holy spirit of religion, peace and friendship seem likely to unite all the house of Israel into one bond of good faith. The Damascus persecution has fallen in a time to put down all petty strife and make us all desire to act and pray for the oppressed.[26]

In response to a threat from the outside, the gap between the acculturated and the immigrants had not closed, but it was bridged.

The quickening sense of mutual concern led to the first proposals for a permanent liaison between Jews in various American cities. In Charleston a resolution was passed calling for the appointment of a "committee of five . . . to confer with the Richmond committee and others in relation to the objects of this meeting."[27] Philadelphia appointed a committee of correspondence to "keep abreast of what other Jewish communities in the United States were doing about the

Damascus Affair."[28] These proposals were never implemented; however, the issue of unity had been raised.

In the course of the activity surrounding the Damascus Affair, Isaac Leeser emerged as the preeminent spokesman for American Jewry. He delivered the major address at the Philadelphia meeting, which was reprinted and widely circulated. In it Leeser articulated an American Jewish ideology: "As citizens, we belong to the country we live in; but as believers in one God . . . we hail the Israelite as a brother. . . . We have therefore met . . . to offer our aid in conjunction with our brothers in other towns both of this country and elsewhere." When the resolutions calling for ongoing communication between cities were not acted upon, Leeser took the initiative in preparing a detailed plan for a national union of American Jewish congregations. The proposal was printed and circulated in July 1841. The only congregation to respond was Beth Elohim of Charleston, which opposed the proposal on the grounds that a union would be hostile to change. Leeser may have been disheartened, but he was not daunted and proceeded at once with other ventures.

The following year he announced his plans for publishing a monthly journal in English. The periodical, *The Occident and American Jewish Advocate*, appeared on April 18, 1843. In his first issue Leeser cited the establishment of Jewish periodicals in Germany, France, and England and the need for "a similar work in this country." He promised "to give circulation to everything which can be interesting to the Jewish inhabitants of the Western Hemisphere" and solicited "the respective presidents and secretaries of our American Congregations [to] send us a condensed account of their first establishment. . . . Such a regular series would serve as the best history of the American Jews."[29] American Jewry not only had a spokesman; it now had a forum for the exchange of ideas and information.

At the time Leeser began to publish *The Occident,* an attempt was made in Philadelphia to establish a German language newspaper, called *Israelite* and published by Julius Stern, a German immigrant of 1837. Two issues are known to have appeared, but the enterprise failed and no information concerning its content has survived. For the next six years Leeser's *Occident* remained the only Jewish periodical in America.

In 1844 I. Daniel Rupp published *An Original History of the Religious Denominations in the United States.* It contained "authentic accounts of their rise, progress, statistics and doctrines written expressly for the work by eminent theological professors, ministers and lay-members of the respective denominations."[30] Rupp reports that in preparing his work he sought "the most prominent divines and lay members of the different denominations," adding, "It would be superfluous to say anything in regard to the contributors— they are too favourably known to their own sects to need it." The contributor of the section on "The Jews and Their Religion" was Isaac Leeser. His role as "the most prominent divine" (indeed the *only* articulate religious leader) of American Jewry at that time was undisputed.

In his essay describing contemporary practice in American Jewish life, Leeser wrote: "We have no ecclesiastical authorities in America other than the congregations themselves. Each congregation makes its own rules for its government, and elects its own minister, who is appointed without any ordination, induction in office being made through his election."[31] His statement details the institutional anarchy that prevailed and confirms the emergence in America of a new variety of religious professional, of which Gershom Mendes Seixas a few decades earlier was a precursor: the Jewish "minister" who was not a scholar-rabbi and had no ordination, nor indeed any set of specified qualifications, but who functioned increasingly as a pastor and preacher in the Protestant mode.

Leeser himself was an example. He conducted religious services, preached sermons, supervised religious education, officiated at weddings and funerals, and performed pastoral duties (he is listed in Rupp's book as "pastor of the Hebrew Portuguese Congregation of Philadelphia"). Leeser's essay makes no mention of rabbis. At the time he wrote, the 1840's, the first ordained rabbis had already come to America, but they had not yet found a recognized place or function for themselves in the new environment. Leeser noted neither their prior absence nor their recent arrival. For American Judaism as experienced and explained by Leeser, the traditional rabbi was at best marginal.

In the traditional Jewish community elsewhere, the role of the rabbi had been primarily juridical and scholarly. He expounded Jewish law and rendered judgments in cases involving civil as well as ritual matters. He also occupied himself with the study and teaching of Jewish texts, especially of Talmud. Even when the dissolution of the autonomous Jewish community and the spread of secular learning undermined the role of the rabbi in Europe, the traditional pattern with its recognized standards of competence continued to exercise an influence. Moreover, men with classical Jewish training and with rabbinic ordination took the lead in exploring a variety of alternatives for the adaptation of Judaism to facilitate the participation of Jews in modern society.[32] Issues were discussed and argued with a view to their traditional as well as scientific justifications, and expertise remained the major criterion for participating in the debate. There could be no leadership position in Europe for Jewish ministers, who were at best amateurs in their familiarity with Jewish sources and modern scholarship.

By way of contrast in America, there was no tradition of

rabbinic leadership, nor was there an institutional context in which a rabbi could be expected to function. A formal Jewish legal system had never been framed; few scholars with the requisite background for serious Talmudic learning had immigrated. Problems relating to the participation of Jews in general society never arose, since Jews had never been excluded. In a land where (Jewishly speaking) there was no law and no learning, there was little call for judges and scholars.

In the interim between the atrophy of the old style of Jewish religious leadership and the consolidation of a new pattern, American Jewish institutions blundered along seeking to retain something of the old ways while adapting to the demands of a new kind of society. Congregations—whether of assimilated native Americans or of struggling immigrants—were autonomous and governed by laymen who were pragmatic in their concerns. Usually, they acted without reference to consistent standards or scholarly criteria. In 1844, 1845, and 1846 German rabbis interested in reforming Jewish thought and practice were holding three landmark conferences where basic issues were debated. During the same years such controversies as arose in Jewish religious life in America were of a totally different order. The German Hebrew Congregation of Philadelphia, Rodeph Shalom, which suspended its chazan (who also served as shochet for a total salary of $100 per year) for a period of three months in 1844 for marrying a couple "without inquiring into their religious status," subsequently reelected him for an additional term of six months (with his salary increased to $150 per year). Isaac Leeser was one of those who intervened on his behalf.

The first ordained rabbi to settle in America was Abraham Rice of Gagheim, Bavaria, who arrived in 1840 at the age of forty. Little is known of his European background, but his

journey to America without an invitation is evidence of lack
of previous success. While in New York, he is reported to
have addressed the Anshei Chesed congregation. Shortly
thereafter Rice met a "landsman" (fellow townsman from
the old country) who invited him to Baltimore, where he
was elected rabbi of the Baltimore Hebrew Congregation.[33]

His difficulties with the congregation began at once. Rice
directed the enforcement of one of its bylaws, that violators
of the Sabbath should not be called upon to participate in the
reading of the Torah. Under pressure from the trustees, he
was compelled to retreat. In a pathetic gesture of defiance
he recommended that when Sabbath-breakers recited the
blessings before and after the Torah reading, the congregation
should not respond with "Amen."[34] In America this with-
holding of the "amen" was the limit of a rabbi's authority.

Strife between Rice and his congregation was constant.
Two years after his arrival, he provoked a confrontation
when representatives of the Masonic and Odd Fellows lodges
began to perform the graveside rites of their orders for a
deceased member of the congregation. Apparently Rice was
taken completely by surprise by the intrusion of what
seemed to him a bizarre pagan ceremonial. His vigorous protests succeeded only in creating antagonism against him. In
reaction to this incident, a group of members of the congregation resigned and organized a reformist society, the Har
Sinai Verein.[35]

In 1845 the increasing affluence of the earliest German
immigrants made it possible for the Baltimore Hebrew Congregation to build its first edifice. The building, including a
"women's balcony screened off with lattice work" (in keeping with strict traditional practice) was designed by Baltimore's leading architect, who had also built an Episcopal and
a Presbyterian church and two Catholic churches.[36] The
dedication of the building became a source of added trouble

for Rabbi Rice, who spoke in German while Samuel Isaacs of New York and Isaac Leeser of Philadelphia spoke in English. The constituency, which was sufficiently prosperous to build a new synagogue, was apparently sufficiently acculturated to want an English-speaking leader. Samuel Isaacs, who was not a rabbi, was offered the post of preacher. Only Isaacs' refusal to move to Baltimore made it possible for Rice to retain his position. Leeser, who purported to be Rice's friend and supporter, and who was ostensibly a fellow traditionalist, contributed further to the problem when he wrote: "We deem it an undeniable truth, that the German language, no matter how eloquent the preacher, must soon become useless as a pulpit language, since the children of the present immigrants will soon know no other than the English language. . . . In saying this we by no means undervalue the learning and eloquence of Rev. Rice . . . but only maintaining that we need another speech for the future Israelites in America."[37] Clearly, familiarity with Jewish sources and rabbinic credentials were of little moment. An English-speaking minister was preferred to a German-speaking rabbi.

For a number of years Rice sought to find a *modus vivendi* for himself as a rabbi in America. He was flexible enough to attempt the elimination of piyyutim (medieval religious poems, which added to the length of the service); yet the congregation that had repudiated his attempt to enforce traditional behavior outside the synagogue rejected his effort to alter traditional ritual in the synagogue, and his proposal to abbreviate the service was defeated.[38] The congregation's inconsistency in supporting permissiveness in private behavior outside the synagogue and rigidity in ritual practice within it must have been as exasperating as it was illogical.

Rice established an afternoon Hebrew school that was a compromise between the inadequate Sunday school and the unattainable all-day school. He urged "the great importance of selecting a spiritual chief or bet din [Jewish rabbinic court], for the purpose of regulating all our spiritual affairs. . . . It is surely necessary to prevent the uninitiated from giving their crude decisions, which are but too well calculated to do permanent injury to our faith."[39] None of his efforts was successful, and in 1849 he resigned his position and opened a dry goods store. He wrote to his teacher and friend in Germany, Rabbi Wolf Hamburger, expressing his desolation:

> I dwell in complete darkness, without a teacher or a companion. . . . The religious life in this land is on the lowest level, most people eat foul food and desecrate the Sabbath in public. . . . Thousands marry non-Jewish women. Under these circumstances my mind is perplexed and I wonder whether it is even permissible for a Jew to live in this land. I am tired of my life. . . . I often think of leaving and going to Paris and put my trust in the good Lord.[40]

America was not a congenial setting for conscientious traditionalist clerics of any sect. Abraham Rice's view had much in common with that of the nineteenth-century Catholic Redemptorist Father who wrote to an arriving Catholic sister: "You are here in Sodom and Gomorrah."[41]

Needless to say, the masses of immigrants did not concur in these gloomy assessments, nor did the new breed of religious leaders who were prepared to function within the emerging American pattern. While Abraham Rice was submerged in despair, Isaac Leeser was writing: "In America, where the constitution . . . secures to every person the enjoyment of life, liberty and the pursuit of happiness without anyone having the right to question him concerning his religious opinion or acts, the Children of Jacob have received a new home."[42] The discrepancy in assessment between these points of view—Leeser reflecting the rapid integration of the Jewish masses and Rice the alienation of a scholarly traditionalist—explains why the masses flocked to America in ever-increasing numbers while emigrating scholars continued to be rare and lonely exceptions.

The few rabbis who came were men whose earlier successes were negligible and whose credentials were frequently questionable. For the most part there is no verifiable record of their experience prior to their arrival in America, and we have only their own testimony (not always reliable) as to their past training and activities. In an era of sparse documentation and poor communications, it is difficult to separate factual achievements from embellished claims.

Leo Merzbacher, generally regarded as the second rabbi to settle in America, arrived in New York in the early 1840's. He was reported to have had both a university degree and rabbinic ordination. An obituary by Max Lilienthal, shortly after Merzbacher's death in 1856, declared that he had his rabbinic degree from Rabbi Moses Schreiber of Pressburg (a distinguished scholar known as the Hatam Sofer) and that he had completed his doctoral studies at the University of Erlangen.[43] Subsequent articles reiterated that Merzbacher was in possession "of credentials of established rabbinical authority and of a full collegiate education."[44] It is not possible to check the claim of ordination, but at Erlangen there is no record of a university degree. The fact that Merzbacher was asked in 1844 by members of Congregation Anshe Chesed to pasken sh'elot (resolve ritual problems in accordance with Jewish law, a responsibility only a rabbi might undertake) has led some authors to conclude that he was in fact an ordained rabbi.[45] Such claims overlook the fact that the minutes of Anshei Chesed always refer to Merzbacher as "Mr." and never as "Rabbi." If Merzbacher was indeed an ordained rabbi, his experience provides additional evidence of the lack of regard in America for traditional authority.[46]

Whether or not he had formal ordination, his scholarly training was superior to that of any Jew in America, with the possible exception of Abraham Rice. Despite his qualifications, he was hard put to find a job. We know nothing of his activities during his first year in America. In 1842 he participated in the founding of Rodeph Shalom, a new German congregation in New York. A history of the congregation, written in 1892, reports, "The dedicatory services were conducted by the Rev. Dr. Merzbacher."[47] Apparently he was associated with this congregation for a brief time, but "the details of his duties are not preserved."[48] The position cannot have been very satisfactory, for in 1843 the Board of Trustees of Congregation Anshe Chesed received an application from "Mr. Merzbacher" requesting them "to assist him to gain a livelihood as lecturer or teacher." No appointment was made at that time, but a committee was asked to take up a "subscription" for his support among the members. Six weeks later the committee reported that forty-nine dollars was pledged. The response may be characterized as tepid.

In November of that year, Merzbacher was asked by the trustees of Anshe Chesed to deliver lectures on several specified Sabbaths and to give religious instruction "several hours a week to children over twelve." It was further stipulated that he would be paid one dollar for a eulogy delivered for a nonmember of the congregation. Merzbacher requested that he also be given the privilege of officiating at weddings ("giving Kiddushin" is the terminology). He declared that he would charge no fees for his services and would take no income away from the officers of the congregation. He stated, however, that he considered it part of his duties as lecturer to give Kiddushin. Action on this request was postponed to the following meeting, at which time the request was denied. Subsequently the question was reopened and a decision was postponed "until after Pesach."[49]

In assessing the significance of the congregation's actions, we must note that Jewish religious law does *not* require that an ordained rabbi officiate at a marriage ceremony. It does require that an officiant be observant and knowledgeable in the laws concerning marriages, and be able to write a wedding contract. Given the low level of piety and learning of both the laymen and the chazanim who generally conducted weddings, it is surprising that a man of Merzbacher's background and education (whether or not he was ordained) would be denied permission to officiate but the rights of less qualified individuals were protected. The incident provides additional evidence of the lack of regard for scholarly credentials or consistent standards. Instead, a blend of primitive piety and opportunistic pragmatism which characterized the developing Jewish religious institutions made it virtually impossible to deal systematically with ideological questions.

"The business of allowing Mr. Merzbacher to give Kiddushin" was finally resolved on May 12, 1844, more than six months after it had been raised. He was given the "privilege," provided: (a) he obtained consent of the Parnass (president); (b) other officers of the congregation received their usual fees; (c) "the chazan has to be present at all chatunot" (weddings—this term, like most references to Jewish rituals, appears in the Minutes in Hebrew script).[50] In this way, a place (carefully circumscribed) was made in congregational life for the rabbi without unduly encroaching on the prerogatives that others had exercised. In America, where the giving of kiddushin could be referred to as "business," problems of religious authority could be settled in the spirit of free enterprise.

In 1845 Merzbacher was elected minister of newly estab-

lished Congregation Emanu-El.[51] Despite the reformist aspirations of this congregation, his position was only slightly
improved. He was still referred to in the early minutes of the
Congregation as "Mr.,"[52] was still required to obtain permission of the officers of the congregation before officiating at a
wedding,[53] was required to obtain committee approval for the
slightest modification in pulpit procedures,[54] and was repeat-
edly in jeopardy of losing his job.[55] During one altercation
the Board of Trustees informed Merzbacher that they "did
not wish to receive further protests, admonitions and rebukes
and would feel themselves necessitated to leave them un-
answered."[56] In 1855 he was instructed to prepare his sermons in manuscript and to have them lying on the pulpit
during his delivery. Whatever the reasons for this stipulation
may have been, the procedure was clearly demeaning. Shortly thereafter the board decided over Merzbacher's strenuous
protests "to advertise for an assistant minister able to speak
English."[57] No assistant had been found by 1856, when Merzbacher collapsed and died while walking home from the synagogue. A contemporary observer commented that during
his lifetime, "he was virtually unknown outside a small
circle."[58] After his death the congregation "erected a costly
and elegant monument over his grave."[59]

The earliest leaders who sought to impose standards or
discipline or to raise the intellectual levels of Jewish life were
faced with frustration and hostility. In his journal Isaac
Leeser continued to denounce the low level of religious leadership and the shabby treatment of qualified leaders who
attempted to assert themselves. He bemoaned the inadequacy
of chazanim who were equipped to do no more than read the
ritual; he condemned "temporal managers" and congregational bossism.[60] In the end, Leeser himself was unable to
maintain his position as minister of Mikveh Israel and in 1850
resigned because of conflicts with his "temporal managers."

All the while, new immigrants added to the size of the community. A growing proportion of earlier arrivals achieved a measure of social and economic integration and acquired an appetite for spiritual and intellectual stimulation. Soon, a small but significant number of better qualified leaders had arrived; they were able to delineate problems and suggest responses. Gradually, the preconditions for a more vigorous communal life took form. The examples and experiences of the initial failures helped prepare the way for the achievements that were to follow.

Later American Jews in their decorous "temples" repressed the memory of the chaotic and strife-ridden beginnings of their institutions. The elegant life styles they eventually achieved led them (as well as later immigrants who encountered them) to accept the myth that they had always been prosperous, cultivated, worldly, and "reformed." By the 1840's the transformation had hardly begun.

6 Religious Reform, 1840–1855

In the last two decades of the nineteenth century, masses of Eastern European Jews arrived in the United States. They encountered a well-established German-Jewish community. It was relatively affluent and acculturated and had espoused a radically reformed version of Judaism. In the absence of visible evidence to the contrary, the new arrivals assumed that this situation had always prevailed. Americanized German Jews, eager to confirm their status and to emphasize the contrast between their own gentility and the uncouthness of the Eastern European newcomers, nourished the notion that German Jews were and indeed always had been a different (i.e., superior) element. This myth entered the canons of American Jewish folklore and has been reaffirmed in scholarly as well as popular treatments. The legend persists: "They came with their ideas for reform. . . . The transferral of German Reform concepts into this country was straightforward and direct."[1]

A revision of this view is in order. In the years prior to 1848 when the controversy over reform raged within Germany, few if any German-Jewish immigrants came to America with ideas for reform. On the contrary, in the period immediately following their arrival in the United States they generally rejected proposals that seemed to be reformist. The compromises they made in modifying their ritual practices in their private lives were dictated by economic necessity, not religious ideology. Their blend of institutional piety and personal laxity demonstrates the lack of a consistent outlook or program among ambitious but poor and untutored immigrants who, in many respects, closely resembled the Eastern Europeans who were to arrive fifty years later.[2] When reform ideologues finally did emigrate from Germany, they were quick to recognize and denounce the religion of convenience which they found in America and which was not to be confused with the reformist principles they themselves espoused.[3]

The dynamics of change in the New World were quite different from those which had prevailed in Germany. There religious change was inseparably linked to emancipation. The implementation of some program of religious reform was viewed as an essential precondition for the entry into general society so urgently desired by the ever-growing Jewish urban population.[4] No such incentive existed in America, where emancipation was taken for granted and where improved status in the general society was more a function of economic advancement than of ideological transformation. In Germany, reform was viewed as a precursor to acculturation and integration. In America, acculturation and integration proved to be the precursors of reform.

In Germany, Jewish religious reformism had radical—even revolutionary—overtones and consequences. It was more than an assault on the traditional Jewish communal structure; it was a challenge to the established social and political order and was understood as such by secular authorities seeking to preserve inherited prerogatives and practices. The frequent repression of Jewish reformist groups (along with all other liberal movements) helped radicalize German reform. The political overtones of religious reformism in a strife-ridden society fostered the development of a movement with an ideological platform and programmatic objectives.[5]

In America precisely the opposite dynamics were at work. Jewish reformism emerged out of the desire not to change the established social and political order but to join it. Examination of the process through which reformism gradually developed in American-Jewish institutions reveals that ideology in the European sense played a minimal role, and a predetermined program was virtually absent. The handful of ideological leaders who later migrated never succeeded in their attempt to create a party based on a philosophy. By the time their platforms and manifestoes were formulated, the work of nondoctrinaire reform was being accomplished by the slow but steady Americanization of the synagogue. By investing the desire for social adjustment with religious significance, they merely provided an intellectual justification for what American Jews were already doing.[6]

Jewish religious reform in nineteenth-century America began with a series of modest ritual changes and shifts in emphasis which were primarily concerned with appearances and social conformity. As indicated previously, the earliest reformist attempt was made in Charleston, whose Jewish residents were native born and thoroughly Americanized. The initial proposal to introduce changes in 1825 cited decorum and intelligibility as objectives rather than substantive revision of either faith or practice. Outside influences came from American Unitarianism, which was gaining momentum during this era, not from German-Jewish reform.[7]

Some years after the failure of this effort, reformism again emerged in Charleston, this time within the original Sephardic congregation, Beth Elohim, which had resisted the earlier effort and had remained a congregation of "American aristocrats . . . of Portuguese descent."[8] As was to be the case in numerous subsequent instances, the occasion for introducing reforms was provided not by an ideological debate but rather by the construction of a new synagogue edifice between 1839 and 1841. Moreover, the specific reforms proposed were modest and dealt with aesthetic rather than philosophical issues. Two reforms were instituted: the delivery of discourses in English and the installation of an organ "to assist in vocal parts of the service."[9]

At the time these changes were instituted, Gustavus Poznanski was chazan of Beth Elohim. All available evidence indicates that Poznanski—like other "religious professionals" of the time—was a man of modest qualifications. His role in the congregation was such that he was expected to be servant rather than leader. Although Poznanski was himself an immigrant from Posen, he had associated himself with the Sephardic community and served Congregation Shearith Israel in New York from 1832 to 1836 as "shochet, shofar blower and occasional chazan." He was elected to the Charleston post in 1836 on the recommendation of none other than Isaac Leeser, who noted that when Poznanski took up his position, he was so strict in his religious observance that "he did not partake of a meal prepared for the public celebration of the anniversary of a charitable institution of the members of his congregation."[10] Poznanski clearly did not bring either reformism or religious laxity to Charleston.

In 1839 the Board of Trustees of the congregation approached Poznanski with a request "to have English introduced during divine Service in the Synagogue, either by discourses or prayers." Poznanski replied that "he would consider the subject and endeavor to comply with the wishes of the Board as much as possible."[11]

The following year, thirty-eight members of the congregation petitioned the Trustees to install an organ. The trustees rejected the petition on the grounds that it violated the congregation's constitution. The trustees were, however, overruled by the membership, which voted forty-six to forty in favor of the organ. For a time the two factions used the synagogue on alternate Saturdays: one week the organ was used; the following it was not. At the dedication of the new edifice on March 19, 1841, Poznanski lauded the decision and defended the restoration of instrumental music "on grounds of both reason and scripture."[12] If Poznanski did not foster reforms, neither did he resist them. He seems merely to have maintained his earlier promise "to comply . . . as much as possible," even if this meant alternating modes of worship from week to week.

The dedication ceremony was described in considerable detail in the Charleston *Courier*, which also reported on the content of Poznanski's "discourse." In it he is reported to have declared: "this synagogue is our temple, this city our Jerusalem, this happy land our Palestine." In subsequent years this statement (frequently in a garbled version) was cited as evidence of his repudiation of traditional Jewish messianism and restorationist hopes and his espousal of the principles of German radical reform.[13] An examination of the circumstances indicates that such an interpretation is a distortion of what was unquestionably a bit of patriotic hyperbole.

In reporting Poznanski's remarks, the article in the *Courier* refers to the Damascus Affair of the previous year and acknowledges that these "occurrences of the last year [were] awfully threatening to [the Jews]." As a result, the *Courier* asserts, "their christian countrymen [are] more and more interested in their sojourn, movements and preservation as a *nation* (italics added)."[14] In the light of these comments, the force of Poznanski's statement becomes clear. He was not engaging in a theological discussion, nor was he probing the issue of Jewish "nationhood" (a concept the *Courier's* sympathetic report does not question). His expression of "a noble and generous enthusiasm" for America was an affirmation of confidence in the face of anxiety. In the words of the *Courier*:

> In dwelling on the plenitude of civil and religious privileges, enjoyed by the House of Israel in this land of liberty and equal rights, he kindled with a noble and generous enthusiasm, and declared, in behalf of himself and all grateful Israel that "this synagogue is our temple, this city our Jerusalem, this happy land our Palestine, and as our fathers defended with their lives *that* temple, *that* city, and *that* land, so will their sons defend *this* temple, *this* city, and *this* land.[15]

Poznanski's rhetoric is somewhat overheated and probably reflects the insecurity of a threatened minority. Since his intent seems to have been to stress the willingness of Charleston Jews to defend their city and their country, however, no one was likely to take issue with the affirmation or regard it as a reformist deviation. At the time the address was delivered, there is no indication that any of the traditionalists in the Charleston congregation or elsewhere objected. Taken out of context and viewed in relation to later controversies concerning Jewish nationalism, however, Poznanski's words appeared to be far more radical than they actually were. Closer scrutiny indicates that the problem of Jewish nationhood and restoration was never raised in 1841. No move was made to modify the text of prayers or the observance of holidays (such as the fast of the Ninth of Ab, which laments the destruction of the Temple in Jerusalem). Poznanski's declaration exemplifies the universally accepted determination of Jews to be "at home" in America. It does not indicate that they felt the repudiation of traditional texts and forms to be the price that had to be paid for the attainment of this sense of belonging.

Two years after the dedication of the new building, Poznanski attempted to exercise some leadership by proposing
modifications in synagogue ritual. In an address to the congregation on the first day of Passover in 1843, he suggested
that the customary observance of the second day of the festival (which is not stipulated in the Bible but was introduced
later for Jews outside Palestine because of the problems of
determining the calendar in ancient times) was no longer
necessary.[16] The Board of Trustees of the congregation
promptly reminded Poznanski that he was only a chazan,
that he had violated the constitution of the congregation, and
that he should inform the trustees "whether he intended in
his future lectures to propose or advise innovations of the
established form of service as observed by us and all other
congregations of Jews throughout the world." After an exchange of letters in which Poznanski expressed his pique, he
agreed, "with the sole view of restoring peace and harmony
in our Congregation," that he would recommend no further
innovations. Shortly thereafter, he resigned his post.

Congregation Beth Elohim continued to vacillate between
affirmation of tradition and acceptance of modest changes in
the format of the ritual. In 1841 a number of dissidents with-
drew in protest over the use of the organ and organized a
new congregation. In 1843 a meeting of the remaining members (ostensibly the more reformist element) rejected the
suggestion that the second day of festivals be eliminated. A
resolution affirming that "the established service of this Congregation embraces all the Mosaic and Rabbinical laws" was
also rejected, by a vote of twenty-seven to twenty-four. Subsequently no consistent program of reform was undertaken
in the congregation. Not until 1879 was the women's gallery
removed and seating arranged so that men and women could
sit together. Until that year, the congregation continued to
elect a shochet to oversee ritual slaughter of meat. Even at

that late date, a new prayer book prepared by the rabbi of the congregation was not accepted until after he declared to a committee his belief both in the coming of the Messiah and the resurrection of the dead.[17]

Although Beth Elohim in Charleston was the first American synagogue to take a few reform steps, it would be an error to designate the congregation in the 1840's as "reformed" or to ascribe the changes in its ritual to influences imported from abroad. No consistent principle infused the minor changes that were introduced. The minimal clerical encouragement for reforms came from a chazan of limited influence who became an advocate of modest change only after a period of residence in South Carolina. The Charleston experience demonstrates, however, that the erosion of traditional knowledge and the process of social integration combined to create an appetite for the Americanization of religious practice. Without intending to set an example or to create a model, Beth Elohim in fact became a paradigm, which congregations in other communities would follow when they reached a comparable stage in their development.

The first congregation in America to be organized as a self-declared reform body was Har Sinai, formed by German-Jewish immigrants in Baltimore in 1842. Unfortunately, few of the early records of this congregation have been preserved. The Minute Books between September 10, 1846, and May 30, 1873, are missing, and the earliest documents extant date from 1873. Occasional references in journals and personal recollections recorded many years after the fact provide only fragmentary information about the early development of this congregation. It was apparently established by members of the Baltimore Hebrew Congregation, who were also members of Masonic and Odd Fellows lodges and were angered by Rabbi Rice's unwillingness to allow these fraternal order to perform their graveside rituals.[18] This circumstance indicates that the founders of the congregation were not recently arrived from Germany but were, in fact, immigrants of an earlier period who were sufficiently Americanized to join such lodges and to be accepted by them. One of the leaders of the group was Joseph Simpson, who is known to have settled in Baltimore about 1828. Only after fourteen years in America did the reformist inclination manifest itself in him.

Initially Har Sinai called itself a Verein (German for association or club), rather than Kahal (the usual Hebrew name for congregation). This terminology follows some German precedents in which reformist associations existed outside the recognized communal framework. It also implies intellectual aspirations that are not necessarily a part of an ordinary synagogue organization. Whatever the intention, the Verein attracted very little support within Baltimore's German-Jewish community. Only seven persons attended the first meeting.[19] For many years the group struggled to sustain its existence in the face of widespread hostility within the German-Jewish immigrant community. "There was decided prejudice against the Har Sinai Verein . . . a prejudice which did not abate for nearly two generations."[20] When Isaac Mayer Wise visited Baltimore in 1864, he reported that Har Sinai (numbering eighty-five members at that time) was the smallest of the four "organized" synagogues there.[21] As late as 1878 the question of dissolving the Congregation was seriously considered. Apparently even when German-Jewish immigrants were prepared to consider introducing reforms, they remained chary of Reform.

The negative attitude toward Har Sinai becomes even more remarkable when we discover how modest the initial reforms were. Men and women continued to sit separately; dietary laws were observed, as were the extra days of festivals. It was primarily the introduction of an organ which marked this congregation as different from others. A history of the congregation published in observation of its seventy-fifth anniversary commented: "The form of Judaism followed by the Har Sinai Verein would be today considered Orthodox or very conservative . . . Men wore their hats and sat apart from the women. The Sabbath was generally observed and, among many of the Har Sinai Verein members, strictly observed. . . . Dietary laws were kept. On Friday nights and Saturdays the 'Shabos Goy' [non-Jew hired to perform tasks forbidden to Jews on the Sabbath] would attend to the lights and the fires."[22] In 1845 the congregation rejected the suggestion of its lay reader and decided to continue the observance of the Fast of the Ninth of Ab.[23] Once again the essential conservatism and traditionalism of the German-Jewish immigrants, even the few who affiliated with the handful of reform congregations, is unmistakably evident.

Har Sinai did not adopt a consistent reformist program until 1855, when the congregation invited the well-known reformer David Einhorn to leave Europe and become its rabbi. Even then the strife between the rabbi and others—in and out of the congregation—indicates the difficulty of maintaining principled positions in the American setting. During the riots of 1861 Einborn was forced to flee Baltimore because of his outspoken opposition to slavery.[24] The congregation would permit him to return only on condition that he refrain from commenting "in the pulpit on the excitable issues of the time."[25] Einborn never returned to Baltimore, and thereafter Har Sinai never exercised a discernible influence on the development of American-Jewish life. American Jewry's first self-declared reform congregation never became a success in its own development or as a model for others.

The only other congregation that unequivocally identified

itself as "reform" prior to 1850 was Emanu-El of New York. Myer Stern, who wrote a history of the congregation in 1895, reported that the founders had "not connected themselves with any existing Congregations already organized, for in their homes in Europe they had acquired a broader view of the requirements of their religion than obtained among their brethren here."[26] No evidence is adduced to support his statement. In view of Stern's filiopietistic attitude and the lack of scholarly method which characterizes his and other works of the period, his statement merely reflects what a later generation chose to believe about its esteemed ancestors.

Closer investigation suggests that the founders of Emanu-El were little different from other immigrants at the time of their arrival. They belonged to the element that moved most rapidly toward economic success and social adjustment in America. They were also aggressively involved in identifying and pursuing the new opportunities being created by expansion in commerce and industry. Their entrepreneurial intelligence and energy distinguished them from their contemporaries, whose aspiration in all matters was more modest. The venturesomeness that enabled many of them to rise from peddler to investment banker also affected their religious endeavors.

One of the founders of Emanu-El was James Seligman. He came to America in 1838 and joined his older brother, who was traveling with a pack on his back in rural Pennsylvania. Like all peddlers, the Seligman brothers found it impossible to observe the dietary laws; however, their letters home assured their father that Jewish law was being faithfully observed.[27] As more Seligmans arrived in America, and as their resources grew, the family opened a number of stores, first in Alabama and later in St. Louis, Watertown (New York) and San Francisco. By the time James settled in New

York City to establish a branch of the business there, the family was well launched on the course that eventually led to its phenomenal success.

In the mid-1840's the Seligmans and others like them had not yet achieved a level of financial success or social integration that would gain them acceptance among the established Jewish elite of New York. Shearith Israel and even Bnai Jeshurun undoubtedly regarded such individuals as parvenus and pushy foreign upstarts. At the same time, this aspiring and able group found the existing congregations of German immigrants too petty to provide a proper environment for its rapidly developing sense of self-esteem. The solution was to establish a congregation which, while new and German, would be appropriately high toned. Emanu-El was born out of this need. It rapidly became the gathering place for the emerging German-Jewish elite.

The new congregation had its origin in a "cultus verein" in which—if later reports are accurate—ritual questions were entirely tabooed. A report on the verein in the *Occident* refers to it as the "Mendelssohnian Society," named after the German-Jewish philosopher.[28] In April 1843, after eighteen months of existence, the society numbered thirty-three members and decided to organize itself as a formal congregation called Emanu-El. At its first meeting the amount of $28.25 was subscribed by those assembled. Contributions ranged from the twenty-five cents of Mr. I. Oppenheimer to $2.50, from a Mr. Reutlinger. James Seligman (who was a member of the committee of five empowered to provide needed articles for the synagogue) contributed $1.00.[29] The founders of Emanu-El were men on the move, but in the early days they still had a long way to go in their quest for affluence.

Like most other immigrant congregations, Emanu-El's first meeting place at Grand and Clinton Streets was a rented room. Men sat in the front and women separately in the rear.

capped by the "frequent turnover of ministers, teachers and sextons, each newly arrived functionary a law unto himself about method and curriculum." Despite the difficulties of maintaining traditional practices, "there is not an iota of evidence to suggest that [the members of Congregation Beth El] were originally impelled by a desire to modernize Jewish worship." In 1853 the congregation published a revised set of by-laws which reiterated the requirement that all prayers should be in Hebrew and should follow the "Polish minhag." The most significant evidence of acculturation and rising expectations up to this date was the adoption of the requirement that members of the congregation who wished to be called to the Torah must wear hats rather than caps— a token of the transition from lower-class to middle-class status.[6] As elsewhere, the precursor of the desire for reform was the concern for respectability.

The first congregation in Chicago, established in 1846, was Kehillat Anshei Maarav (Congregation of the Men of the West.) The corrupt spelling of the name in surviving records provides evidence of the low level of Hebrew learning and points to the garbled Yiddish pronunciation of at least some of the founders.[7] Lack of learning did not imply lack of piety, however. The memoirs of one of Chicago's early settlers contain the following report: "The families had all brought with them their old country piety. . . . On holidays it was customary to close all places of business, and in the wholesale as well as in the retail district one could observe notices in the windows and doors of every Jewish business house with the inscription "Closed on Account of Holiday!"[8] In this synagogue "the ritual [Minhag Ashkenaz] was transplanted in its entirety from the old country. . . . The traditional Sabbath was scrupulously kept by the members." In 1851 the congregation outgrew its rented second-story quarters and built its own edifice, oriented so that worshipers

At this stage there is no evidence that such a modification was considered, much less adopted. At most, the use of "temple" in Emanu-El's minutes seems to indicate an attempt to find an appropriate English term for a place of worship. Most congregations continued for many years to refer to Jewish practices and institutions in Hebrew terms, which were written in their minutes either in Hebrew script or in transliteration. In an effort to translate such terms into English, congregations were confronted with the prospect of using words with Christian or at least churchly connotations. The word "temple" avoided this dilemma. It was a non-denominational English word that had the added attraction of being closely related to the German "tempel." It must therefore have seemed an appropriately dignified and elegant reference for the new congregation.

Aside from these relatively modest matters of style, there were few changes in the early conduct of Emanu-El to indicate a deviation from traditional Jewish practices. In keeping with the "aesthetic views of the new congregation," a few German-Jewish hymns were introduced; an attempt was made to temper the raucous behavior that characterized the observance of the carnival festival of Purim; some marginal readings from the prayer service were omitted.[34] The rest remained as it had been.

In 1847 a group of members of Emanu-El proposed the fusion of four German congregations in New York into one large synagogue.[35] The proponents of the scheme argued that there was no need for four separate German congregations in the city. They envisioned a place of worship seating twelve hundred people and a school for eight hundred children. Since the other three congregations involved were firmly traditional, what more convincing evidence could be adduced to demonstrate that at the time of this proposal the ritual changes instituted or envisioned were not yet so drastic as to have created a schism between Emanu-El and other congregations. Given the fact of institutional competitiveness and the growing proliferation of synagogues in the nineteenth century under the American free enterprise system, it is not surprising that the proposal was not accepted. That it was even considered is testimony to the slow pace of initial reform.

Meanwhile, changes in the economic status of Emanu-El and its members were rapid and visible. In the first year of its existence, the synagogue was whitewashed twice.[36] Only two years later the congregation purchased a church on Chrystie Street for $12,000. One member contributed $1000 of this sum; $3630 was raised at the initial meeting.[37] A chandelier for the new edifice was purchased for $175.[38] Shortly thereafter, the salary of the minister was raised to $600 and that of the cantor to $350. In 1854 the congregation again moved uptown, to Twelfth Street. Emanu-El's second building was a church that had been purchased for $30,000 plus an annual ground rent of $500. By this time the Seligmans had begun their banking activities.[39] Other members of the Board of Trustees of Emanu-El were only slightly behind them in expanding their economic horizons and social aspirations.

The reforms that were gradually introduced reflected the changing status of the constituency. As Emanu-El grew increasingly prosperous and respectable, it sought an appropriately elegant edifice and properly decorus service. When the first building was purchased, an organ was installed. The traditional marriage contract continued to be used, but in May 1848 an English translation was appended. In that same year, a hymn book was printed containing German hymns. Two years later the custom of making offerings when called to the reading of the Torah was abolished.[40] Three years thereafter, the practice of calling individuals to the reading of the Torah was eliminated altogether and the reading was done by the officiants. The traditional services with occasional omissions were still conducted in Hebrew, and women were still seated in the gallery, but by then the spontaneity and pious enthusiasm of small-town immigrants had given way to the propriety of comfortable American burghers.

When the congregation moved uptown in 1854, the pace of change accelerated. Family pews were introduced; a revised prayer book was prepared which, though still in Hebrew, abbreviated the traditional service. The pressure for English lectures grew, since the members who were "patriotic in all things . . . desired that the language of the land should be heard in their shrine."[41] In April 1855 the congregation advertised for an assistant minister able to speak English as well as German. Within the next six months the use of the tallis (prayer shawl) and the celebration of the second days of festivals were discontinued.

By this time the reforms instituted were substantial, although they were still piecemeal, haphazard, and primarily concerned with decorum and appearance rather than ideological consistency. Even in the late 1850's Emanu-El was far from the radical changes that later came to characterize Reform Judaism in America. Borrowing the terminology of twentieth-century American Jewish life, Grinstein concludes that "from its formation until 1864, Temple Emanuel of New York may be considered a 'conservative' congregation."[42] Although many of the ritual practices in a congregation identified as conservative in the mid-twentieth century are comparable to those at Emanu-El in the early 1860's, great differences would be found in outlook and in ideology. The conservative movement in American Judaism did not come into existence until after the beginning of the twentieth century and any attempt to identify earlier developments with this movement is subject to numerous qualifications. Nevertheless, it is appropriate to say that the conduct of

Jewish ritual at Temple Emanu-El up to and beyond 1860 closely resembled the normative practices of conservative congregations in the midtwentieth century.

The experience of Emanu-El affords an important insight into the character of the German-Jewish experience in America. Even in this most advanced of congregations, the immigrants were barely concerned with intellectual or theological issues. Their interest in reform was not imported from Germany; it evolved as they became acculturated and as they consolidated their newly acquired affluence. In attempting to retain links with the old ways while rapidly integrating themselves into the new society, they developed a pattern of pragmatic pruning in which the balance between continuity and change was continually readjusted. As their position and their outlook changed, so did their sense of the appropriate form of Jewish expression.

The role of Jewishly educated intellectual leadership in determining the patterns of change was minimal. Most congregations did not have access to qualified leaders in shaping policy. Emanu-El, which had a rabbi, never permitted him to exercise a vigorous leadership role. Control was firmly in the hands of lay leaders who permitted neither traditionalist scruples nor reformist dogmas to impede the process of social adaptation.

Moderate and expedient as the reformism of Emanu-El was, it never exercised a direct influence on the totality of Jewish life, nor did Emanu-El attempt to assert leadership. The congregation convened no conferences, published no brochures, made no effort to disseminate its ideas or practices or to encourage others to follow them. If Emanu-El served as a model at all, it was as an example of success rather than reform. Prior to 1860 only a handful of congregations declared their commitment to reform. In New York City only one other congregation had even begun to consider minor ritual changes.[43] The overwhelming majority proceeded at their own pace and charted their own courses. The ultimate triumph of reform among them was not the result of influences from the outside. It occurred when the members of these congregations experienced the same changes in status which altered the outlook of the members of Emanu-El. The catalysts were Americanization and upward mobility.

7 Emerging Options, 1840–1850

S H O R T L Y after his arrival in America in 1842, Abraham Kohn was wandering the back roads of New Hampshire with a peddler's pack on his back. Among the comments on American life which he recorded in his diary were a number dealing with his perception of religion. He found America to be "like an adolescent youth. . . . Her knowledge of religion, history, and human nature is, in truth, very elementary. . . . American history is composed of Independence and Washington; that is all! On Sunday the American dresses up and goes to church, but he thinks of God no more than does the horse that carries him there."[1]

Whether or not Kohn was accurate in his assessment of the religious climate among the native Americans he encountered, the religious institutions established by immigrants in the 1840's entered a period of vigorous expansion. In 1845 German-Lutheran immigrants organized a new synod, the German Evangelical Synod of Missouri, Ohio, and other States. The synod established a newspaper, colleges, seminaries, and a system of parochial schools. Soon thereafter, two additional synods were formed.[2] The Roman Catholic Church also experienced a period of rapid growth, and by 1850 dioceses had been organized in almost every city of considerable size. In May 1852 the First Plenary Council of the nation's Catholic hierarchy was held at Baltimore. Despite the fact that only nine of the thirty-two bishops in attendance were native born, the Americanization of the Church was unmis-

...y in progress.[3] The constituencies of both groups continued to face problems resulting from their own poverty and marginality, but both demonstrated growing strength and self-confidence. They were establishing themselves in the New World without having to repudiate their old ways.

The general experience of the Jews coincided with that of other immigrant groups, but the details of their adjustment took a somewhat different course. As individuals, Jews advanced socially and economically more rapidly than most other immigrants. The very occupational patterns that had made them economically surplus pariahs in Europe uniquely qualified them to take advantage of the opportunities available in America. Their commercial skills and entrepreneurial initiative were urgently needed in the developing society and often yielded generous rewards. Their mercantile occupations brought them into contact with a cross-section of the American population and speeded the process of acculturation. Their relatively small numbers and their dispersal throughout the country in search of economic opportunity fostered integration into the general society. For the most part, they speedily overcame both the poverty and the sense of alienation which characterized the early immigrant experience in America. Initial hardship and depression gave way to comfort and confidence.

At the same time, Jews were lagging behind other immigrant communities in the development of group life. When it came to institutional consolidation, the Jews were uniquely handicapped. Many of the reasons have been discussed: the absence of a transferable communal framework, the lack of authority, the paucity of religious or intellectual leadership, the difficulty of maintaining the traditional Jewish regimen in a non-Jewish environment. In addition, the factors that made for individual success compounded the problems of communal development: rapid acculturation, small numbers, and dispersal. During the era when immigrant Lutherans were successfully organizing synods, parochial schools, colleges, and seminaries, American Jewry were just beginning to consider the institutional requirements of group survival in America. While Catholics were consolidating their religious structure on local and national levels, Jews were spawning a chaos of small, autonomous, and frequently competing congregations and organizations which betokened much energy but little cohesion. The impulse to maintain the continuity of the tradition was strong; the means of effecting the transplantation were inadequate.

The decade between 1840 and 1850 saw initial congregations organized in Boston (1842), Buffalo (1847), Chicago (1846), Cleveland (1841), Detroit (1850), Hartford (1847), Memphis (1850), Mobile (1844), Montgomery (1847), Newark (1848), Norfolk (1846), Pittsburgh (1848), Rochester (1845), Syracuse (1846), Wheeling (1849), and Wilkes Barre (1845), as well as in numerous smaller towns such as Columbia (South Carolina), Danville (Pennsylvania), Augusta (Georgia), Vicksburg (Mississippi), Donaldsville (Louisiana), and Lafayette and Fort Wayne in Indiana.[4] Without exception the new congregations repeated the experiences of the synagogues founded in the previous decade as they attempted to recreate the religious practices of the small European towns that had been left behind.

A few examples illustrate the general experience. Congregation Beth El of Buffalo, established in 1847, was concerned about the provision of kosher meat and a cemetery. Its first functionary was a shochet and mohel who was "in and out of office many times." As was the case everywhere "the scarcity of Jewish scholars in America . . . militated against any serious pursuit of learning among them."[5] Although an attempt was made to provide Hebrew education for the young, and a day school was inaugurated, efforts were handi-

and dispersal. During the era when immigrant Lutherans were successfully organizing synods, parochial schools, colleges, and seminaries, American Jewry were just beginning to consider the institutional requirements of group survival in America. While Catholics were consolidating their religious structure on local and national levels, Jews were spawning a chaos of small, autonomous, and frequently competing congregations and organizations which betokened much energy but little cohesion. The impulse to maintain the continuity of the tradition was strong; the means of effecting the transplantation were inadequate.

The decade between 1840 and 1850 saw initial congregations organized in Boston (1842), Buffalo (1847), Chicago (1846), Cleveland (1841), Detroit (1850), Hartford (1847), Memphis (1850), Mobile (1844), Montgomery (1847), Newark (1848), Norfolk (1846), Pittsburgh (1848), Rochester (1845), Syracuse (1846), Wheeling (1849), and Wilkes Barre (1845), as well as in numerous smaller towns such as Columbia (South Carolina), Danville (Pennsylvania), Augusta (Georgia), Vicksburg (Mississippi), Donaldsville (Louisiana), and Lafayette and Fort Wayne in Indiana.[4] Without exception the new congregations repeated the experiences of the synagogues founded in the previous decade as they attempted to recreate the religious practices of the small European towns that had been left behind.

A few examples illustrate the general experience. Congregation Beth El of Buffalo, established in 1847, was concerned about the provision of kosher meat and a cemetery. Its first functionary was a shochet and mohel who was "in and out of office many times." As was the case everywhere "the scarcity of Jewish scholars in America . . . militated against any serious pursuit of learning among them."[5] Although an attempt was made to provide Hebrew education for the young, and a day school was inaugurated, efforts were handi-

faced to the east and including a gallery for women.[9] In 1853 a day school was established "where Hebrew was taught in addition to the common English branches."[10] That same year, Abraham Kohn, erstwhile peddler in the farm country of New England and now a successful merchant, became the president of the congregation. (It was said that he had made the move to Chicago because the Millerite millennial movement in 1843 caused his New England customers to stop buying supplies in anticipation of the end of the world.)"[11]

The experiences of Beth El in Buffalo and Kehillat Anshei Maarav of Chicago are, with minor variations, typical of all the first congregations established in new communities during this period. In Detroit a day school was established in 1850, the first year of Congregation Beth El's existence. German as well as Hebrew and English was included in its proposed curriculum.[12] In Rochester a similar day school was founded only after Congregation Berith Kodesh obtained a building in 1856.[13] Without guidance or direction, the same general pattern of organization and practice emerged wherever Jewish immigrants settled.

At the same time that initial synagogues were being established in newer areas of settlement, the number of congregations was increasing in older, larger communities. Between 1840 and 1850, nine new congregations were formally organized in New York, in addition to the six already in existence. In Philadelphia the number grew from two to five. Albany, Baltimore, Cincinnati, New Orleans, and St. Louis, each having had one, soon had three. In the 1850's the pace of proliferation accelerated in the wake of continued immigration, and every large city soon contained two or more congregations.

The precise reasons for the organization of new congregations usually remain obscure, since the documentary sources are meager and totally devoid of analytic discussion. The conflicts that led to secessions frequently focused on the rite that was to be followed. Immigrants placed great stress on recreating local traditions brought over from Europe. If the initial congregation followed the Minhag Ashkenaz (German rite), the seceders organized a congregation that followed the Minhag Polin,[14] and vice versa.[15]

A typical experience is described in an account written in 1889 by Solomon Schindler, the (reform) rabbi of Temple Adath Israel in Boston, describing the secession of that congregation from Boston's first synagogue, Ohabei Shalom, in 1854.

> The first settlers had come from all parts of the old country; some, as we have seen, from Bavaria, others from the eastern provinces of Prussia, others from Poland, and others again from Holland. They all had brought with them a strong love for the religious customs which prevailed in the lands of their nativity. . . . Every one of them desired, therefore, to have such a mode of worship established in the synagogue as would remind him of his own youth. Differences of opinion arose, and after the animosity had kept on growing for a few years, the storm finally broke loose when the congregation was about to engage a new minister. It is a pity that authentic records concerning this quarrel cannot be found and that all information had to be collected from the testimony of partisans who would not yield an iota of their right. The testimony collected is so contradictory that a jury would not admit it as evidence; still so much can be gleaned from it that those who called themselves Germans, because they hailed from the southern part of Germany, rose in opposition to those members whom they called Polanders because they had hailed either from Poland or from the eastern provinces of Germany. The German

faction was led by the president and officers of the congregation; still they were in the minority. The Polanders, forming the majority of the congregation, were marshalled by ambitious men out of their own midst. The Germans favored a minister who had come from the same part of the country from which they had come; the Polanders' choice was a man of their own nationality. The dissension grew hotter and hotter until the minority bolted. Leaving to the majority all the property which they had acquired, inclusive of the burial ground, they took with them nothing but the little account-book and the Shofar which happened to be in the possession of their president, and formed a new congregation. . . . Services were still kept in all these congregations in the old orthodox style.[16]

Another common source of friction, frequently linked to the quarrel over the rite, was the tension between newly arrived immigrants and their predecessors who were already somewhat acculturated. For example, Bnai Israel, the first congregation in Cincinnati, followed the Polish minhag. When a second congregation was organized in Cincinnati in 1840, the reason stated was that "the mode of worship in the established synagogue of our beloved brethren, K. K. B. Israel [Kahal Kadosh Bnai Israel] in this city is not in accordance with the rites and customs of the German Jews."[17] The credibility of this assertion is undermined by the fact that in its earliest meetings the new congregation, Bnai Jeshurun, also followed the Polish minhag. The more probable reason for the schism lies in the fact that the older congregation was known as the "English Congregation" both because its founders had included some "English" Jews and because its members (or at least its leaders) were sufficiently acculturated to be able to use the English language. As late as 1853, when Isaac M. Wise first visited Cincinnati, he described Bnai Israel as "English and very aristocratic." Thirteen years before, the newer German-speaking immigrants had undoubtedly been intimidated by the snobbery typical of early settlers toward those who arrived later.[18] The response of new immigrants in Cincinnati and elsewhere was to organize a congregation of their own. Although the social and linguistic distinctions ultimately disappeared, the institutions that had been created because of them survived.

When the noted German reformer Rabbi David Einhorn arrived in America in 1855, he concluded that the institutional fragmentation he found in the New World resulted from more trivial motivations. The multiplicity of congregations existed, he wrote, because "somebody wants to become a president, another wishes to be a treasurer and a third desires to play the role of a chazan."[19] To a doctrinaire intellectual like Einhorn, the relatively minor differences in ritual and in accent among the various congregations appeared to be of no consequence. He saw petty personal ambition as the only reason for the proliferation of institutions which tended to reproduce the same essential patterns in an ever-increasing number of settings. Whether or not Einhorn's judgment is valid, it is clear that the growth in the number of congregations was rapid and the modification of patterns or practices was gradual.

Some needs of the expanding Jewish population were not fulfilled by the establishment of new synagogues. No individual congregation could provide the educational materials and social services that were lacking, yet the development of cooperative arrangements among congregations seemed to be impossible. Ironically, the growth in Jewish population which increased the need for coordination intensified the difficulty of effecting collaboration. Only the specter of anti-Semitism raised by the Damascus Blood Accusation moved

American Jewry to consider joint action.[20] When the anxiety subsided, the interest in cooperation waned. Isaac Leeser's 1841 proposal for a "union of all Israelites residing in America" had included detailed suggestions for an "ecclesiastical authority," schools, and a union of congregations.[21] Without the pressure of impending calamity, there was little incentive to act on this proposal.

In the absence of unity, some other means had to be found to transcend the handicaps imposed by institutional fragmentation. In the mid-1840's the growing urgency of unmet needs and the increasing sophistication of the acculturated among the immigrants led to a number of experiments in supracongregational action which opened new options for communal development.

One of these was the formation in 1844 of a German Hebrew Benevolent Society in New York which drew leadership from across congregational lines and assisted impoverished German-Jewish immigrants without regard to their synagogue affiliation.[22] A similar organization called The Hebrew Benevolent Society had been formed in the 1820's by the Ashkenazim who seceded from Bnai Jeshurun.[23] Although in theory a communal organization, this society had remained the virtual monopoly of the congregation.[24] By the 1840's the resources of the group no longer sufficed to cope with the growing needs of newcomers for assistance. Moreover, the old society was controlled by individuals who were so Americanized that they were viewed as unresponsive by the newer immigrants, who were prospective beneficiaries, as well as by those who were prospective donors. A need was felt for a charitable organization that would be more sensitive to the particular problems and aspirations of the recent arrivals.

As the newer immigrants progressed in their own acculturation, the distinction between the two "benevolent societies" became less significant, and by 1849 they united their fund-raising efforts in an anniversary fund-raising dinner. A complete union of the two organizations was not achieved until after the panic of 1857 had created a fiscal crisis that forced a reevaluation of the charitable activities of New York Jewry. By that time, differences of language and status among the leaders of the two groups had faded, and the two societies were fully merged in 1859.[25]

The development of a major, autonomous, philanthropic agency did not eliminate all other charitable associations within or outside of synagogues. The Lyons-DeSola directory of 1854 listed forty-four Jewish organizations in New York, including a Bachelors' Hebrew Benevolent Loan Association, a Young Men's Hebrew Benevolent Association (for the distribution of fuel during the winter), a North American Relief Society (for the indigent Jews in Palestine), and one group (attached to Congregation Rodeph Shalom) with the intriguing name Hebra Ahavat Nashim (society for the love of women).[26]

By 1859 the number may have been even larger. The merger of the Hebrew Benevolent Society and the German Hebrew Benevolent Society had demonstrated the possibility of creating a voluntary charitable organization outside the synagogue with a wide base of communal support and responsibility for a broad spectrum of social needs. The model was followed in other cities and became the basis for the growing philanthropic enterprise of American Jewry in subsequent decades. Next to anti-Semitism, charity was the concern most likely to elicit a cooperative response.

As might be expected, collaboration in cultural and educational matters was more difficult to achieve. In 1845 Isaac Leeser attempted to contend with the problem of cultural poverty by initiating the establishment of an American Jewish Publication Society, which would make it possible "to obtain a knowledge of the faith and to defend it against the assaults of proselytemakers on the one side and of infidels on the other."[27] Leeser waged a single-handed effort to provide material on Jewish subjects in English. In his journal he reprinted literary and historical essays. In 1845 he published an edition of the Pentateuch with an English translation printed parallel to the Hebrew text.[28] He recognized, however, that his individual endeavors could not meet the growing need for books, especially for use in Jewish schools. Since no existing agency was able to deal with the problem, he formed a voluntary association of individuals which he hoped would "place a mass of good reading within the reach of even the poorest family."[29]

During the six years of its activity, the Society was never able to attract adequate fiscal or intellectual support. It did succeed in publishing a series of books under the general title of "The Jewish Miscellany." In addition to volumes such as *The Jews and Their Religion* and *The Spirit of Judaism*, the series included historical fiction, most of which was reprinted from works previously published in England. In 1851 a fire destroyed the plates and books of the Society and ended its brief existence.

Although the actual content of the material produced was of limited significance, this experiment in responsible voluntarism served as a useful prototype for future developments. The voluntary society made it possible to undertake tasks that no individual synagogue or local congregation would or could consider. It provided a means for engaging complex problems that transcended the scope of the existing institutional framework. Leeser's initiative suggested a practical way of circumventing the handicaps of disunity. Thus even in failure the first Jewish Publication Society showed the potential utility of an alternate form of social organization.

In 1843 a group of Americanized immigrants in New

York had initiated a venture of another kind which was new to the Jewish institutional pattern. They founded an independent secular Jewish fraternal order outside any synagogue and unrelated to the preexisting model of communal or congregational committees. They named the new organization Bne B'rīth (Sons of the Covenant; hereinafter the contemporary spelling "Bnai Brith" will be used.).[30] In some respects their innovation represented a more radical break with the past than any of the changes introduced in the synagogues by the so-called reformers.

The new organization was consciously modeled after fraternal orders which the immigrants encountered in America. Secret rites, special regalia, passwords, and mottoes were part of its prescribed practice. At the same time, it remained Jewish. Its very name, "Bnai Brith," is a synonym for "Jews." Moreover, the terminology its founders used in their ritual was related to Jewish history and folklore; their emphasis on mutual aid was a carryover from the traditional Jewish communal pattern; their program included efforts to encourage the dissemination of Jewish culture.[31] The establishment of Bnai Brith created a new mode of Jewish identification in the American setting. It was a secular organization, yet it had Jewish religious overtones. It remained a membership organization responsible only to its own constituency; yet it soon began to assume obligations involving the welfare of the broader Jewish community. Bnai Brith was an American response to the vacuum created by the absence of an organized communal framework and the chaos of synagogue autonomy.

The initiative for the establishment of this new instrumentality came from German immigrants who were on the road to acculturation and who were prominent in the post-1820 immigrant community. The prime mover was Henry Jones, a long-time leader of Anshe Chesed Congregation, established in New York in 1828. Some of the founders were also involved in the establishment of Emanu-El. Although German was the language of early meetings and records, the organizers of Bnai Brith had already overcome the initial adjustment to America and were well acquainted with the problems that faced the newcomers. The response of the immigrant multitudes was spectacular. By 1851 Bnai Brith had 700 members in New York City alone. Five years later the membership passed 1000. In 1850 the first English-speaking lodge had been established in Cincinnati. The transition to English proceeded rapidly thereafter.

Their aims, as stated in the preamble to their constitution, were grandiose:

> Bnai Brith has taken upon itself the mission of uniting Israelites in the work of promoting their highest interests and those of humanity; of developing the mental and moral character of the people of our faith; of inculcating the purest principles of philanthropy, honor and patriotism; of supporting science and art; alleviating the wants of the poor and needy; visiting and attending the sick; coming to the rescue of victims of persecution; providing for, protecting and assisting the widow and the orphan on the broadest principles of humanity.[32]

The aspiration exceeded the fulfillment; in the course of the following decades, however, Bnai Brith did undertake projects that treated many of the concerns alluded to in this statement.

In part the incentive for the organization of Bnai Brith seems to have come from difficulty experienced by some Jews in gaining admission to Odd Fellows Lodges "on account of their religion."[33] The rapid growth of the organization was, however, due to the function it served in providing for its members a degree of security, psychological as well as fiscal. During these years of rapid urban growth in America, governmental programs to alleviate socioeconomic deprivation were virtually nonexistent. The Hebrew Benevolent Society had been designed to assist only the destitute, and its resources were often inadequate even for these. Moreover, the prospect of having to ask for charity was appalling to the average immigrant. Synagogues were too small and unstable and too preoccupied with their institutional requirements to provide reliable assistance through their mutual aid committees. An increasing number of immigrants were affiliated with congregations only sporadically; many were not affiliated at all. As a result, the fraternal order, with its broad appeal across congregational lines, its large membership, and its concentration on mutual aid and fellowship was able to fulfill an urgent need. In the increasingly large and impersonal urban setting, it restored some elements of reassurance comparable to those once provided by the extended family and village community.

In an age when death or even illness in a family could mean disaster, the importance of the role of such an organization cannot be exaggerated. Lodges maintained sick-benefit funds for members and funds for widows and orphans. The payment of dues and modest fees provided a form of insurance through which a member's widow received $30 toward the cost of her husband's funeral and thereafter $1 a week for herself, 50 cents a week for the first child, and 25 cents a week for each subsequent child. Aid to children continued until they reached the age of thirteen. The society insisted that children up to that age be sent to school. On the death of a member's wife, a benefit payment of $15 toward funeral expenses was made. In the words of Bien, "the Order was a promoter of material welfare providing a system of material aid in case of sickness or misfortune."[34]

Lodge membership also conferred a sense of community

on families seeking roots in an alien environment. Special committees visited the ailing; funerals were attended en masse. In addition, the lodge provided a psychological shelter for hard-working immigrants whose self-respect was constantly assaulted by the harsh reality of their everyday life. As Grinstein observed:

> The very meetings with their secret passwords, inner and outer guards, regalia, rosettes, initiations and ceremonies of various kinds, made the German Jews eager for admittance. The immigrant might peddle his way through life or toil with his hands, or engage in retail trade; once a week, however, he forgot that he was a stranger in a land he did not understand and that did not understand him. He went weekly to the place of his lodge meeting where he was ranked according to his degree; once there, once he donned his regalia, he was of the inner circle.[35]

Secrecy and ritual, Bien observed, "proved to be a great attraction to uncultured minds." In time, affluence and acculturation diminished the appeal of such practices, and Bnai Brith shifted its emphasis to more sophisticated cultural, political, and philanthropic activities; by 1890 the regalia, secrecy, and benefits had been abandoned. But in the 1840's and '50's the appeal of its fundamental programs made Bnai Brith the first national Jewish organization with branches in all of the major American cities. By 1860 three similar orders had been established, and the existence of a Jewish institutional option unrelated to the synagogue was an established fact.[36]

One of the objectives of the founders of Bnai Brith was cultural improvement. Although this endeavor never became a central part of the program of the Order, it was on the agenda of the leadership. In an 1852 address to Zion Lodge. No. 2 of New York, Henry Jones "confessed frankly" that "the founders of the Order saw very well the demoralized condition and the low intellectual status of the Jews. . . . The founders knew that the heart of the Jew was sound, that his faults arose from want of education and instruction." Jones continued by praising the establishment of the lodge, which was "composed of brethren who knew how to speak the German language correctly. . . . You do not appreciate sufficiently," he added, "the gain afforded by the thorough knowledge of the height and depth of a language."[37] He concluded with an exhortation to his audience "who are able to speak well to warn, teach, inspire . . . [and] instruct the inexperienced."[38] Jones's appeal was not for the preservation of German—it was for the spread of literacy.

Jones's remarks provide telling evidence of the limited educational background of the masses of German-Jewish immigrants in the midnineteenth century. They also reflect the growing determination of the leadership element to raise the cultural level of American Jewry. Shortly before Jones delivered his address, several Bnai Brith lodges in New York had organized the Maimonides Library Association. By 1855 this association is said to have had one hundred and fifty members and a collection of eight hundred volumes. It also sponsored weekly lectures in German and English and occasional musical programs.[39] The contribution of Bnai Brith to the intellectual development of American Jewry remained modest, but the involvement of a fraternal order in such activities indicates both the special needs of the Jewish immigrant community and the quasi-religious character of this secular organization.

The development in the 1840's of charitable educational and fraternal organizations outside the framework of the synagogue signified an attempt by immigrant Jewry to reconstitute a viable mechanism for continuity in the American setting. A pattern took shape without any clearly preconceived plan or long-range objectives. Like much of America's social and political development, the Jewish pattern evolved as a result of pragmatic responses to new problems that were deeply felt but not clearly understood. The unintended result was a transformation of Jewish identity. As the means for identifying as a Jew were enlarged and as the options for dealing with communal concerns were broadened, the distinction between religious and secular in American Jewish life became increasingly blurred. The European unified communal structure, which had been shattered by the traumas of modernization and transplantation, could never be replicated in the United States. In its place a far more complex and diversified entity began to emerge.

8 Prosperity and Provincialism, 1845–1854

New societies and congregations were formed amongst them and their moral progress would have been equal to their material, had not a spirit of jealousy and intolerance begotten of provincial antipathies and prejudices prevented union and cooperation.

THUS did Julius Bien (himself an immigrant), who served for thirty-five years as international president of Bnai Brith, describe the state of American Jewry in the late 1840's.

Bien's contrast between material progress and moral backwardness is a persistent theme in the discourse of this period. Moral is not meant to impute debauchery or dishonesty to the immigrants; it refers to assertiveness and lack of polish—in Bien's terms, jealousy, intolerance, and provincialism. The implied individualism might be an asset in the struggle for initial success in the world of business, but it was a social embarrassment to those who had acquired a degree of respectability. It was also an obstacle to the creation of stable and decorous institutions. In 1844 Leo Merzbacher, denouncing "selfishness, passion and partisanship" in congregations, recommended the "establishment of societies of the betters—those infused with a higher moral instinct."[1] Merzbacher, whose target was manners, not morals, had not been in America long enough to recognize that the selfish, passionate, and partisan of one decade were the "betters" of the next.

The continuing influx of new immigrants contributed to the rough-and-tumble character of the German-Jewish community for some time. Quarrels on synagogue boards and in committees were common.[2] Occasionally, vigorous disputes ended in physical violence. In one notorious incident none other than Isaac M. Wise was assaulted on the pulpit on the morning of Rosh Hashanah. In the ensuing brawl the sheriff and his posse had to be called.[3] The practice of civility and experience with democratic procedures were felt to be sorely lacking by the "betters," who were increasingly impatient with the unruliness of their fellow countrymen.

Before long it became clear that the chaotic, self-governing congregation was to be a training school in propriety. As early as 1840 a long-established congregation like Rodeph Shalom of Philadelphia had instituted a schedule of fines for members "who will not behalf [*sic*] orderly."[4] As the decade progressed, the demand for decorum became a universal and recurrent theme. By 1848 Bnai Jeshurun of Cincinnati (founded in 1840) had passed an extensive proposal "to prevent disorder" in the service. Among the abuses prohibited was "the loud kissing of tzitzit [fringes on the prayer shawl]." It was also decreed that only the president might call for order, and he was constrained to do so "in a quiet fashion."[5] (Apparently one source of disorder was the cacophony of loud calls for order.) Knesseth Israel of Philadelphia (founded in 1847) was even more rigorous. In 1852 it passed a series of regulations requiring "orderly dress." No one was to be admitted who was not wearing a "hat" (a regulation directed against those wearing caps and other types of head coverings regarded as undignified. Worship with an uncovered head would have been unthinkable). In addition, members were to enter the synagogue "with decency and without noise" and to proceed without delay to their seats. Other behavior subject to fines included "walking around," standing together, conversation with neighbors, jokes, or "making fun."[6] (Philadelphia was never a city to tolerate levity). The promulgation of such regulations is evidence that the proscribed behavior existed. It also suggests a growing determination to eliminate conduct that was seen as a vestige of foreign, lower class, and uncultivated origins.

The quest for "moral" uplift was reinforced by the arrival in the late 1840's of a number of immigrants with scholarly training and leadership experience. One of these was Max Lilienthal, a native of Bavaria and the first rabbi with unquestioned credentials and prior reputation to settle in America.[7]

For unknown reasons Lilienthal, who held both a rabbinic and a university degree,[8] never officiated as a rabbi in Bavaria. He did, however, publish accounts of his scholarly research in the *Allgemeine Zeitung des Judentums*, at that time the only Jewish journal in Germany. In 1839 Lilienthal, then twenty-three years old, had been appointed director of a new Jewish school being established in Riga with the ostensible cooperation of the Russian government. For the next six years he devoted himself to the task of creating a modern Jewish educational system in Russia. The project ended in disaster when the Russian government intensified its repressive policy against Jews and it became apparent that the government intended to use the schools to promote conversionist efforts.[9] In 1845 he left Russia dismayed and disgraced.

By this time several members of his family had already emigrated to America. Lilienthal joined them, arriving in November 1845. The appearance in the New World of so well-known a figure created a stir. A week after his arrival, when he was invited to speak before the Anshe Chesed Congregation in New York, the notice in the daily press announced: "Dr Lilienthal, the chief rabbi of Russia will give a lecture in the Synagog Anshe Chesed next Saturday.'"[10] On the following Sabbath, Lilienthal spoke before two other German congregations, Shaarey Hashamayim and Rodeph Shalom. Unlike Rice and Merzbacher before him, he received a warm welcome. In part this response may be attributed to Lilienthal's superior qualifications. It was also due to the rising aspirations and capacities of the immigrant group.

Lilienthal's presence inspired a promising experiment in interinstitutional cooperation. Within a few weeks the three German congregations that had invited him to speak joined in electing him their rabbi. In a letter announcing this fact he signed himself "chief rabbi." This endeavor, evidence of growing sophistication and social maturity, provided a promising model for overcoming some of the problems of institutional fragmentation in American Jewish life.

In the first flush of enthusiasm, consideration was given to inviting even Bnai Jeshurun to join the Union;[11] Emanu-El, impressed (or threatened) by the venture, submitted its own proposal to unite the four German congregations.[12] The enthusiasm was short-lived: for reasons not entirely clear the experiment came to an end after two years. In February 1848, after a quarrel with Lilienthal over a relatively trivial matter, the Board of Anshe Chesed declared "a vacancy of the office of raby [*sic*],"[13] signifying its withdrawal from the Union. The enterprise that began with a bang ended with hardly a whimper.

The minutes of the Union from December 1845 to March 1846 survive.[14] These minutes, together with reports in the press and references in congregational minutes, offer some insight into the details of the experiment as well as the state of the community as a whole. The sources reveal that in his early years in America, Lilienthal was opposed to religious reform. In his inaugural sermon he expressed his disapproval of the innovations introduced by the reform rabbis in Germany. He affirmed his intention to promote "decorum," but committed himself to preserving traditional practices.[15]

The proceedings of the Union show that in his initial endeavors Lilienthal wholeheartedly adhered to this commitment. His first act was to organize a "Chevrah Shas" (Circle for the study of Talmud).[16] In addition to preaching and overseeing children's education, he supervised the kashrut (ritual fitness) of meat as well as the qualifications of the Shochtim (ritual slaughterers); he resolved sh'elot (ritual questions) for members of the three congregations according to the traditional Codes of Jewish law and also answered "questions [Fragen] which related to Jewish life."[17] More remarkable, he was responsible for the reintroduction of the ceremony of halitza, in which a deceased man's widow released his brother from the Biblical obligation to marry her. Lilienthal wrote the appropriate documents and arranged for the purchase of a shoe to be used in the ceremony.[18] The only change in liturgy which Lilienthal proposed was the elimination of the prayer for monarchs (hanoten teshua) and the substitution of a modified prayer, more suitable to American political circumstances. There is no indication in the sources of the period that there was ever any controversy between Lilienthal and his congregations over issues of doctrine or ritual practice.

During his brief tenure as "chief rabbi," Lilienthal further undertook to strengthen both unity and tradition. In April 1847 he organized a Beth Din—a Rabbinic Court to render "beneficial service to the Jewish congregations of America."[19] In deference to the autonomy of American congregations, Lilienthal stipulated that the Beth Din would not assume any "hierarchical authority" but would act "only in an advisory capacity." To serve with him as members of the Court, Lilienthal invited Isaac M. Wise, who had arrived in America a few months earlier; Dr. Hermann Felsenheld, who was a teacher at the Union School; and a Mr. Kohlmeyer, who had been a rabbinical student. At its first meeting the Beth Din declared itself interested not only in rendering decisions according to Jewish law, but also in preparing text books and prayer books to improve Jewish education and Jewish worship. A second meeting never took place.[20] The American Jewish setting was too anarchic to support even a modest experiment with authority.

A source of constant conflict was the dominance of laymen and their unwillingness to relinquish or even share their control of the affairs of religious institutions. In the absence of recognized rabbinic leadership, the board of each congregation had come to act autonomously. The individualism and assertiveness of these immigrants was reinforced by the prevalent American attitude that deprecated expertise of all kinds. When a man of Lilienthal's stature arrived, he was granted the exalted title of "Sein Hochwurden Herr Rabbiner" (literally, His Reverend Sir Rabbi). However, laymen continued to exercise close supervision over his activities.

Despite his well-known record and prior reputation, Lilienthal was required to produce proof of his rabbinic ordination.[21] He was forbidden to lecture outside the synagogues of the Union, visit a school, certify a shochet, or even answer a sh'elah without the approval of Union officials. Festive occasions, such as Lilienthal's installation, were determined by the board down to the minutest detail.[22] Even the seat that Lilienthal was to occupy in each of the three congregations was specified. Subsequently an act as simple as ordering a book of liturgical music by Vienna's famed Cantor-composer Solomon Sulzer led to "a bitter war of words." In the view of the officers and trustees, the "Hochwurden Herr Rabbiner" was expected to serve, not lead.

No doubt Lilienthal found these constraints increasingly

abrasive. The incident that led to the dissolution of the Union reveals that by late 1847 the relationship between Lilienthal and at least one congregation had become one of mutual hostility. According to the account in the minutes of Anshe Chesed, a member of the congregation had sought men for a minyan (quorum for a prayer service) to bensh (bless) a sick child. He found Lilienthal and others at a meeting. Lilienthal objected to "the breaking up of the meeting for this purpose, observing that there were yehudim enough in the neighborhood." In spite of the fact that the requisite men were found and the minyan was held, charges against Lilienthal were brought to the board. Lilienthal refused to defend himself and left a board meeting in anger. He was subsequently "declared guilty by a majority of the board" and was suspended for three weeks from his services to this congregation . . . for reason of the charge brought against him by Mr. Nordlinger as also for . . . insults given to the Board of Trustees."[23] Subsequent attempts to bring about a reconciliation served only to reveal the extent of Lilienthal's grievances and the firmness of the Board's determination to protect its honor. The union of congregations that began as an example of growing responsibility and sophistication disintegrated in a demonstration of lingering pettiness and immaturity.

In the course of his brief tenure Lilienthal apparently drew some conclusions about the feasibility of institution-building within the free enterprise system. He proceeded to establish a private Jewish day school, which he operated for a number of years with considerable success. This Hebrew Union School became known as the best institution of its kind in America and drew students from many cities outside New York. The man who had undertaken the task of achieving unity now chose the alternative of going into business for himself.

A year after Lilienthal settled in America, a second rabbi arrived who was to assume a significant leadership role. He was Isaac Mayer Wise, a native of the village of Steingrub on the Bohemian-Saxon-Bavarian frontier, "being one mile distant from the Saxon and three miles from the Bavarian line."[24] It is difficult to confirm the details of Wise's early years, since we have only his own account, marked by exaggerations, inaccuracies, and anachronisms.[25] Wise's explanation of his family name as a translation of the Hebrew title chacham, which had been bestowed upon his grandfather, is implausible.[26] His claims to have studied with various European rabbinic authorities and to have been present as a visitor at the rabbinic conference in Frankfurt in 1845 are unsubstantiated. Even the exact date of his ordination was never specified by him; and his claim to possess a university degree is apparently without basis in fact. In 1854, when Isaac Leeser was engaged in a quarrel with Wise, he challenged him to produce "the diploma which constitutes Dr. Wise a doctor of divinity."[27] Wise never responded to the challenge.

A liberal but critical review of the available material enables us to determine the basic features of his background. Wise was born in 1819, son of a melamed (village school teacher). He had a traditional Jewish education, supplemented by some formal secular education and by a good deal of informally acquired general knowledge. He grew up in a small town and received training in one or more of the Yeshivot (Talmudic academies) in Bohemia. As a young man he was caught up in the turmoil that resulted when the Austrian government insisted that no one could be ordained rabbi who did not have a university degree. Wise proceeded to learn to read and speak "in pure German, instead of the *Juedisch-Deutsch* that had been his vehicle of expression until then."[28] He also acquired the equivalent of a gymnasium education—largely by self-study—and may have studied at the universities of Prague and Vienna. For a period of three years he served as rabbi in the provincial town of Radnitz. According to his account, he experienced difficulties with both secular and rabbinic authorities and in 1846 emigrated to America.[29]

Lacking both reputation and credentials, Wise did not find a ready acceptance of his rabbinic talents awaiting him. In fact, the early advice he received from acquaintances whom he consulted here was "either to peddle or to learn a trade."[30] Shortly after his arrival, Isaac Leeser described him as a "young schoolmaster who also preaches and is said to possess some Hebrew learning."[31] Yet Wise's attributes compensated for his initial handicaps: he was energetic, ambitious, and ideologically flexible; he was also an effective orator and organizer. In contrast to his comparatively passive predecessors, he was aggressive and seemed to thrive on controversy. In view of his lack of standing in Europe, he had no inhibitions in repudiating dependence on old-world leadership. He found the American environment entirely congenial and emerged as the champion of American Judaism.

Wise's writings are so full of contradictions that it is difficult to discover the truth about his early attitudes and actions. Late in his life, in 1895, he wrote that he had arrived in New York "with a finished plan of action ready for immediate execution. It was mapped out on paper ready to be submitted to the masters in Israel."[32] Earlier accounts provide no evidence to support this claim. Neither his experience in Europe nor his early work in America revealed a substantive commitment to the principle of reform, much less "a finished plan."

The *Reminiscences* that Wise chronicled in 1875 (which also project his later reformist commitments back to an earlier period) present a different picture of his attitude at the time of his arrival. Concerning his first holiday in America, he wrote: "the old Rosh Hashanah melodies, which appealed none the less strongly to me, brought back the sounds I had learned to love in my youth." His trial sermon, delivered in Albany a few months later, was of the old-fashioned genre which evoked "sobbing" in the [women's] gallery . . . so audible that I felt compelled to stop."[33] His earliest quarrels with his congregation were waged not over his deviations from tradition but rather over his insistence that his congregants close their stores on the Sabbath.[34] If at that time Wise harbored radical ideas, they did not reveal themselves in his deeds or his public utterances.

In the period following his arrival in America, he appeared to be a modern traditionalist whose approach was similar to that of Lilienthal and Leeser. Like them, he was interested in secular culture and in the "scientific" study of Judaism. He was also committed to fostering decorum and dignity in Jewish worship but not to any radical changes in ideology or practice. In 1847, when Leeser visited Albany "to make the acquaintance of Dr. Wise," Leeser reported that he "was gratified to hear the desirable progress of our brothers there both in prosperity and in religious improvement." Leeser praised Wise as the "eloquent preacher at the head of this kahal [congregation]" whose efforts had produced a gratifying contrast to the formerly reported state of indifference." Wise himself boasted that "the Sabbath was observed as strictly in the Bethel Congregation in Albany as in Wilna and Brody [in Lithuania]." When Wise wrote to Leeser in December 1849, he addressed him as "my best friend in this world of flattery and falsehood."[35]

One of Wise's first endeavors in Albany was the establishment of a day school in which secular and religious subjects were taught in English and Hebrew. Instruction in German was notably absent. A news item in the *Occident*, Spring 1847, reports on progress demonstrated by the pupils at a public examination. After showing their proficiency in spelling, reading, arithmetic, and geography, the students were examined by Wise "in reading the Prayer Book and Pentateuch." The account concludes with a comment by Leeser giving "much praise . . . to the Rabbi for his labours in teaching the scholars the true way of becoming what they ought to be."

Within the congregation, Wise introduced a few modest changes having to do with music and decorum. A letter from Albany to the *Occident* in February 1847 (p. 600) addresses that journal as the organ of "useful reform and religious enlightenment" and reports improvements in the music at Beth El. The letter expresses the hope for a "better mode of public worship" which will "lead our brothers in the land . . . in the paths of righteousness and strengthen them in the observance of his commandments." A year later Leeser, reporting on the achievements of the school in Albany, commented (p. 417): "This by the by, is the right way of *reforming*. . . . We also learn that the choir of the Synagogue Beth El is progressing fast to a degree of perfection and the service is conducted as it should be, on the old Jewish platform, nevertheless with solemnity and edification." According to Wise's own testimony, the only issue that created conflict during his early years dealt with the length of his contract—hardly an ideological concern.[36]

When Wise wrote his *Reminiscences* in the 1870's, he alleged that he had desired to introduce reforms in the late 1840's but had been discouraged by lack of support. He describes his 1848 behavior as follows:

> I became at once exceedingly amiable, obliging, tractable, polite, careless and sociable. The people came in great multitudes to the synagogue on the following Fall holidays to hear me preach. I declaimed charmingly;

hysterical women wrote me anonymous love letters;
eccentric men looked upon me as a demigod, for I did
not mention reform or progress, but uttered rhapsodies
on Israel's greatness and Israel's imperishable treasures.
The Fall of 1848 found me a half-dead apostle of peace,
submissive, humble and despairing.[37]

Given Wise's penchant for self-dramatization, this ex post
facto rationalization can be discounted. It is particularly un-
convincing because his conduct showed no overt signs of
despair or resignation. It was precisely at this moment that
the self-styled "half-dead apostle of peace" advanced an ambitious proposal for a union of congregations which thrust
him into an active and controversial role. Whatever the inner
dynamics of the man, the fact remains that during this period
Wise, according to his own testimony, "did not mention reform or progress."

While repressing any commitment he may have had to
radical reformism, Wise lost no time after his arrival in the
United States in demonstrating his energy and his passion for
Americanization. He set out at once to perfect his English
and soon became sufficiently proficient to speak at a public
meeting against attempts to convert Jews to Christianity.[38]
He spent long hours in the library reading works of philosophy, history, and comparative religion. He cultivated personal relationships with Christian clergymen, local business-
men, and political leaders. During his very first year in
Albany he became a member of an Odd Fellows lodge. In
his *Reminiscences* he declares that he found the "feature of
secrecy repugnant" and that he disliked the "saloon politics.
[I] could not drink the three cent beer [and] could not
endure the card-playing and spitting." Despite his ostensible
antipathies, however, he "organized a new lodge and went
through all the offices."

Wise reports that as early as 1848 he consulted with William Seward in Albany and "went to New York and consulted with Horace Greeley." By 1850 he claimed close friendship with Senator Seward, who accompanied him to the White House to meet President Zachary Taylor and then took him to Daniel Webster's home. Wise reported that he dined with Webster and even visited John Calhoun "shortly before his demise."[39] In 1852 Wise became the first Jewish clergyman to be invited to deliver a prayer at the opening of a session of the New York legislature.[40] Isaac Mayer Wise was clearly a young man bent on making a reputation.

His advancement in Jewish circles was less spectacular, but not for lack of drive. Within months of his arrival, he was invited by Lilienthal to serve as a member of the projected Beth Din. Wise "proposed a Minhag America for divine service . . . which would promote harmonious development of the young congregations." The new rite was to treat with the prayer service "according to the Din" (Jewish law), but was also to be based upon "scientific principles [i.e., the assumptions of Jewish historical scholarship] and the demands of the time."[41] The plan did not materialize, so that it is not known what specific suggestions Wise intended to present. Without having to clarify his intentions, he nevertheless succeeded in projecting himself onto the national scene and in establishing himself as an aspirant to leadership who was both orthodox (acting according to Din) and progressive (responding to the demands of the time). American Jewry was being made aware of the fact that there was "a man in their midst."

Wise was not discouraged by the failure of the Beth Din and proceeded to confer with Leeser and Lilienthal about a proposal for a union of congregations. In December 1848 he published a call "To the Ministers and other Israelites" in the

Occident (p. 431). Wise's approach was cloyingly modest: "Brethren, though I am a stranger among you, unknown and unimportant—though I am aware that there are men among you much better than myself, 'whose little finger is thicker than my loins'—though my years are but few in number and among you are men gray-haired and highly experienced—notwithstanding all this, I make use of the Reverend Editor's permission to express publicly my views." The proposal which followed, embellished with numerous Biblical and Talmudic quotations and analogies, points to the problems of standards and credentials in such matters as the dietary laws, marriage and divorce, and education. He particularly stressed the danger of missionary activities and concluded with a call for a conference of "ministers and laymen and all who have an interest in the promulgation of God's law . . . to bring together all men of zeal and piety, of wisdom and knowledge to consider what should be done for the union, welfare and progress of Israel."

Lilienthal associated himself with Wise's call. Leeser, citing his own previous initiatives and suggestions, supported the proposal and dismissed fears of "ill-digested reforms." Positive responses were also received from S. M. Isaacs, chazan of Shaarey Tefillah in New York, and James Gutheim, chazan of Bnai Jeshurun in Cincinnati. A subsequent circular described a modest agenda and announced that Leeser would convene the conference when twenty congregations had answered the call. Nine congregations responded of which only one was in New York, and no meeting was ever held.[42]

The failure of the attempt cannot be attributed to any single factor. Congregations as dissimilar as Mikveh Israel in Philadelphia and Bnai Jeshurun of Cincinnati had chosen delegates. Congregations as dissimilar as Shearith Israel and Emanu-El of New York had ignored the invitation. Neither positive nor negative responses revealed any commitment to a point of view. The major impediment seems to have been a combination of apathy and anarchy. In 1849 many separate Jewish organizations—religious and secular—were growing in numbers and in strength. But the incentive for the entire community to come together for common purposes was lacking.

Wise's efforts had brought him notice but not acceptance. He was rebuffed not only by the Sephardim (who continued to look down on all Germans) and by the older German immigrants (of Congregation Bnai Jeshurun in New York), but also by the more intellectual elements among the recent immigrants. He failed to secure any support from the membership of Emanu-El or from a newly formed group known as Lichtfreunde (Friends of Light).[43] German Jewish intellectuals on both sides of the ocean continued to regard Wise as a pretentious upstart. He complained that Ludwig Philippson (editor of the *Allgemeine Zeitung des Judentums*) "gave me . . . a blow whenever he could" and that "the German Jewish journalists . . . have always treated me shamefully." Like Leeser, Wise lacked the intellectual credentials to be recognized as a Jewish leader anywhere but in middle America.

In his own synagogue Wise also experienced difficulties. In 1850 a quarrel arose between him and the president of the congregation which led to a brawl on the pulpit and a split in the congregation. The only description of the affair is Wise's late account, which implies that his reformist position was at the root of the controversy. Such details as are available indicate that it was the usual blend of the petty and the personal, as well as the perennial antagonism between lay leaders and rabbis, which produced the rift. The president who attacked Wise had been his close friend and supporter and had joined the congregation "because of his sympathy with the reforms that had been adopted."[44] Those who defended Wise were "the Poles and Hungarians who thought only of me [and] struck out like wild men." This division of forces does not substantiate the claim of a conflict between orthodoxy and reform. Whatever the causes of the schism, the incident reflects the lingering immaturity and instability of Jewish institutional life at this time. Piecemeal changes were in process, but a basic transformation was not yet imminent.

Unlike Lilienthal, Wise did not withdraw from congregational life. Despite his characterization of himself as "submissive, humble and despairing," he was not easily discouraged. He organized a new synagogue and spent the next four years acquiring skills and experience which enabled him to reassert his leadership with increased effectiveness.

During the years that Wise was embroiled in strife in Albany, Isaac Leeser was encountering difficulties with his congregation in Philadelphia. In 1850, after twenty-one years of service to Mikveh Israel, Leeser's association with the congregation was terminated. Since Leeser did not write his Reminiscences we know little about the details of the conflict. Clearly reform was not an issue. The dispute seems to have centered on the terms of Leeser's contract and "Leeser's refusal to be dominated by an inflexible system of government [i.e., rigid control of the congregation by laymen]."[45] In 1851, when a new chazan was elected, Leeser was still a candidate for the post and received about one third of the votes cast.[46] Thereafter, he continued his editorial work and his writing, but his influence in American Jewish life waned.

Ironically, the growth in strength and numbers of American Jewry at the beginning of the 1850's was accompanied by the repudiation of virtually every religious leader of standing. Lilienthal, Wise, and Leeser lost their posts; Abraham Rice resigned his position in Baltimore and went into business;[47] Leo Merzbacher was in serious jeopardy (in February

1852 Emanu-El declared its pulpit vacant).[48] The advocates of orthodoxy, reform, and compromise were equally vulnerable. In the emerging American-Jewish pattern, congregational life continued to be dominated by laymen, and rabbis were frequently reminded of the precariousness of their position. The gifted and persuasive might aspire to prominence but not to authority.

Wise said that there was "antipathy at that time in America to rabbis and preachers in general, just as there was a prejudice against cultured people of any kind, because they were looked upon as impractical and helpless. He also characterized the role of the "Mighty Parnass" (congregational president): "The parnass was an autocrat in the congregation. He was president, shamash [sexton], chazan, rabbi. He ruled the quick and the dead. He was the law and the revelation, the lord and the glory, the majesty and the spiritual guardian of the congregation. He suffered no rival; all were subject to him."[49] In time, lay leaders became more refined and sophisticated, but they did not relinquish their prerogatives.

In 1849, when the status of rabbis in America was at a particularly low ebb, Congregation Bnai Jeshurun of New York invited Morris Raphall of Birmingham, England, to occupy its pulpit. Raphall was the first Jewish clergyman to come to America in response to a congregational invitation. His salary of $2,000 per year[50] contrasted sharply with I. M. Wise's $250 per year plus $9 for each pupil in his school; Merzbacher's $200 in 1845, raised to $600 in late 1848; and Lilienthal's budgeted salary from the three congregations of the Union, $1,000 per annum (surviving congregational minutes indicate, however, that after a few months at this level, the salary was reduced).[51] Raphall's presence is reported to have made Bnai Jeshurun "the leading house of worship among New York Jews."[52]

Like most of the Jews of this time who came from England, Raphall was not a native Englishman. He was born in Stockholm in 1798, where his father is reported to have been a banker to the King of Sweden. He apparently moved about a good deal during his youth and is said to have earned a "Doctor's degree" at the University of Erlangen.[53] There is no record of his having received rabbinic ordination or even a classic rabbinic education. He settled in England in 1825 and for a number of years edited an English language magazine called *The Hebrew Review, or Magazine of Rabbinical Literature*. In 1841 he became preacher of the Birmingham Hebrew Congregation and Headmaster of the Hebrew School there. During his stay in Birmingham he earned his reputation as an orator and as "the foremost expounder of the Jew to the non-Jew in England."[54] It was this reputation which made him so attractive to the most Americanized Ashkenazi congregation in America.

Raphall's well-paid appointment indicated the direction in which American Jewry was moving. The importance of "lecturing" (which among Jews was not yet known as "preaching") grew with the movement toward Americanization and the quest for respectability. Before long, all reputable congregations sought lecturers who spoke English and who were able to represent Judaism to the non-Jewish world. A new type of Jewish religious leadership developed, focused on the pulpit lecture and the public presence. Bnai Jeshurun, which considered itself an orthodox congregation, led the way in introducing this form of Protestantization.

Raphall's words and deeds, however, had little impact on American Jewry. He is said to have snubbed and insulted both Leeser and Lilienthal, neither of whom was invited to his installation.[55] He undertook no significant tasks, made no noteworthy contributions, and proved to be extremely flexible in his ideological positions.[56] Nevertheless, he was considered the most successful rabbi of the time. He was certainly the most widely known;[57] he delivered the eulogy at Mordecai Noah's funeral, and in 1860 became the first Jewish minister to deliver a prayer at the opening of a session of Congress.[58] The contrast between the acceptance of Raphall and the harassment of his contemporaries demonstrated that oratory and image were valued, while learning and inventiveness were resented. The leading rabbi was the one who chose not to lead.

The close of the decade brought a new surge of immigrants. Only a few had actually participated in the revolutionary ferment of 1848 and 1849 in central Europe,[59] but many had broader cultural backgrounds than the earlier arrivals. They found American Jewry in a state of flux, lacking in direction or program but increasingly prosperous, full of energy, pursuing a variety of options to secure communal survival. Out of the chaos a direction for future development was emerging.

9 Progress and Prospects, 1850–1860

IN an address delivered on January 25, 1852, Henry Jones, President of the Maimonides Library Association of Bnai Brith, described "the progress made during recent years . . . and the prospect that has been opened. . . . Time is measured no longer by hours and minutes, by the oscillations of the pendulum, nor by the sun dial, but by flashes of the magnetic telegraph and the revolutions of the steam engine. These are the mighty levers which move mankind in the onward march of events, of development and progress. We must keep abreast with this progressive movement."[1] Some time thereafter in a lecture to the same Association, Julius Bien, president of the Order, was even more rhapsodic in his assessment: "*Science* is the *Messiah* of the human race, leads to human happiness and leads toward the realization of the brotherhood of man.' "[2]

Henry Jones and Julius Bien were not average citizens, but neither were they wild-eyed visionaries. They were responsible, thoughtful men who saw and welcomed the changes that were taking place and who were eager to take advantage of the opportunities that were opening before them. Both had arrived in America as immigrants from Germany and had participated actively in the affairs of the nascent Jewish community. Both became recognized as leaders in the community primarily because of their rapid adjustment and their identification with an American outlook. In an era when "the central body of American religious thought assimilated the concepts of progress and perfectibility,"[3] men like Jones and Bien represented the vanguard of those who were articulating the Americanization of American Jewry.

The substantial scientific and technological innovations of the decade of the 1850's made the messianist optimism of Jones and Bien plausible. The development of the telegraph revolutionized communication. The spread of railroads brought cheap, safe, speedy transportation of persons as well as produce within reach of virtually every village. The number of miles of track increased from 9,000 in 1850 to 20,000 in 1860. While the great leap forward in industrialization did not occur until the following decades, the transition from commercial to industrial capitalism was under way, and increases in production of all kinds were phenomenal. (One of the advances that had an immediate impact on the Jewish community was the development of the sewing machine, which was perfected in 1851.) The American credo of bigger and better emerged not as an article of faith but as a conclusion based on heady experience.

In the 1850's the sense of growing opportunity stimulated a flood of immigration which exceeded anything even America had seen. Almost two and a half million immigrants entered the United States during the decade. Of these almost 700,000 originated in the German states.[4] During the three years between 1852 and 1854, over half a million Germans emigrated; in 1854, 53 percent of the immigrant arrivals in the United States were German.[5] While there are no statistics on the proportion of these who were Jews, contemporary accounts estimate that the American Jewish population grew from 50,000 in 1844 to 200,000 in 1860.[6] In 1858 a Jewish associate of Abraham Lincoln reported that "in the free states there are 50,000 Jewish votes."[7] These figures are no more than unsubstantiated guesses, but they clearly reflect a considerable increase in population.

No amount of economic growth and progressivist optimism could completely alleviate the stresses and strains of change and especially the problems created by the influx of so many aliens. Inevitable tensions and anxieties provided fertile soil for a nativist backlash. As early as 1835 anti-foreign parties had arisen in New York and other cities. In the mid-1850's nativist sentiments coalesced into the Know-Nothing party, which flourished for a brief period and then disappeared as rapidly as it had arisen.

Even in their brief heyday, the Know-Nothings, though hysterically anti-Catholic, were not particularly anti-Jewish. The "few expressions of anti-Jewish prejudice on the part of Know-Nothing supporters were typical . . . of similar sentiments among supporters of the Democratic party."[8] Although most of the more recent immigrants opposed the Know-Nothings, some Jews—especially in the native-born community—were sympathetic to them. Isaac Leeser did not support the party but he did counsel neutrality, stating that "the new party has not displayed, as a portion of its doctrine, any marked hostility to our religion."[9] Toward the end of the decade, when the Know-Nothings were in eclipse, there was cooperation between Know-Nothing leaders and Jewish communities in protesting the abduction of a Jewish child by papal authorities in Rome (the Mortara case). In general, the Jews were of little consequence to the Know-Nothings and the Know-Nothings were of minor concern to the Jews.

The other major disruptive issue during the 1850's was the debate over slavery. The decade began with the futile Compromise of 1850; ten years later South Carolina passed the Ordinance of Secession. In the intervening period the political strife that was to culminate in the outbreak of the Civil War was continuous. Once again the Jewish group was not directly involved in the conflict and was only marginally affected by it. A small number of Jews in the South, most of them descendants of the old Sephardic community, were slave owners. A handful of German-Jewish immigrants were ardent abolitionists. The large majority—including Wise, Lilienthal, and Leeser—were moderates who favored peace and union. When, in 1860, Morris Raphall at Bnai Jeshurun delivered an address defending the Biblical basis of the institution of slavery, his trustees passed the following resolution: "We the Board of Trustees, respectfully suggest to Dr. Raphall the impropriety of any intermeddling with politics, as we firmly believe such a course to be entirely inconsistent with the Jewish clerical character, calculated to be of serious injury to the Jews in general and to our congregation in particular."[10] The board did not condemn Raphall's position, only the fact that he took a public stand.

In Baltimore the board of David Einhorn's congregation was equally unhappy with his abolitionist preachments. After his flight from Baltimore in 1861, a condition for his return was that "in future there would be no comment in the pulpit on the excitable issues of the time."[11] As for the "moderate" Isaac M. Wise, the board of his congregation in Cincinnati voted on April 14, 1860, "to notify Rev. Wise that the Board disapproves of all political allusions in his sermons and to discontinue same."[12] Prior to the outbreak of the Civil War, the Jewish population sought with considerable success to avoid becoming embroiled in the growing controversy.

The energies of Jews as individuals and as a community were primarily devoted to the tasks of continuing their adjustment to life in the New World. Those who had arrived during previous decades strove to consolidate their gains and to build on their accumulating experience. Newcomers who had to begin at the bottom of the ladder found their way somewhat eased by the lessons learned from their predecessors and by the assistance that could be expected from fellow Jews who had already overcome their own initial hardships.

The newcomers of the 50's rarely found themselves total strangers in a strange land; wherever they went, they found *landsleute* who had preceded them; usually they found a synagogue (or at least a minyan) already in existence. In the early '50's such quasi-communities could be found as far afield as the mining camps of California. Jewish immigrants to America now had an address of their own.

A common assumption about the German immigration after 1848 is that it consisted largely of "Forty-Eighters," political activists who had participated in the European up-risings of 1848 and 1849 and who had fled to America fol-lowing the failure of the revolutionary movement. The myth originated in the romance of a number of refugees from the revolution who did emigrate, and has become fixed in popu-lar imagination. Careful investigation of the facts has led students of immigration to conclude that the size of the emi-gration "was directly little affected by the political events of 1848 and 1849. The most dramatic political events of the Revolution occurred among people and in places where there was little Auswanderung [emigration] before, during or after 1848. . . . The handful of Baden republicans . . . who created this legend are not numerically important, nor are they in any way representative; they were *emigres*, not *Aus-wanderer*."[13] The huge increase in immigration between 1851 and 1854 resulted from renewed economic pressures in Eu-rope and the growing attractiveness of American opportun-ity. In the early 1850's, a larger proprotion of the emigrants —Jews as well as non-Jews—"swarmed to the sea from inland areas including Bohemia and Posen." In 1855 when condi-tions in Germany improved and reports of an "economic pinch and nativist agitation in America became known, the tide was sharply interrupted . . . [and] the mid-century emigration [from Germany] was over."[14]

The circumstances of the general German immigration are

equally applicable to German Jews. Detailed study has disclosed only a small number of German-Jewish immigrants who were participants in the revolutionary events of 1848-49.[15] Contemporary accounts mention the excitement among American Jews concerning the episodes and speak in general terms about immigrants who came after the failure of the revolution, but there are few direct references to political refugees. Later accounts frequently allude to "the higher class of German Jewish immigrants who came here in 1848 and thereafter,"[16] and during the course of the decade a small number of better educated individuals did arrive in America. The basic character of the emigration did not change, however, and contemporary sources continue to refer to "the demoralized condition and low intellectual status" of the immigrants. Increasing numbers came from Bohemia and Posen, but "the later immigration seems to have continued closely along the lines of the former."[17]

Despite the fact that the European revolutions did not succeed, political conditions for Jews in some German states improved. Subsequently, agitation for Jewish religious reform in Germany which had been most pronounced in areas where the civil status of Jews was upgraded, rapidly subsided. David Philipson, the historian of the reform movement, attributed the decline in "religious concerns" to the involvement of German Jews in political issues. His interpretation is highly questionable, but the facts are indisputable. In the 1840's when reformist energy was at its height in Germany, interest in reform was minimal in America. During the 1850's, at the very time when the agitation for reform was growing in American Judaism, the movement in Germany became dormant.

On both sides of the ocean the attitude within the Jewish community toward immigration became somewhat more ambivalent. In Germany, although a number of societies to assist (and even promote) emigration were formed after 1848, there were also protests that it was not proper "to desert fatherland, friends and brothers [and that] even if some time is still to elapse until our salvation is realized and even if many struggles and sufferings still await us, we want to hold fast and loyally to our fatherland." A contemporary account summarizes the sentiment, reporting that "more mature deliberation has forthwith cooled off and downed the enthusiasm of the movement [for emigration]. As gladly as I and all of my brethren and colleagues in Israel will proffer our hands for the realization of the call 'Up, and to America,' nevertheless, we also hear the counter-call: 'Remain in this country and find sustenance in faith and reliance.' "[18] For the most part, the people who wrote these accounts vacillated; if they moved, it was generally to the rapidly growing cities within Germany.[19] Emigration to America continued to emanate from the villages, where the encroachment of modernization was disrupting the old way of life.

In America expressions of anxiety about the "distressed Israelites . . . flocking in great masses" were taken up by those who had themselves arrived not too long before. Isaac Leeser's response to the news that emigration societies were being formed in Bohemia was less than enthusiastic: "The majority, we fear, will be poor." Max Lilienthal wrote in his "open letter in *Die Deborah* that "the Polish Jews who have come mostly from East Prussia have the characteristics of a chameleon." In 1855 Bnai Brith organized a short-lived Hebrew Agricultural Society not because any of its members had shown interest in becoming farmers, but "in order to employ the newly arrived emigrants and generally the working man out of employment."[20] (It should be noted that the recording secretary of the Society was a gentleman named Mr. H. American.)[21] For social as well as economic reasons, it seems that at least some of those who had already overcome the initial problems of adjustment would have preferred to direct the newcomers away from their neighborhoods and their occupations. Since the immigrants of the 50's were no more interested in agriculture than their predecessors, the Society expired in 1856 without achievement. The latest arrivals were accepted and assisted, but not without some unease and embarrassment on the part of the recently hatched Americans.

The newest wave of immigrants repeated the experience of earlier decades. Many began as peddlers. New synagogues were founded in which familiar faces, dialects, and melodies provided a sense of being at home for those who still felt strange in the new environment; but by this time, styles and standards were being set by those who had come earlier and whose successful adaptation spurred them to emphasize how much at home they were in America. It was Henry Jones, Julius Bien, and others like them who prescribed the pattern.

Between 1850 and 1860 the number of congregations in New York increased from fourteen to twenty-seven.[22] While the newcomers were organizing thirteen new synagogues, the earlier institutions were moving to larger quarters, fostering decorum, sponsoring lectures, increasing their use of English and striving to find ways to demonstrate their integration into the general community.

In January 1844 Congregation Anshe Chesed of New York, still housed in rented upper-story quarters, had hesitated before assuming the trivial expense of painting the walls and floors of its meeting room.[23] Six years later the same congregation dedicated a handsome building expressly constructed for use as a synagogue. Printed invitations and a printed program were prepared for the ceremony at which an orchestra of twenty musicians played an introductory symphonic selection. Two cantors and a choir of eight sang appropriate psalms and prayers. Drs. Lilienthal and Schlesinger spoke in German, and Rev. S. M. Isaacs in English; Leo Merzbacher pronounced the blessing for the welfare of the United States government. Among the guests were the Honorable Caleb Woodhall, Mayor of New York, "some aldermen and a great many other persons of distinction."[24] Six years had brought a remarkable improvement in the social and economic status of this congregation and its members.

Not to be outdone, Bnai Jeshurun sold its old building in 1850 and constructed a new edifice "uptown" (on Greene Street) in 1851. The synagogue, which was of the "perpendicular style of Gothic architecture," was erected at a cost of $50,000. The rabbi of the congregation, Morris Raphall, delivered an address (in English, of course) at both the cornerstone laying and the dedication. On both occasions, "the Mayor and other city officials" were present.[25]

Less affluent congregations emulated the style if not the scale. Emanu-El, still relatively young but advancing rapidly, dedicated a remodeled church building (purchased at a cost of $30,000, plus an annual ground rent of $400) in 1854.[26] Its older building, in a location described as "not the most savory one," was sold to Congregation Beth Israel (reported to have been founded both in 1843 and 1846 and to have consisted of Polish Jews). For Beth Israel the move was obviously a mark of improved status and rising expectations. Rodeph Shalom dedicated its new building in 1853 with "Rev. Dr. Merzbacher," "Rev. Dr. Raphael" and "Rev. Dr. Isaacs" in attendance (of whom the latter two were English speaking.)[27]

Everywhere else in the country a similar development was in progress. In Philadelphia, Congregation Knesseth Israel (founded in 1847) dedicated a remodeled church in 1853. Congregation Bnai Israel did likewise in 1856. Rodeph Sholom (which had remodeled its church structure in 1846) contented itself with building a chapel on its newly acquired burying ground.

The West did not lag far behind. Kehillath Anshei Maarav in Chicago (founded in 1847) dedicated its new building in 1851, in the presence of "the most influential citizens of Chicago." Rev. S. M. Isaacs of New York traveled all the way to Chicago to deliver the dedicatory sermon (in English). Bnai Israel of Cincinnati dedicated its new building in 1852, with Morris Raphall of New York as the guest speaker. Bnai Jeshurun of the same city, which had consecrated a building in 1848 ("said to be the finest of its kind in this country, the West Indies or England"),[28] purchased a three-story building for its Hebrew-English-German day school in 1856. United Hebrew Congregation of St. Louis dedicated a new building in 1859. The account of the event published in the local press reported that the members reasserted their commitment to "uphold the purity of their faith as they have received it from their own fathers."[29] That same year the members of Congregation Achdut Ve-Sholom (Unity and Peace) of Fort Wayne, Indiana, concluded three years of discussion by voting 8 to 6 to purchase the German Methodist Church for $1,200 and to remodel it for use as a synagogue. Included among resolutions dealing with the dedication (drafted in English but also read to the members in German), was one that read: "The Israelites of Fort Wayne thank their Gentile fellow citizens for contributions towards the purchase of a new Synagogue and for empathy and participation at its inauguration ceremony."[30]

According to the tabulations of the United States census, the value of synagogue property in the United States increased from $418,600 in 1850 to $1,135,300 in 1860. Though the total sum was modest, the relative growth was impressive. The advance suggests that substantial elements in the community had overcome their early difficulties and had acquired the fiscal resources and the social facility to be able to devote their attention to matters beyond the immediate problems of personal adjustment. As Isaac M. Wise wrote in 1854, "The first necessities of life have been provided for and the desire for elevation and improvement is general."[31] The acquisition of a synagogue edifice with the accompanying display of civic recognition and patriotic affirmation became a symbol of belonging in the new society. Jewish immigrants were thereby announcing their conviction that they had become American Jews.

The recurrent participation of English-speaking "rabbis" in the dedication ceremonies represented the growing determination of all segments of the community to speed the use of English in communal affairs. Some congregations—especially those in the West—had been writing their minutes in English from the time of their establishment.[32] When the first congregation was established in St. Paul in 1856, its practice was strictly orthodox, but its records were kept in precarious English. The first entry in its minute book reads: "At a special Meeting called by the Presidend it was moved and second to thake the Room of I. Tronstad at $100 p. year. Payable monthly in advance."[33] By the 1850's the move toward wider use of English was evident everywhere.

Emanu-El in New York—stronghold of reform and of the German immigrant elite—began in 1854 to publish its reports in English as well as German. Later that year the board of the congregation directed its "minister" Merzbacher to offer a course on Judaism "in the English language." In 1855 Merzbacher was asked to speak in English "at times," since "there had long been a desire on the part of the members of Emanu-El to have English spoken in the pulpit." Myer Stern, an early member of the congregation and author of its first history, explains that "patriotic in all things . . . [the members] desired that the language of the land should be heard in their

shrine."[34] When Merzbacher was unable to comply, a committee (of which Stern was a member) was appointed to
secure an "English lecturer." After Merzbacher's death in
1856, the congregation hired an English lecturer in addition
to the new rabbi who was brought over from Germany.[35]
By 1862 Emanu-El was publishing its financial report only
in English and canvassing its members to order English-
language Bibles from England. In 1868 James Gutheim was
elected as "English minister." The next time Emanu-El had
the opportunity to choose a rabbi (in 1873), it selected Gus-
tav Gottheil of Manchester, England.[36]

In Congregation Knesseth Israel of Philadelphia the determination to use English and the movement for reform of
the ritual emerged simultaneously. In 1856 portions of the
minutes began to appear in English and a motion was adopted to translate the constitution into English as well as "pure
German." At the same time the installation of an organ was
approved and the congregation began to refer to itself as
"reform." When the new constitution was printed, German
and English versions appeared side by side. Subsequent correspondence with Congregation Rodeph Sholom was conducted in English. In 1863 a summons to the Congregation
to raise a fund "in aid of our wounded soldiers" was printed
only in English.

The move toward English at Emanu-El and Knesseth
Israel is particularly significant because the principal resistance to the introduction of English came from the intellectual spokesman for reform in America. David Einhorn, who
arrived in America in 1855, had been a leader of reform in
Germany. In America he became the advocate not only of
radical intellectual reform, but also of German language and
culture. "Reform," he wrote in his journal, *Sinai*, "is too
young to be deprived of its carrying case (*Hullë*), the German language." Furthermore, Einhorn maintained there were

few English-speaking teachers who were acquainted with *Wissenschaft*—the scientific approach to Jewish theological and historical problems.

Einhorn's resistance to English had little impact, even in the few self-proclaimed reform congregations. While varying amounts of German continued to be used in almost all synagogues until the 1870's, the pressure for the introduction of English was constant, and the portion of the service conducted in English steadily enlarged. When Einhorn delivered his farewell sermon at Congregation Beth El in New York in 1879, he still maintained that "where the German language is eliminated, there reform of Judaism is nothing more than a glittering veneer." By then he was the last advocate of a cause long since lost. His valedictory sermon concluded wistfully with the announcement of surrender: "Henceforth you will hear the word of God expounded alternately one week in English and one week in German."[37] In the same year Temple Emanu-El abolished German in its pulpit. Einhorn's inability to exercise a decisive influence, even in the radical reform congregations, provides an example of the limited power of even the most forceful rabbis to affect the developing patterns of American-Jewish life. In America, German was seen as a hangover from the past; Americanization was the carrying-case of reform.

Outside the synagogue the transition to English was even more rapid. In 1849 two new journals were established in New York: *Israel's Herold*, a German language weekly edited by Isidore Busch, and *The Asmonean*, an English language weekly edited by Robert Lyon. *Israel's Herold* expired after three months of publication. *The Asmonean* became an influential and widely-read journal and continued publication until Lyons' death in 1858. Unlike Leeser's *Occident*, it did not become an organ of the native-born community. Issues of interest to the immigrant German-Jewish community were debated in its columns. Isaac M. Wise and Max Lilienthal became frequent contributors. The new English-language newspaper became a vehicle for the exchange of ideas and information as well as an instrument for cultivating the knowledge of English. German undoubtedly continued to be the language of the home and certainly remained the primary mode of expression for the newcomers; but in its public expressions, the community increasingly committed itself to the use of English. In 1854 Isaac Mayer Wise moved to Cincinnati and founded American Jewry's third newspaper, an English-language weekly called *The Israelite*. A year later, Wise began publication of a German-language paper of considerably less importance, because, Wise wrote, "no one except the women wished to read German."[38]

Although the Jewish community grew in affluence and self-confidence and the number and size of synagogues increased, attempts to achieve organizational unity or doctrinal clarification continued to be unsuccessful. In an address in 1853 Merzbacher described the problem:

> We have no hospitals, no nurseries, no orphan asylums; not for want of means but for want of harmony; common and higher schools cannot prosper because there is no union; good teachers cannot be obtained because of insufficient remuneration. . . . Literature receives no encouragement because the author who takes pains to write a good book in the interest of Jewish life, the editor who publishes a Jewish paper looks in vain for proper support. . . . The worst part of it is that our dignity is compromised and our position lowered in the eyes of the community by the attitude of congregations who compliment each other with epithets.[39]

Such pleas, however persuasive, produced little cooperative action.

Following the trend of a decade earlier, occasional initiatives were undertaken by autonomous groups in response to some of the unmet needs enumerated by Merzbacher. In 1852 Sampson Simson, a native of New York (who was a graduate of Columbia College and who had once served as confidential clerk to Aaron Burr), assumed leadership in establishing a hospital. Ignoring existing societies and congregations, he founded the "Jews' Hospital in the City of New York." A "Jews' Hospital Society" had been organized in Cincinnati in 1850, but the New York project advanced rapidly and became the first full-scale hospital under Jewish auspices in America. In 1855 a building erected at a cost of $30,000 was completed and began to receive patients. In the early years of its existence, German Jews were excluded from the board of the hospital, and only individuals from the old Sephardic and English community participated in its governance. (Since there were few Jewish physicians in America at that time, most of the hospital staff were non-Jews.) The hospital was established not through unified action of the community but by the action of a small group on behalf of the community.

As previously indicated, autonomous charitable agencies were formed originally in an attempt to circumvent the fragmentation of Jewish religious life. In the absence of overall unity, the voluntary agency provided a means for collaboration across established congregational lines to meet specific social needs. In time the growth of an increasing number of charitable institutions independent of each other and totally detached from the synagogue created an additional galaxy within the amorphous Jewish universe and added new obstacles to the achievement of unification. In the 1850's, despite "the want of harmony," the one area in which the community was able to secure a measure of cooperation was in philanthropic services. At the close of the decade the Hebrew Benevolent Society and the German Hebrew Benevolent Society in New York were consolidated, and they established the Hebrew Orphan Asylum.

In the area of education the problems were more intractable and the response less efficacious. In the same year that Sampson Simson founded the "Jews' Hospital," he obtained a charter for a "Jewish Theological Seminary and Scientific Institution." Even though Simson deeded a tract of land to the corporation, the proposed seminary never became a reality. His personal eccentricity, his estrangement from the German-Jewish community, his lack of Jewish knowledge, and the absence of any recognized intellectual leadership precluded implementation of the plan.

The quality of education in Jewish institutions became increasingly questionable. Most congregations continued to maintain day schools in which Hebrew as well as English (and sometimes German) were taught. In 1854 in New York alone there were seven Jewish day schools with 857 pupils attached to congregations, and a number of private schools under Jewish auspices. The perennial shortage of qualified teachers and textbooks generated, however, a continual stream of complaints and criticisms. The educational system was in a "constant state of flux as a result of movement of teachers [who] had no tenure; the school committees were constantly hiring and firing them."[40]

Conditions of employment were so bad that teachers served only for a short period following their arrival in America but left as soon as they could find other jobs. Frequently the teacher was expected to serve as chazan, shochet or secretary of the congregation in addition to his classroom duties. In Buffalo the congregation offered to pay a salary of $200 per year to a teacher who would also agree to collect the synagogue dues.[41] In 1853 when Bnai Jeshurun, one of the wealthiest and best acculturated congregations in New York, engaged "the most famous Hebrew teacher in the city at that time," it proposed that care of the mikvah (ritual bath) be included as one of his tasks.[42]

Bnai Jeshurun had opened its Educational Institute in 1852 with an enrollment of 140 pupils and an announced curriculum of "Hebrew: Reading, Writing, Grammar, Translation of Prayers, Scripture and Bible History; English: Reading, Writing, Ciphering, English Grammar, Geography, Penmanship, and Elocution." Girls were to be taught needlework, and arrangements were to be made for teaching French, German, Spanish, Algebra, Drawing, Latin, and Classics. In 1854 a "splendid building" was erected (at a cost of $8,600 for the edifice and $5,000 for the land) and "Inauguration Exercises" were held in the presence of such dignitaries as Chief Justice Oakley; Judges Campbell, Woodroff, and Dan; Rev. Drs. Osgood, Raphall, and Burchard; Mr. Redfield, Collector of the Port of New York; and Commodore Uriah P. Levy of the U.S. Navy. Despite the public display, the school closed in 1855 "after a career of three years, and only a year and a half in the new building." When Bnai Jeshurun resumed its educational endeavors in 1861, it contented itself with establishing a Sunday School.[43]

The closing of a sumptuously housed school is indirect though dramatic testimony of the deterioration of educational standards. More direct information is provided in the records of numerous congregations. The minute books of Congregation Beth El in Buffalo for the 1850's "are filled with complaints about the religious school. In addition to the frequent turnover of ministers, teachers, and sextons, each newly arrived functionary was a law unto himself about methods and curriculum."[44] At Knesseth Israel in Philadelphia the school report in 1857 was "very unsatisfactory." Because of irregular attendance, some of the students had not yet learned the Hebrew alphabet. In this instance the blame was placed on the parents rather than the teachers, and it was resolved that students who attended irregularly would be expelled so that the progress of other students would not be impeded.

The reports from Rodeph Shalom in Philadelphia are even more graphic. A teacher was reprimanded for "beating the children." Rules for the school were revised to stress "order, respect, propriety and obedience"—all of which were presumably lacking. Neither beatings nor rules solved the problems of maintaining discipline. In 1854 a detailed list of complaints includes such offenses by students as "firing shooting crackers . . . intending to imitate a circumcision, and making water in the school room in the presents of girls."[45] Classroom conduct had deteriorated to a ribald state.

Such problems were indicative of the growing gap between the subject matter taught in Jewish schools and the life experience of the students. The level of Jewish observance outside the synagogue continued to erode. "In reality," Merzbacher declared in 1853, "there is no one here who has not changed greatly in the observance of ancient regulations."[46] Inside the synagogue, attendance faltered and attention wavered. Parents who were themselves ill-educated and less and less observant of Jewish rituals could not communicate their visceral affection for the old forms to a new generation that had no memories of the fullness and warmth of the tradition. In the 1850's the belief in God was not yet widely challenged, but the sense of the "nearness of God in the intimate acts of daily life" was waning. If, as Julius Bien proclaimed, "Science is the Messiah," the kingdom being ushered in was not that of the God of Israel.

10 Transformations in Process, 1850–1860

IN the 1850's traditional ideas and practices were unmistakably fading among American Jews, and integration into American society was rapidly accelerating. Nevertheless, ideological reform did not make significant gains. Most congregations were ambivalent, vacillating between their determination to maintain tradition and their desire to introduce changes that would reflect the rising aspirations and new life styles of the membership. Weinryb, discussing the disorganization, insecurity, and alienation that accompany immigration, described the characteristic inconsistency of immigrant behavior: "resistance to change and willingness to give up old ways and mores, clinging to group identity and the urge for assimilation, pride in association with the group back home and the drive to shed all group identity and submerge in the new country, religious piety and laxity."[1] Such incongruity of attitude and behavior was manifest everywhere. There were few willing or able to break completely with the past; there were fewer yet who were able to adhere to it.

Confusion and contradiction reigned. In the late 1850's United Hebrew Congregation in St. Louis adopted a motion to seek a "minister and lecturer" (instead of a shochet) who knew English as well as German; a committee was appointed "to revise the prayers so as to omit what can be dispensed with," and at the same time a resolution was passed to "preserve and advance in the path of Orthodox Judaism [and] to strive to the utmost of their ability to uphold the purity of their faith as they have received it from their own fathers."[2] Rodeph Shalom of Philadelphia narrowly defeated a motion to consider "alterations in the present minack," but discontinued sale of Mitzves [synagogue honors] as inconsistent with the progress of time. Shortly thereafter the rabbi of the congregation, Bernard Illowy (who was reputed to be orthodox), was brought to trial before the board of directors for a series of charges that included among others "honing razors for shaving," dining without ritual washing or wearing a head covering, tying up his lulob on the first day of the Feast of Tabernacles, and eating a goose that was not cleaned in accordance with Jewish dietary law.[3] The charges were dismissed, however, and Illowy left the congregation shortly thereafter. The quandary was not dispelled.

In Anshe Chesed of New York the imminent dedication of a new building in 1850 raised the question whether the cantor must continue to face the ark when conducting the service or whether he might be permitted to face the congregation. The individuals consulted agreed that the cantor might face the congregation, but they could not agree on further ritual modifications. After considerable discussion it was decided not to proceed with changes in the minhag. Later that year the cantor of the congregation approached the Board "for the purpose of inquiring about the service of Tisha B'av [the fast of the 9th day of the month of Av]" namely to know how many kinnot [lamentations] shall be said, if all or only a few."[4] The Board opted for a few. Some years later piyyutim (liturgical poems) were eliminated, and the service was thereby shortened on all holidays. In this manner changes were made even though change was resisted.

Bnai Jeshurun of Cincinnati provides even more striking illustration of mixed feelings and muddled practices. As late as 1850 members of the congregation were still "staying up

Shebuous [Pentecost] for reading and learning according to our wholly law of Germany." They also dismissed a shochet whose ritual practice did not satisfy their strict standards. Early in the 1850's occasional English prayers and lectures were introduced, and a Rev. A. L. Rosenfeld of the "orthodox Portuguese" congregation of Charleston, South Carolina, was elected "Chazan and lecturer." The new chazan was soon brought to trial for a number of alleged violations (largely ritual), including having kept a Christian cook and having slaughtered his own poultry without being a shochet.[5] Rosenfeld was acquitted but left the congregation shortly thereafter. His replacement was none other than Isaac Mayer Wise. The profound inconsistency of a congregation that will "cavil at the heterodoxy of one rabbi in respect to matters that were utterly trivial and then promptly select in his place one [who] was on the side of a progressive and rapid liberalization of Judaism" is sufficient to bewilder even the congregation's most avid apologist.[6]

In the context of the times, the sequence of events in Cincinnati is not altogether surprising. Individuals (rabbis as well as laymen) and congregations meandered from issue to issue without clear commitments. The general objective was to become an American while remaining a Jew, to participate in the spirit of the age while preserving the legacy of the ages. Precisely how the symbiosis was to be achieved was a matter for continuous pragmatic reformulation. In 1861 Sinai, a radical reform congregation, was finally established in Chicago with an explicit platform repudiating most traditional beliefs and practices. Even then, "objections were raised by some members . . . that in the building [which had been purchased] the congregation would have to sit with their faces toward the northern wall, while a Jewish congregation, for religious purposes assembled, in accordance with law and custom, should turn their faces toward Mizrah, that is: towards the east."[7] Even among the radicals the attachment to the past was not wholly eradicated.

Of all the Jewish leaders of the mid-nineteenth century, the man who found the amorphous American Jewish community most congenial was Isaac Mayer Wise. Ideologically he was the embodiment of pragmatism and flexibility. From the time of his arrival in America he had presented himself as both progressive and traditional, stressing whichever aspect of his approach seemed appropriate to the situation. A letter addressed to Wise in 1859 attests to his success in maintaining his dual image. The letter was written by Rabbi Benjamin Szold, a conservative and disciple of Zacharia Frankel, who arrived from Germany in that year. "Your tendencies are generally mine," he wrote to Wise. "I, too, like you, am against the fresh reform. . . . People are still debating whether I am orthodox or reform. . . . I am like you . . . neither of the two or both at the same time."[8]

During the course of the preceding decade, Wise had founded a new congregation in Albany where modest reforms in liturgy and ritual were introduced. In 1853 he was elected rabbi of Bnai Jeshurun in Cincinnati. In accepting the position he repudiated "the stories set afloat among your community in regard to my disbelieving in the immortality of the soul, future reward and punishment and the final redemption of Israel [as] positively not true."[9] During his trial sermon Wise himself tells us that he "said not one word about principle." Instead, "I scattered so many blossoms and flowers upon the congregation from the pulpit . . . that there were enough bouquets to go around and everyone went home bedecked."[10] His first address to the congregation was delivered in English and his second in German. Small wonder that he was such a great success with his congregants!

The changes made in synagogue practice were trivial and

in keeping with the statement that "order and decorum in the House of God should be our first aim."[11] Piyyutim were eliminated. The number of Mi-she-berachs (special prayers of petition recited on behalf of individuals) was reduced to one "with only three names mentioned in it." The sale of Mitzvot was modified, "for while it does bring in money, it also disrupts the service." A compromise was adopted in which fixed standards of fees were established for Mitzvot, thereby serving to insure both decorum and fiscal soundness. The board reaffirmed the resolution that no member who did not keep his business closed for the Sabbath could be a candidate for president or vice-president of the congregation.

During the ensuing years Wise himself notes that "reforms were taking place quietly in the B'ne Yeshurun congregation." A choir was organized, and an organ was introduced. In 1857 Wise produced a revised prayer book which he called *Minhag America* (American rite). The revision omitted prayers for the return to Palestine and for the restoration of the Davidic dynasty and the sacrificial cult, but beyond this the revision contained "as little change as possible . . . in the order of the prayers and in the typical prayers."[12] When the traveling journalist I. J. Benjamin visited the congregation in 1860, he found that men and women were still seated separately and that on the New Year and the Day of Atonement, the traditional prayer book was still in use. "Perhaps," he wrote, "they were afraid that God was awake on those days and they might be the worse for it in God's judgement."[13]

In most matters, Wise—like the vast majority of Jewish immigrants—was prepared to compromise and to improvise in his religious principles as well as practices, but he was unwavering in his commitment to one goal: Americanization: "The Jew must be Americanized, for every German word reminds him of the old disgrace. . . . The Jew must become an American in order to gain the proud self-consciousness of the free born man." Once this conclusion was reached, Wise "began to Americanize with all my might. . . . We must be not only American citizens, but become Americans through and through outside the synagogue." This passion enabled him to become the interpreter of American Jewry's aspirations and architect of its institutional structure.

Wise had begun to stress the importance of an American Judaism almost from the moment of his arrival. In 1846 he had proposed the creation of a Minhag America and, shortly thereafter, a union of American congregations. In the intervening years there had been no progress in achieving doctrinal or structural unity, but de facto unity of purpose had been achieved regarding one issue. American Jewry was united in its determination to become fully American.

Wise's post in Cincinnati provided him with an institutional base of operations and financial support. He quickly launched several enterprises intended to fill the institutional vacuum and provide a framework for American Jewry with himself as the central figure. Within a year he established two newspapers (the major one in English, the subsidiary in German), laid plans for the establishment of a college, and convened a conference of congregations intended to create a unified American Jewish religious system.

Soon after his arrival in 1854, Wise began publication of an English language weekly called *The Israelite*. Leeser in Philadelphia wrote: "A weekly paper has begun to appear in Cincinnati under the direction of the well-known Mr. Wise, falsely called Israelite. It will in all likelihood prove a creature of a day and will soon go the way of all flesh." Despite this prediction, Wise's paper was far more successful than Leeser's *Occident*, since Wise made his paper "simple and popular; for I wanted to write for the people—i.e., for my people. This would not give scholars any reason for particular admiration." Wise never won any admiration from scholars ("abroad the paper was unknown"), but he did succeed in attracting a large following among the upwardly mobile, rapidly Americanizing Jewish burghers who were "his people."[14]

In the second issue of the *Israelite*, he proposed a "Union of Judaic Congregations" and in the following issue called for the establishment of an "institute of learning." Pointing out that most colleges and universities in the United States were supported by religious sects, he urged: "Let us educate our ministers, here in our own College and we will soon have American ministers, American congregations, and an American Union of Israel for religious and charitable purposes. Let us have American trained teachers and they will educate for us American citizens."[15]

In October 1854 Wise convened a meeting in Cincinnati at which the following series of resolutions was adopted: (1) the organization "of an association to be known as the Zion College Association;" (2) the establishment by this association of "an university in the city of Cincinnati, the theological faculty of which shall be that of Judaism"; (3) the payment of an "admission fee of $1 and the subscription of $2 per annum," to be required of each member of the association. The *Israelite* reported that "one hundred and thirty men joined the society on the spot." On November 3 of the same year he informed his readers that "the plan of the Zion Collegiate Society had been received very favorably by men of vast influence in Eastern cities. We have received numerous private letters from influential men, assuring us that they will make an attempt in the different cities to have similar societies formed for the same purpose."

Wise and his supporters realized that support from other communities besides Cincinnati was of utmost importance in the success of their endeavor. "The members of the above association are aware of their being alone unable to accomplish the magnificent task they propose to themselves. . . . The association, therefore, hope that similar societies for the same purpose will be organized in all the large cities of the Union."

In order to gain such support, he publicized the provisions made by the Cincinnati group for participation of other communities in the management of the college:

> The scholastic departments, and the buildings, libraries, etc., appertaining thereto, shall be governed by laws and regulations made hereafter by the representatives of this association and the sister societies having the same object in view. . . . This and every other sister society should be entitled to one representative for every twenty-five members of such a society. With this comes the obligation, that this and every other society should contribute fifty dollars to the fund of the university for every representative.

Wise commented, "These laws are just, granting equal rights to all societies hereafter forming and we believe, it may justly be expected that such societies may soon be organized among our brethren abroad." Wise was bent on enlisting the aid of all the Jews of America for this project. To achieve this end he seemed willing to make concessions on matters that he deemed unimportant, but he was adamant that the administrative control of the institution be in his hands, and that the location of the institution be in Cincinnati.

Sampson Simson, who had founded a Jewish Theological Seminary Association in New York in 1852, responded to the announced formation of the Zion Collegiate Association by soliciting Wise's support for *his* organization. He described *its* purpose as the "perpetuation of the ancient and orthodox Jewish faith, its customs, rites, and ceremonies."

Wise replied: "We are quite sure that the two plans to effect *the same end* [italics added] will finally be merged into one." In answer to a question whether he was orthodox or reform, he replied: "I am neither . . . I am a historical Jew." When a letter to the *Israelite* inquired about the orientation of the new college and its leaders, Wise replied: "I can assure you, dear Sir, that I consider myself an orthodox Jew." But when the editor of *The Asmonean*, Robert Lyon, criticized him for ignoring the existence of other Jewish college associations in New York and Philadelphia, Wise stood his ground. Lyon asserted that there was room in America for more than one college and hoped "that our children will at no very distant day see an Israelite College in every state of the Union." Wise replied: "We beg leave to differ. . . . We hope that at no distant day, to see *one* grand and complete Israelite college for *all* states of the Union. . . . We go in for Cincinnati [as its site] on account of its central location, and the readiness of its brethren to make great sacrifices for this national cause."

The Zion Collegiate Association inaugurated its campaign to win broad backing by printing two thousand copies of a circular in German and English "to be distributed among our co-religionists in this country." The circular reiterated and publicized Wise's previously expressed views "that there is but one university required for these United States. Cincinnati is, therefore, according to our best judgment the best situated for this institute, because, (a) We have in this city four flourishing and well-organized congregations, the members of which are willing to make great sacrifices to effect this grand purpose. (b) The city of Cincinnati has a central location. (c) It contains the largest number of Israelites next to New York."[16]

In May of 1855 Wise undertook a trip to the East, to rally support for the college plan and to organize branches of the

Zion Collegiate Association. The testimony of his New York backers indicates that in order to gain the support of the Easterners, Wise was forced to assure them that the "when and the where, that is to say, the place where the insititute should be located, and the time when it would be called into existence as well as the manner in which it would be managed would be left to the decision of a convention of delegates of the sister societies."

Wise won approval for his plan among groups of Jewish citizens in Baltimore, Philadelphia, New York, Albany, and Syracuse. The program he had outlined in talks he gave throughout the East was interpreted by his supporters to imply a retreat from his stated intention of establishing a college in Cincinnati. This impression was dispelled upon his return home. In the *Israelite* of August 17, 1855, he asked that the Jews of Cincinnati "prepare for the great work" of the opening of "the first Hebrew college in the United States and England." This was followed by a meeting of the Zion Collegiate Association, at which time the decision was taken to open the college. A board of directors was elected and the Association decided to defray "all of the expenses incurred during the first year of the existence of the college."

Wise was euphoric: "We rejoice unrestrained in this brilliant success." He further called upon the sister associations in Albany, Philadelphia, Louisville, New York, Baltimore, and Syracuse to "act speedily" and to "support this most necessary measure," and reminded them that "all sister societies shall have the right to add one director to the Board of the college for every hundred dollars annual contribution to the funds of the college. Plans were made to open Zion College in Cincinnati on November 1, 1855.

In his editorial of October 12, 1855, Wise described the soon-to-be-opened school in a somewhat different manner. In this article he distinguished for the first time between the college about to be opened and a university to be founded at some time in the future. "The university, the theological faculty of which is to be that of Judaism . . . can be realized only after a college preparatory to the university is in existence and has prepared students for the professional studies of the university. . . . The college and the university which is sure to follow will be the pride of humanity."

The New York branch of the Zion College Association condemned Wise's unilateral action as a "breach of the covenant whereon all the Associations were founded," and severed relations with him. Wise defended himself by maintaining that the university was the goal "which the united Associations pledged their honor to establish and support," whereas Zion College being established by the Cincinnati Association was merely to be an academy which would fill "the vacuity between the best of our common schools, and a university after the pattern of similar institutions in Germany." He declared that the Cincinnati Association, which called upon other cities for help, recognized that "they should have the same claim on us whenever they would be prepared to establish a similar institute in some eastern city, which must be done if the university should prosper." If such was really Wise's intention from the first, he had not made it clear to his adherents outside Cincinnati, nor had he indicated it in any of his writings. His haste in launching the institution resulted in the loss of any support beyond his own city and Louisville.

Zion College opened on November 26, 1855, with an enrollment of fourteen students and a faculty of seven instructors. The event was celebrated with a banquet at which "the elite of Cincinnati was present," and the speakers included "the governor of the state, the late Chief Justice, Salmon P. Chase, Judge Carter and others."[17] Wise was elated: "We laugh at all obstacles thrown in our way, because they are ridiculous. . . . We go on. There is no stop." After one year the school closed without explanation. In April 1857 a meeting of the Zion Collegiate Associates was held to settle the debts and dispose of the property of the association.[18] In his *Reminiscences* Wise commented: "American Jewry was not ripe for such an undertaking." This judgment is probably correct, although if Wise had been as tractable and as politically astute regarding matters of control and location as he was in his ideological orientation, the project might have succeeded.

At the same time that Wise was pressing for the establishment of Zion College, he called a conference of ministers and delegates of the "Israelite Congregations" to meet in Cleveland. The purpose of the conference was to organize a "Union of American Israel," to establish a "regular synod consisting of delegates chosen by the congregation and societies," to discuss a plan for Minhag America and to plan "for scholastic education in the lower and high branches of learning."

The conference met in October 1855. In addition to Wise himself, Lilienthal, Merzbacher, and Leeser were among those present. Once again, Wise attempted to straddle the ideological issues. His opening address was a masterpiece of ambiguity. He stated that "the Bible is the revealed word of God, given to us by divine inspiration," and the Talmud "contains the logical and legal development of the Holy Scriptures, and that its decisions must bind us in all matters of practice and duty," but that the "illiberal assertions of the Talmud are not the kind referred to and have no binding force on us." After much discussion the conference adopted a compromise that affirmed the immediate divine origin of the Bible and the Talmud as the "traditional, legal, and logical exposition of biblical law."[19]

In contrast to his amiability on ideological issues, Wise was unyielding in his personal ambitions. He had himself elected president and proceeded with actions that alienated even those who might have been inclined to support him. His unilateral inauguration of Zion College further antagonized potential allies. There were few in any camp who were prepared to accept the absolute hegemony of the sage of Cincinnati. Personal animosities and sectional rivalries added fuel to the persisting centrifugal tendencies at work within American Jewry. While the old immigrant antagonisms between "Poles" and "Germans" subsided, new rivalries between East (New York, Philadelphia, and Baltimore) and West (Cincinnati, Cleveland, and Louisville) arose. Americanization provided new foci for controversy. As a result, a second conference was scheduled but was never convened.

Following the failure of the Cleveland Conference, both Wise and Leeser found themselves under attack from orthodox as well as reform factions. Both men were regarded by their more principled colleagues as opportunistic pseudo-intellectuals. Leeser was censured by Raphall and others who ostensibly objected to his compromise with reformers; his critics took even greater offense at the claims to leadership put forward by the representative of midwestern "yokel-dom." It was inconceivable to them that Shearith Israel and Bnai Jeshurun of New York and Mikveh Israel of Philadelphia would accept the leadership of upstarts who were not only parvenus and greenhorns but Western primitives to boot! In 1859 a segment of the older Jewish establishment in the East initiated its own attempt to assert communal leadership when it founded the Board of Delegates of American Israelites. Then it became the turn of Wise and the Midwest to protest the claims of the "discredited aristocracy" and to refuse cooperation.

Wise was even more severely opposed from another quarter. In 1855 David Einhorn had immigrated to America to become the rabbi of Har Sinai, the reform congregation of Baltimore. With his arrival, radical and doctrinaire reform acquired a vigorous and caustic advocate. Einhorn was forty-six years old at the time. He had been a brilliant student in both traditional Jewish learning and secular university studies. He became a leader of the radical faction at the German rabbinical conferences of the 1840's and was one of the best known reform leaders in Europe. In 1852 he had left his post as rabbi of Mecklenburg-Schwerin to accept a position with the newly formed radical reform congregation in Pesth, Hungary. Shortly afterward the reform temple was closed by order of the government, and Einhorn was without a position for three years.[20] It was then that he accepted the invitation to come to Baltimore.

In his very first sermon, Einhorn articulated his philosophy of intellectually consistent reform and rejected piecemeal efforts to achieve decorum by modifying old practices: "Experience has shown that all persuasion and pleading in favor of tradition—to galvanize dead forms into life—are ineffective. . . . Even the praiseworthy attempts to bring back something of the old charm by establishing outward harmony must and will remain fruitless because at bottom they serve merely to hide the decay within."[21] Ritual laws, he declared, were only "signs of the covenant [which] must necessarily change with different stages of culture, national customs, industrial, social and civil conditions, in short with the general demands of the inner and outer life. As little as the ripe fruit can be forced back into the bud or the butterfly into the chrysalis so little can the religious idea in its long process from origin to maturity be bound to one and the same form. . . . The evil which threatens to corrode all the healthy bone and marrow must be completely eradicated. . . . We [must] remove from the sphere of our religious life all that is corrupt and untenable. . . . Judaism has arrived at the critical stage when it must part company with dead and obsolete ceremonies."[22] Einhorn arrived with a fully developed and ideologically coherent point of view. Nothing that he found in America caused him to change his thinking or modify his program. He was not a man to "scatter blossoms and flowers" upon a congregation.

Within weeks of Einhorn's arrival the Cleveland conference adopted its compromise platform affirming the divine origin of the Bible, acknowledging the Talmud as the traditional legal and logical exposition of the Biblical laws, and calling for the establishment of a synod. Einhorn lost no time in denouncing the agreement. In a statement (in which he was joined by members of his congregation) he declared: "We appreciate peace in Israel as a precious boon but a peace which necessarily degrades Judaism . . . appears to us too dearly bought. . . . May the free American Israel keep a strict watch on hierarchical movements which would again forge its chains though under the most charming lullabies of peace."[23] Shortly thereafter he established a monthly German language magazine called *Sinai* and began an uninterrupted series of polemics against the "foul peace of Cleveland,"[24] against "so-called reformers" in general, and against Wise and Leeser in particular. "The real culprits," he wrote, "are the so-called reformers. . . . Reform is something quite different from the elimination of [one or another of the prayers which are listed]."[25]

Wise, no mean polemicist himself, condemned Einhorn as "a Deist, a Unitarian, and a Sadducee and an apostle of deistical rationalism. . . . Einhorn, you should not have so far forgotten that your father was a Jew. . . . Reclaim publicly your false representations of Judaism and your slanders of the Jew." He climaxed the attack by calling Einhorn "an enemy of the Jews and Judaism."[26] The implacable hatred between the two men continued throughout their lives, and the conflict between pragmatism and principle was exacerbated by their rival claims to leadership.

Though Wise was no intellectual match for Einhorn, the latter was no tactical match for Wise. Einhorn was unable to adjust to America and as a result never became comfortable here, nor was he widely accepted. When he attacked Leeser's *Catechism for Younger Children,* he wrote, "Only in America could such a man who hardly knows the first elements of the Jewish religion embolden himself to write a book on this subject."[27] He was expressing his contempt not only for Leeser but also for the level of intellectual life in America, which he labeled "a land of humbug." His attitude extended even to the members of his own reform congregation. When he was forced to leave Baltimore during the riots of 1861 because of his abolitionist views, members of his congregation invited him back on condition that "for the sake of your own safety as well as out of consideration for the members of your congregation [you do] not comment from the pulpit on the excitable issues of the time." Einhorn's reaction was that "there is nothing more loathsome, indeed, than this riffraff of bacon reformers."[28]

Given the circumstances of American Jewish life and the characteristics of Einhorn's outlook and temperament, he never developed a large or loyal following. His congregation in Baltimore was the smallest of the four organized congregations there. In 1861 when he became rabbi of Congregation Knesseth Israel in Philadelphia, the minutes of the congregation report that "Dr. Einhorn is very dissatisfied with the attendance in the synagogue and would expect more visitors to listen to his instructions."[29] In 1862 he found it necessary to suspend publication of his journal. The radically reformed and predominantly German prayer book[30] that he had prepared in 1856 was not used anywhere except in his Baltimore congregation. Emanu-El, the exemplar of radical reform, continued to rely on the far more conservative prayer book prepared by Merzbacher a year earlier.[31] Even those who admired Einhorn were not willing to go along with his prescriptions.

Einhorn's experience with American congregations must have been continually frustrating for him. Despite his passionate commitment to German language and culture, his Philadelphia congregation moved steadily to increase the use of English in the synagogue. When a new building was dedicated in 1864, the board directed that songs be sung in German *and* English and that the sermon be delivered in English. Despite his firm commitment to thoroughgoing ritual reform, the extra day of holidays was not eliminated until 1864, five years after this move had been taken in Wise's congregation. Shortly before Einhorn left Philadelphia in 1866, the board was still passing regulations providing fines for "all chatting" and "coming into or leaving the Temple during the sermon." Even Einhorn was unable to change the American pattern in which "the ultimate decision in all matters of reform . . . was not in the hands of the minister."[32] He persistently complained that the pattern of change everywhere was determined by "the riffraff of bacon reformers." Ultimately many of his ideas were accepted, but they did not lead the way to principled reform, they merely provided an ex post facto intellectual justification for a patchwork of practices that had been accepted for pragmatic reasons. Concerning his influence in his lifetime, it was said that "outside a small circle, the name of Einhorn was unknown."[33]

Toward the end of the 50's another attempt to establish a unified organization of American Jewry was undertaken. This time the native Jewish community in New York took the initiative in response to an infringement of Jewish rights. In 1859 the English Jewish members of Congregation Bnai Jeshurun and its offshoot, Shaarey Tefilah, reacted to the

infamous Mortara case (see below) by calling for the formation of a permanent "Board of Representatives of the Jews of
America."

Other instances of discrimination during the decade had
provoked some remonstrance but had not led to unified
action. The provisions of a proposed treaty between the
United States and Switzerland in 1850 had elicited widespread concern. The first article of the treaty stipulated that
"on account of the tenor of the Federal Constitution of
Switzerland, Christians alone are entitled to the enjoyment
of the privileges guaranteed by the present article."[34] For a
variety of reasons—perhaps including Jewish protests—the
treaty was rejected.

In 1855 a revised version with less offensive verbiage but
equally discriminatory provisions was passed despite widespread protests. When an American Jewish merchant was
actually expelled from Switzerland in 1857, all segments of
the community were aroused. Wise wrote in the *Israelite*:
"Agitate! Call meetings! Engage the press in your favor!!!
Israelites, free-men and citizens! Let not the disgrace of the
treaty between the United States and Switzerland remain
upon the history of our country."[35] Leeser in the *Occident*
and Einhorn in *Sinai* joined in the protest. Meetings were
held in a number of cities.

In Baltimore a committee was appointed to "communicate
upon the subject with similar committees in other cities" and
a convention was called to meet in Baltimore on October 26,
1857. As a result of confusion and apathy (and probably
antagonism between Wise and Einhorn), two meetings were
held in Baltimore—both poorly attended. Einhorn's congregants were active at the first meeting; Wise was chairman of
the second. Two delegations proceeded to Washington to
present memoranda to Secretary of State Lewis Cass and
President Buchanan. Einhorn wrote in *Sinai*: "We feel satis-

fied that the Israelites of the United States may feel implicit confidence in the Executive and that their rights as citizens of the United States will be zealously maintained." Wise reported a similar conclusion: "No doubt was left in the minds of the delegates but that this matter is settled as far as we are concerned."

In this instance there was no change of policy, and the discriminatory provisions remained in force until the Swiss cantons changed their laws in 1872. The willingness of Jewish leaders to present their concerns to government officials attested to the sensitivity of American Jewry to the issue of Jewish rights and to their growing political confidence and sophistication. It also revealed the continuing difficulty in achieving unified action even when the entire community was in agreement.

In 1858 the Mortara episode aroused more widespread agitation and more lasting consequences. It concerned a Jewish child in Rome who had been baptised by his Catholic nurse without the knowledge of his parents and was forcibly abducted by papal guards.[36] Reaction was worldwide. Sir Moses Montefiore, President of the Board of Jewish Deputies in England, addressed an appeal to American congregations "to cooperate with the Jews of England, Holland, and France, in the adoption of such measures as in your judgement may be expedient, by appeal to your government, and otherwise, to seek to obtain the restoration of the child . . . and also the prevention of similar outrages for the future."[37]

The response of American Jewry was typically anarchic. Wise and Lilienthal arranged a meeting in Cincinnati and addressed communications to the Secretary of State as well as to the Pope. In Philadelphia five congregations planned a joint protest meeting and considered a plan for action drafted by Isaac Leeser, but Mikveh Israel, clinging to the vestiges of Sephardic exclusivity and preeminence, declined to participate and addressed its own letter to the Secretary of State. A flood of similar petitions followed from numerous cities, among them Savannah, St. Louis, Richmond, Baltimore, Charleston, Chicago, Syracuse, and Washington. The largest protest gathering in the country was held in San Francisco, where a number of Protestant clergy participated in addressing an assembly of over three thousand people. The growth of American Jewry in numbers, in geographic extent, and in influence was dramatically evident. Equally evident was the lack of communal cohesion.

In New York a semblance of joint action was achieved when a number of congregations (including Shearith Israel, Bnai Jeshurun, Shaarey Tefilah, and Emanu-El) cooperated in sponsoring a mass meeting attended by two thousand. The success of this venture prompted new efforts to form a more permanent body to deal with common problems. The initiative was taken by the "English" congregations. In March 1859 the trustees of Shaarey Tefillah and their minister, S. M. Isaacs, proposed the election of delegates to a permanent Board of Representatives of the Jews of America.

The organizers were undoubtedly influenced by the model of the Board of Deputies of British Jews which had been formed in England in 1840 following the Damascus blood libel. They also may have been affected by the impending formation of the *Alliance Israelite Universelle* which came into being in France as a result of the Mortara case. Unfortunately, American Jewry was too fragmented at the time to be able to emulate its brethren in either England or France, and the effort to achieve unity here was only partially successful.

In November 1859 an organization calling itself the "Board of Delegates of American Israelites" was formed. Shearith Israel of New York and Mikveh Israel of Philadelphia declined to participate, as did Emanuel of New York. The aristocracy and arrivistes stood aloof from communal ventures. In addition, Isaac Mayer Wise and David Einhorn both denounced the effort and refused to cooperate. Wise, the advocate of union but not enthusiastic about one in which he and "his people" would be relegated to a minor role, charged that the Board wanted to destroy reform. Einhorn denounced the "Portuguese Jews" and warned that a union of any kind would attempt to retard the progress of reform. In all, twenty-four congregations were represented, eleven from New York City and thirteen from the rest of the country. The only community west of the Alleghenies which sent delegates was New Orleans.

Isaac Leeser supported the formation of the Board of Delegates and was elected as one of its vice-presidents. He sought without success to transform the group into an ecclesiastical body that would "expound Jewish law for all American Jews," promote Judaism through publications and schools, establish a school to train rabbis, convene a "synod of ministers," and undertake other similar ventures.[38] He was accorded some recognition, but his ideas were ignored. Instead the Board announced much more limited objectives:

1. To obtain and collect all possible statistics, information respecting the Israelites of America and have same duly arranged for easy reference.
2. To appoint a Committee of Arbitration for the purpose of settling disputes, which may arise between congregations belonging to the Union and between individuals and public bodies on congregational matters—with a view of preventing a resort to law. As an objective of this Committee is to be simply the preservation of peace, nothing further than offering of advice is contemplated.
3. To promote religious education; first by encouraging local schools in the congregations belonging to the Board;

second by establishing a High School for the training of young men so as to qualify them to become ministers and teachers.

4. To keep a watchful eye on occurrences at home and abroad and see that the civil and religious rights of Israelites are not encroached upon and call attention to proper authorities to the facts, should any violation occur.

5. To keep up communication with similar central Israelitish bodies throughout the world and, in fine, to establish a thorough union among all Israelites of the U.S.[39]

In its actual functioning, the Board restricted itself even further. It dealt with the defense of Jewish rights and response to anti-Jewish discrimination. During the Civil War it was active in seeking the appointment of Jewish chaplains and was concerned with General Grant's order expelling Jews from the Department of Tennessee in 1862. Thereafter its importance and effectiveness waned. Its leadership never succeeded in attracting the support of German Jews who constituted the bulk of the community. When a union of congregations was ultimately formed in 1873 on the initiative of Isaac M. Wise, the Board of Delegates was superseded. In 1874 the Board began discussing a merger with the new Union of American Hebrew Congregations, and in 1878 it became a committee of the Union designated as the Board of Delegates on Civil and Religious Rights.[40] Thus the first semisuccessful effort to achieve unity among American Jews marked the last attempt of older elements in American Jewry to assert leadership.

As the decade of the 1850's drew to a close, American Jewry was gaining in vigor and self-confidence. No substantial organizational framework had been built to reconstitute a structured Jewish community. No ideological formulation had been accepted to revitalize the Jewish religious tradition. Nevertheless, unstructured community and undefined religion were alive and full of optimism about the future. The sense of belonging in the American setting created an atmosphere of enthusiasm which submerged anxieties and apprehensions. "Judaism here [in America]," wrote I. J. Benjamin, "is full of hope and is advancing toward an exalted and prosperous future."

Formal commitment to reform was still minimal. When Benjamin completed his tour of America in 1861, he reported that "in a land that numbers more than two-hundred Orthodox congregations, the reform congregations number eight." Among the eight were a number that would be considered, by twentieth-century standards, conservative. No congregation had as yet begun to worship with uncovered head; all congregations still conducted services in which the greatest portion of the liturgy was chanted by a cantor in Hebrew. The direction of change had been clearly established; the actual movement was tentative.

Without formal changes in ideology, ritual practice, or institutional structure, a basic transformation in the self-image and the outlook of the midnineteenth century Jewish immigrant had taken place. Isaac Mayer Wise spoke for the entire group when he wrote in 1859: "For our own part, we are Jews in the synagogue and Americans everywhere." As a result of this metamorphosis a new form of Jewish experience would be created, in keeping with the new vision of Jewish identity.

11 The Synthesis

"FROM its formation until 1864," writes Grinstein, "Temple Emanu-El of New York may be considered a 'conservative' synagogue."[1] If this judgment is valid, only a single congregation in all America (Har Sinai) could be considered "reform" prior to 1860. Using somewhat less stringent criteria, Benjamin reported in 1861 that there were eight such congregations.[2] Whichever view is accepted, the number of reform congregations prior to the Civil War was small, and the extent of their reforms was limited.

By 1870, however, there were few congregations in America in which substantial reforms had *not* been introduced and in which an accelerating program of radical revision was *not* in process. Even some of the surviving old-line Sephardic congregations, like Mikveh Israel in Savannah and Beth Ahaba in Richmond, had succumbed.[3] Consolidation of institutional reform on a national scale was not accomplished until the mid-1870's, and vestiges of traditional practices persisted in many congregations for a decade or more thereafter; but in the brief span of ten years, the modest tendency toward reform became an irreversible tide. Moreover, the development was so rapid and so thorough that when Isaac Mayer Wise predicted that "within twenty-five years all the world will have accepted Reform Judaism," he was regarded as naive and overly optimistic but not insane.[4]

Among the factors that contributed to the pace of the change was the drastic reduction in the influx of immigrants who might have reinforced the ranks of traditionalism. Immigration from Central Europe had fallen off sharply after 1854, and during the Civil War years it virtually ceased. The suspension of immigration and the nationalist fervor generated by the war helped to speed the Americanization of all foreign groups. As Hansen has observed: "The four years of bloody strife destroyed not only the Old South but also, in a less obvious way, the varied immigrant America' of the North . . . Dreams of the past gave way to realities of the present . . . When the war ended, foreign languages and foreign customs had not disappeared, but ideals had changed. All who lived in America, alien-born and native-born, were resolved to become one people."[5]

What was true of immigrants generally was even more evident among Jews. Their ties to the old country had always been more tenuous than those of other ethnic minorities; their desire for acculturation had always been strong. The experience of having shared in the trials of America during the war transformed the wish to belong into a feeling of belonging. Jews served as soldiers and even as chaplains; they organized benefits; sewed garments, and wrapped bandages.[6] When General Grant issued an order in 1862 expelling Jews from the Department of Tennessee, they appealed directly to President Lincoln, who promptly revoked the decree. Even this disquieting episode strengthened their conviction that any obstacle to their full acceptance could be overcome.

With the coming of peace, relatively few German Jews were among the new immigrants. A trickle from the Russian Empire and Rumania found its way to America in the 1870's, but this group did not assume significant proportions until after 1881.[7] During the decade following the Civil War, American Jewry attained a degree of homogeneity and acculturation it had not known since the beginning of the Central European immigration in the 1820's.

Immigrant integration into American society was given further impetus by phenomenal economic growth and the upward mobility that accompanied the acquisition of wealth. The war and the favorable climate created by governmental policy in the North had provided an enormous stimulus for industrialization. Manufactured products almost doubled in value between 1860 and 1870, and still greater gains beckoned on the horizon. Some individuals accumulated fortunes; many attained a level of affluence far beyond their dreams of a few years before.

In 1853 a Scottish immigrant named Andrew Carnegie earned $35 a month as a telegraph clerk; in 1859, his monthly salary was $125; by 1868 his annual income was $56,110 and he had begun to accumulate a fortune that defied description. John D. Rockefeller, the son of an itinerant peddler in small village communities, in the post-Civil War years assembled holdings that exceeded even Carnegie's capital. In the booming war and post-war economy no Jew became a Carnegie or a Rockefeller, but many acquired great wealth. Their industriousness enabled them to contribute to and profit from the expansion in manufacturing and trade. The Seligmans, who had begun their careers as peddlers, established an investment banking house in 1864. During the Civil War they placed about $200 million in war loans in Germany, England, and France, and subsequently played an important role in financing the expansion of railroads in America. The Lehmans, the Kuhns, and the Loebs followed a similar pattern. The dry goods stores of the Gimbels, the Strausses, the Bloomingdales, and the Altmans grew to become department stores. Simon Guggenheim became a mining magnate.[8] The manufacture of ready-made clothing—from Levi Strauss's copper-riveted blue jeans to Hart-Schaffner and Marx's well-tailored suits—became virtually a German-Jewish monopoly.[9] No city of size was without its group of well-to-do German Jews who became community pace-setters and assumed leadership roles in Jewish as well as nonsectarian institutions. The number of individuals who achieved the exalted status of millionaires was small, but relative affluence was general.

In the wake of this growth of wealth and power, a mood of high enthusiasm swept over America. "The first week of April 1865 was a time of unparalleled optimism for those fortunate enough to be living within the loyal portion of the United States."[10] Subsequent crises and class conflicts tempered the mood but did not dispel the atmosphere of confidence which prevailed, especially among those who were rapidly advancing. "Progress" might be impeded, but it could not be stopped. Man's faith in himself, his reason, and the power of his technology was unassailable. In an age not yet conscious of the hazards of unlimited power, the thought that everything was now possible was exhilarating.

The progressivist outlook suffused every aspect of society, including religion. Doctrines that "in the decade prior to the Civil War [were] considered little more than infidel, in the light of postwar developments . . . would scarcely cause comment in liberal circles."[11] Darwinism and Biblical criticism were widely accepted, or at least accommodated. A prominent clergyman like Henry Ward Beecher modified his message and his style. Phillips Brooks made the goodness and nobility of men as children of God an essential article of his faith. Octavius Frothingham moved from orthodox Unitarianism to Transcendentalism to non-Christian theism. In 1867 he became the first president of the newly established Free Religious Association.

Contemporary Jews were among the elements of society which were well disposed to participate in the new social and intellectual order. Their eagerness to liberate themselves once and for all from the burden of persecution and isolation fired their enthusiasm for the new progressive vision and the universalist perfectionism it promised. The voice of authority that might have raised the demands of tradition was absent; the anchorage of firmly established institutions which might have resisted change was nonexistent. Most Jews willingly embraced the new ideas.

Among those who addressed the first meeting of the Free Religious Association were not only Ralph Waldo Emerson and Lucretia Mott but also Isaac Mayer Wise and Max Lilienthal. That Wise and Lilienthal would be invited to such a gathering, and accept the invitation, underscores the transformation that had taken place within American society and American Jewry. Socially, the Jewish group was moving from the margin to the mainstream. Its presence in the roster of American religious denominations was now acknowledged and, at least in liberal circles, accepted. Ideologically, Wise and Lilienthal had shifted from esoteric particularist concerns with sale of mitzvot and preparation of halitza documents to involvement in universal issues embracing the future of mankind. Wise, who had been assaulted on the pulpit of an impoverished Albany congregation in 1850, shared a rostrum in Boston with Emerson in 1867 and declared his conviction that reason could lead man to perfection. Emerson was elected a vice-president of the Association; Wise became a member of the Board of Directors.

Changes in the religious and communal life of American Jews in the decade of the 1860's and thereafter corresponded to changes in society at large. "Everywhere there were signs of expansion and prosperity in churches. Where once there was a simple frame meeting house, there now stood a majestic edifice testifying to the affluence of its congregation. Robed choirs, strengthened by professional singers, marched with dignity to their stations . . . and ministers . . . devoted more attention to conducting their services 'decently and in order' . . ."[12]

The description applies as readily to synagogues as to churches. In the 1860's there was hardly a congregation in America which did not build a large and sumptuous new edifice. According to the United States census of religious bodies, the value of synagogue buildings increased from $1,135,300 in 1860 to $5,155,235 in 1870. The tabulation, though incomplete, suffices to indicate the scope of the expansion. The highest percentage of growth took place in Illinois, where the value of synagogue property increased from $3,000 in 1860 to $271,500 in 1870.[13]

Emanu-El of New York—by now the spiritual home of investment bankers and merchant magnates and the wealthiest congregation in America—dedicated its new edifice on Fifth Avenue and 43rd Street in 1868 "with imposing ceremonies." The sale of pews yielded $708,575, leaving a surplus of over $86,000. Myer Stern, who served as auctioneer, was rhapsodic: "Never before in the history of any Jewish congregation was there such a wonderful success shown as with this new structure . . ."[14] The congregation, which had collected $28.25 at its first meeting twenty-three years earlier, had come a long way. Shearith Israel, which had built its new edifice on 23rd Street in 1860 (at a cost of $99,935.01), was left far behind.

The other congregations in New York could not match the grandiosity of Emanu-El, but on a more modest scale all reflected advancing affluence and rising aspirations. In 1862 there had been only one synagogue above 28th Street. By 1865 there were "nine commodious houses of worship" in this uptown area.[15] The new construction followed the uptown movement of the Jewish population.

The same pattern was repeated everywhere. A special

meeting of Knesset Israel of Philadelphia in December 1863 was informed that the cost of the proposed new building had risen from $45,000 to $60,000. This did not deter members from subsequently installing upholstered seats and decorating the temple with fresco paintings.[16] Rodeph Shalom began planning for its new building in July 1867. As a result of a number of delays (including the need to lay an extra foundation because of the discovery of quicksand on the site), the dedication was delayed until 1871. The building, finally erected at a cost of $151,700, "soon became a landmark in the City of Philadelphia."[17]

In Cincinnati, Isaac M. Wise displayed his talent for rhetoric and public relations by endowing the proposed construction of a new building with special significance: "The honor of Judaism in Cincinnati and throughout the West required that K.K. Bnai Yeshurun, hitherto the banner bearer of Reform and progress on this side of the Alleghenies, should come out of Lodge Street into the broad daylight of a more suitable locality."[18] In 1863, when the proposal for construction was first discussed, "temple" was used for the first time in reference to the synagogue. The plans for the new edifice, large enough to seat 2,000 persons, were described in the *Israelite* of May 6, 1864, as "Byzantine style with two steeples and several minor towers. The building will be truly grand both in design and dimensions." The original expenditure for the building and the ground was to have been $72,000; when it was dedicated in 1866, its cost was calculated at $263,525. A daily paper marveled: "Cincinnati never before had seen so much grandeur pressed into so small a space."[19] This spectacular architectural specimen, later called the Alhambra style (the design and ornamentation suggest other nomenclature, such as Baroque neo-Bohemian Byzantine, or perhaps Harem Hieratic), still stands on Plum Street in Cincinnati, a monument to the penchant for display which characterized the nouveau riche of America and American Jewry in the gilded age.

The building epidemic of the 1860's was a highly visible manifestation of the attitudes and aspirations of the new breed of American Jewry. In his sermon at the dedication of the new Plum Street Temple, Wise explained that there was a distinction between a synagogue and a temple. The worship that was to be conducted in the latter was to be "in gladness not in perpetual mourning." On the same occasion Max Lilienthal spoke of "a new covenant of a new brotherhood. . . . Let the light of love and brotherly understanding kindled in our flourishing Queen City of the West shine brightly and lustily throughout the land. Let link to link be added to the chain of love that unites us so harmoniously in our growing gigantic West . . . Let there be light, light that enlightens the mind, warms our hearts, fosters our affections."[20] Both men stressed that the new sumptuousness of the synagogue edifice was a sign of Israel's redemption in a transformed world. American Jews had moved from mourning to gladness, from ostracism to brotherhood, from darkness to light.

Given the changed climate, reforms in ritual and practices which had been resisted but a short time before were now avidly welcomed. Primary emphasis was still on the decorum and dignity that would reflect the new station of the erstwhile aliens. But more drastic changes which affirmed their eagerness to belong were also readily accepted. The modifications in doctrine and belief which were implied in these reforms were hardly noted.

Even so-called conservative congregations like Bnai Jeshurun in New York introduced substantial innovations. In 1868 the reading desk was removed to the upper end of the synagogue and a committee was appointed "for the purpose of preparing a system of changes [because] the spirit of the present age demands a reform of ritual as now practiced in our Congregation."[21] A number of major modifications of the ritual were adopted: "Wearing of shrouds on Rosh Hashono and Yom Kippur, except by officiating officers [was] abolished."[22] In 1875 a resolution calling for the introduction of family pews and an organ was adopted, and a choir of male and female singers was organized. In 1878 the congregation joined Isaac Mayer Wise's Union of American Hebrew Congregations."[23]

As might have been expected, Emanu-El in New York moved more quickly. Prior to the Civil War inhibitions against a radical break with the past had still prevailed. In 1859 strong opposition was aroused by a suggestion that members remove their hats during the services. A compromise was adopted, permitting hats to be removed if members wished to do so, but only during the sermon. For the next few years members apparently wore or refrained from wearing hats according to their inclination. In 1864 the Board adopted a resolution stating that "it is an offense to harmony and decorum that part of the Congregation have . . . their heads covered and part have their hats off." The Board therefore recommended a "binding law that all attending divine service at Temple Emanu-El have their heads uncovered." The resolution was ratified with only one dissenting vote. In five years the inhibitions had vanished.[24]

Removal of hats during worship was a significant step. The covering of heads is not an important issue in Jewish law, but the practice had for long been of symbolic importance and served as a visible distinction between Jewish and Christian worship. Its abrogation became a sign of a decisive break with the past, connoting a desire to emphasize conformity with American behavior and to discard observances that were distinctly Jewish. The balance had been tipped in favor of assimilation over continuity, and Emanu-El was the first congregation to take this decisive action. Most others hesitated before making what was viewed as an irreconcilable break with tradition, but in time almost all followed suit. In another two decades worship with uncovered head would become the hallmark of reform.[25]

Isaac Mayer Wise's congregation rejected a move in 1871 to permit worship with uncovered head. In 1872 a disturbance was reported when a member uncovered his head during the service. The majority of the congregation still opposed the practice but voted to allow Christians who attended services to keep their heads uncovered. In 1874 it was decided that "whereas the Rev. Dr. I. M. Wise on several occasions clearly stated in his sermons that it is not against the Mosaic Law to worship with uncovered heads . . . therefore the Board of Trustees respectfully recommends to the general meeting that henceforth worship with uncovered heads be the mode practiced by this congregation." By 1875 the Committee on Order and Decorum was instructed to enforce the rule strictly and to ask "any visiting stranger to uncover his head."[26]

The precise details of change varied from place to place, but the basic direction was universal. Respectability and Americanization were the goals; decorum, reform of ritual, and English were the means. A small congregation like Achdut Ve-Sholom in Fort Wayne, Indiana, had in 1859 "declared on oath that it would never alter or change our orthodox principles."[27] In 1863 the congregation adopted an extensive list of regulations dealing with decorum and propriety. Among the proscribed practices were changing of seats, praying aloud, singing or loudly humming, conversation during services, and shaking of the lulav (palm branch—during the festival of Succot). It was specified that no one would be allowed in the synagogue on Yom Kippur without shoes.[28] None of these changes explicitly violated orthodox principles; they show, however, that reminders of the old ways were clearly a source of embarrassment. Two years later the congregation adopted the Einhorn reformed prayer book despite vigorous opposition. The dissident minority offered to accept numerous changes in an attempt to reach a compromise, but the radical reform of the liturgy passed by a vote of 32 to 12. The time for half measures was apparently over—even in Fort Wayne.

The congregation in Akron, Ohio, was not established until 1865. Two years later a resolution was offered to adopt the "Minnick America" (a corruption of "Minhag America"). In subsequent discussions the secretary was instructed to find out "what *Minnick America* is"! Three months later a motion to adopt the Minnick America was defeated. Before the year was out, it was unanimously resolved -that "Minhag America" (spelled correctly this time) be accepted, and reform was well under way.[29] The members did not understand the specific details of what was involved, but they recognized that the change would lead them in the direction they wanted to go.

In addition to elegant edifices and decorous services, affluent, respectable congregations of all denominations desired clergymen whose intellect and demeanor would reflect their newly acquired status. It therefore "became increasingly important to have a minister of high social standing; Episcopalians and others frequently imported them from Europe."[30] So did American Jews. Samuel Adler had come to Emanu-El in New York in 1857 and Benjamin Szold to Oheb Sholom in Baltimore in 1858. In 1866 Marcus Jastrow and Samuel Hirsh both accepted invitations to come to Philadelphia, the former to Rodeph Sholom, the latter to Knesseth Israel. Kaufman Kohler arrived in 1869, serving first at Beth El in Detroit and two years later at Sinai in Chicago. Some of these men were regarded as conservatives, others as radicals. All were university graduates and cultured gentlemen who were committed to modernization of Jewish belief and practice. Like their upper middle class Protestant contemporaries, all were "princes of the pulpit."[31] The most persistent demand their congregations made on them was that they learn to sermonize in English.

The handful of rabbis of this period who have been characterized as conservative were in fact reformers who favored substantial changes in ritual and ideology, but resisted what they regarded as precipitate transformations. Men like Szold in Baltimore and Jastrow in Philadelphia were able to delay the abrogation of some traditional practices, but they did not succeed in stemming the tide of reform even in their own congregations. The Oheb Sholom Congregation of which Szold was the rabbi eliminated the second day of festivals in 1867 and abolished head-covering during worship in 1869.[32]

Rodeph Sholom in Philadelphia was somewhat slower in effecting changes; with Jastrow's approval, however, the congregation did introduce an organ, shorten the Torah reading, and abolish the practice of calling laymen to recite the blessings for the Torah reading. It also introduced a new prayer book (prepared by Szold, with revisions and an English translation by Jastrow), which eliminated references to the restoration of the Temple and the return to Zion. In 1878 the congregation joined Wise's Union of American Hebrew Congregations. Jastrow's successor was one of the early graduates of the Hebrew Union College, who described him as follows:

> In the building of this synagogue in 1869 and the creation of a new and revised ritual, he championed the cause of Reform. A wholesome conservatism advocated by him, acted as a check on the precipitate transformations urged by many. Changes were to be the product of growth and ripeness.[33]

Rodeph Sholom did not lead the way, neither did it lag far behind. It soon became as much a reform congregation as any other.

The conservatives differed from the more radical reformers over the proper pace for ritual change, but their fundamental theological outlook was similar. Szold recommended that his congregation "omit from reading in the Torah verses concerning sacrifices [because they are of] no significance to us today."[34] His prayer book—like Einhorn's—denationalized Judaism, eliminated prayers for the restoration of Zion, and transformed the Fast of the Ninth of Av into a day of affirmation of Israel's universal mission. "We do not unduly lament over the Temple that is destroyed," he wrote. "We mourn not despairingly over the downfall of Jerusalem . . . Thou has given us another home in place of that which we lost in the Land of our fathers."[35] For the conservatives no less than for the radicals, Judaism had become an American denomination whose practices were a matter of personal judgment and selection rather than authoritative decision. The binding validity of the tradition had been abrogated, and the view of Israel as a nation in exile repudiated.

Even Sabato Morais, chazan of Sephardic Mikveh Israel, was forced to concede that in order to "preserve historical Judaism . . . concessions for which we are unprepared may be demanded." In order to achieve an "American Judaism more conformable to our changed circumstances," Morais acknowledged the need for a simpler prayer book which would

> expunge what relates to the ordinances followed by the Ancients in the performances of sacrificial rites; strike out what relates to Mishnaic and Talmudic lore; reduce the number of Psalms now to be daily rehearsed; avoid as far as practiceable, the reiterating of a supplication,

confession, or sacred song; eschew the utterance of all
sorts of denunciations; compare philologically long-
established rituals; study to discover in them what is
more correct in diction, select what is more chaste in
style, more exalting in ideas . . . Then endeavor to fill
up a portion of the space made empty by the expurga-
tory process with compositions suited to our existing
wants.[36]

Morais resisted more substantive changes (such as eliminating
hope for the Messianic restoration), not on the basis of their
theological sanctity, but rather because of the pragmatic need
to preserve the unity of Israel. He recoiled at the thought of
"suffering my house of prayer to become a strange place to
my fellow-believer from another land." Even for Morais an
Israelite abroad had become no more than a fellow believer.
The concessions he was prepared to make illustrate the extent
to which the reformist outlook had penetrated the remaining
conservative enclaves in American Jewish life in the 1870's.
Not until the new immigration of East European Jews began
after 1881 was the prospect rekindled for the survival of a
more traditional form of Judaism in America.

During the course of the decade between 1860 and 1870,
the conservatives embarked on a final effort to create an institutional structure that would maintain a somewhat more traditional version of Jewish practice. In July 1867 Maimonides
College was established in Philadelphia under the leadership
of Isaac Leeser. The project was jointly sponsored by the
Hebrew Education Society of Philadelphia and the Board of
Delegates of American Israelites; its purpose was to train
rabbis to serve American Jewish congregations. The sponsors
never provided more than token support for the institution
and Leeser's death in 1868 ended whatever slim prospects for
survival it may have had. Maimonides College continued to

exist on paper for a few years under the leadership of Marcus Jastrow, but it never attracted students, faculty, or lay support. The college expired in late 1872 or early 1873 without ever having graduated or ordained a student.[37]

The radical reformist rabbis were no more successful than their conservative colleagues in their attempt to exercise a decisive influence over the development of American Judaism. In 1865 the radicals—led by David Einhorn, at that time serving as rabbi of Beth-El in New York, and Samuel Adler, Rabbi of Emanu-El in New York—organized the Emanu-El Theological Seminary Association. A year later an attempt was made to broaden the appeal and enlarge the base of support, and the association was renamed The American Hebrew College of the City of New York. The response was negligible, and the proposed seminary never came into existence. The Association's only achievement was to provide scholarships that enabled several students to study in Germany.

In 1869 Einhorn convened a conference of rabbis in Philadelphia to formulate a statement of principles which would serve as a platform for the reform of Judaism in America. Twelve rabbis—most of them recently arrived in America—attended. The brief credo that was adopted disavowed the hope for a restoration of Zion or for a personal Messiah stressing Israel's "universal mission" and the goal of a messianic age that would "realize the untiy of all rational creatures and their call to moral sanctification."[38] The statement repudiated the belief in bodily resurrection and affirmed the desirability of conducting worship in the vernacular rather than in Hebrew. Ironically, the document was issued in German, illustrating the personal dilemma of its German-speaking framers as well as the extent to which they were out of touch with the aspirations of the community they sought to influence.

The Philadelphia conference had no discernible impact, and a proposed second meeting was never held. By 1869 pragmatic piecemeal reformation was well under way, and Einhorn's platform neither hastened nor impeded the emergence of the pattern that was evolving as a response to the American environment.

The task of consolidating an institutional framework to sustain this emerging American-Jewish religious pattern fell to Isaac Mayer Wise—pragmatist, entrepreneur, and Americanizer *par excellence*. Wise had been present in Philadelphia in 1869 but was virtually ignored. Following the failure of the Philadelphia conference, he convened a rabbinical conference in Cincinnati in 1871 which was "distinguished not for declarations of principles but for action for the cause of Israel." The resolution adopted there made no reference to points of view—reform or traditionalist. In the broadest possible terms the statement called upon the congregations

> to unite themselves into a Hebrew Congregational Union with the object to preserve and advance the union of Israel; to take proper care of the development and promulgation of Judaism; to establish and support a scholastic institute . . . for the education of rabbis, preachers and teachers of religion; to provide cheap editions of the English Bible and textbooks for the schools of religious instruction; to give support to weak congregations and to provide such other institutions which elevate, preserve and promulgate Judaism.

The declaration was ideologically vague, but it was organizationally specific. It stipulated that "whenever twenty congregations with no less than two thousand contributing male members shall have declared . . . their resolution to enter the H.C.U., the said community shall convoke the synod to meet at such time and place as may be most satisfactory to the cooperating congregations."[39] None of the Eastern radical reformers participated in the conference. Their absence did not affect the organizational process; their dissent was no more consequential than their affirmation.

In 1873 thirty-four congregations met in Cincinnati to form a Union of American Hebrew Congregations in which "no questions of religious belief or practice should be discussed." Two years later this Union became the sponsoring organization of the Hebrew Union College, with Isaac M. Wise as its president. The groundwork had been laid for the emergence of an organized religious denomination and a professionalized American Jewish clergy.

Initially, only midwestern and southern congregations affiliated themselves with the Union, but within a few years the eastern seaboard congregations joined as well. The hostility of the eastern rabbis to Wise and to his brand of reform was disregarded by congregational leaders who discovered that the upward mobility of Jews in all sections of the country had minimized the social distinctions between east and west. In the late 1870's the Union absorbed the old Board of Delegates of American Israelites, once a stronghold of Eastern conservatism, and became the constituent body of virtually all of American Jewry. The growing homogeneity of American Jewry had made it possible to overcome surviving personal antagonisms, sectional rivalries, and vestigial doctrinal differences. For a few years it seemed as though an increasingly unified American Jewry had achieved a generally accepted American Jewish pattern.

The new American Judaism of the 1870's was not an importation from abroad and not the creation of rabbis. In every instance in which rabbis—of whatever point of view—deviated from the popular tendency, their ideas were ignored. Isaac Mayer Wise's initial moderation and his lifelong stress on Sabbath observance were disregarded. Einhorn's insistence on German as the language of reform and on principled consistency in establishing a reform program was rejected.

Individuals who felt themselves to be a part of the total society sought Jewish institutions that were attuned to that society. The masses selectively took from each leader the views which most effectively reinforced the changes that were in process. They culled from various sources the points of view that provided a rationale for the pattern that had emerged in practice. Without any formal action or specific reformulation, Jewish doctrine had been redefined to conform to the presumed dictates of reason. Jewish ritual practice had been modified to reflect the tastes of an increasingly respectable acculturated constituency: it was decorous, dignified, and readily intelligible to any American audience. Jewish institutions—especially the synagogue had been redesigned in keeping with what was perceived as the American mode. American Jewry believed it had found the synthesis through which it would participate in the inauguration of the messianic age which seemed to be at hand.

The systematic explication of a reform platform was undertaken after the reformation had already been achieved. In 1885 Kaufman Kohler, son-in-law and spiritual heir of Einhorn, convened a conference of rabbis in Pittsburgh. By that time the major problem was no longer to introduce changes but rather to counteract growing religious indifference among the acculturated and the "fading of household virtue." The resurgence of orthodoxy in the wake of the new immigration of the 1880's was acknowledged but was not yet viewed as a serious threat, and indeed among the Americanized element it was not. Kohler proposed adoption of a platform "broad, compassionate, enlightened and liberal enough to impress and win all hearts and also firm and positive enough to dispel suspicion of agnostic tendencies or of discontinuing the historic thread of the past." He hoped that the platform would provide a rallying point for those who had broken with the traditional Jewish code of law."[40]

Isaac Mayer Wise, ever suspicious of intellectuals and of doctrinal declarations, was a reluctant participant. He debated with himself whether to go or "to maintain a kind of armed neutrality." He went to the conference and was elected president. A few years earlier, Wise, ever the fence straddler, had declared that his Hebrew Union College would be "an orthodox Jewish academy . . . in which the Jewish spirit as it is manifested in our literature shall have control over all exotic and original ideas from whatever source and age they may come."[41] In 1885 he presided at Pittsburgh and acquiesced in a platform that repudiated his lifelong views on the divinity of Biblical revelation and "did violence to all he had been saying and writing for many years" regarding the sanctity of the Sabbath.[42] His role has been described as more of a spectator than an active participant.

The eight-point resolution that was adopted by the seventeen rabbis who assembled hailed "the modern era of the universal culture of heart and intellect [and] the approach of the realization of Israel's great Messianic hope for the establishment of the kingdom of truth, justice and peace among all men." All ceremonies regarded as "not adapted to the views and habits of modern civilization" were rejected. Laws regulating diet, priestly purity, and dress were dismissed as "altogether foreign to our present mental and spiritual state." The traditional hope for national restoration was repudiated: "we consider ourselves no longer a nation but a religious community." Judaism emerged as "a progressive religion ever striving to be in accord with the postulates of reason."[43]

The Pittsburgh platform was not a manifesto or a call to action, and indeed no consequences or new initiatives followed its adoption. Wise, who initially applauded the document, soon declared that the Union of American Hebrew Congregations and the Hebrew Union College had nothing to do with it, and the proposed second meeting of the conference participants never took place. The platform did constitute a coherent summary of the changes in attitudes and practice which had taken place during the preceding decades. The statement of generalized beliefs and intellectual justifications invested the quest for social adjustment with religious significance. According to this version of Judaism, adaptation and progressivist change were not only possible—they were necessary. America became the fulfillment of the Judaic ideal, and the tension between the requirements of the secular society and the demands of the religious tradition were dissolved.

The redefined Jewish tradition and the restructured Jewish identity seemed to provide a framework for maintaining a form of Jewish continuity. By remaining a separate and still somewhat distinctive sect, American Jews retained a degree of marginality. Very few followed Felix Adler into the Ethical Culture Society. The normative reform Judaism that emerged in the United States preserved a link to the Jewish past and to the people of Israel which, under the impact of later developments, could again be redefined and amplified.

The tidal wave of East European immigrants which began after 1881 inundated the Jewish community and transformed the confident reform majority into a defensive minority. In the wake of the radically different values and attitudes of the newcomers and the problems created by their arrival, the process of adaptation and adjustment began anew. A new burst of organizational energy led to new modes of accommodation and to the creation of the complex institutional and ideological panorama of twentieth-century American Jewry.

None of this was foreseen in the 1870's. For a decade American Jewry was united in the confidence that it had solved its problems and that, along with the larger society in which it participated enthusiastically, it was on the road to the achievement of the millennium. The messianic age was believed to be dawning. It would witness, in Philipson's words, "the union of all the children of God in the confession of the unity of God, so as to realize the unity of all rational creatures and their call to moral sanctification."

Notes

INTRODUCTION

1. Maldwyn Allen Jones, *American Immigration* (Chicago, 1960), p. 65.
2. Marcus Hansen, *The Atlantic Migration, 1607–1860* (Cambridge, 1945), p. 120.

1. THE EARLIEST AMERICAN JEWRY

1. *Reminiscences*, ed. and trans. David Philipson (Cincinnati: Leo M. Wise and Co., 1901), p. 57.
2. In Jacob R. Marcus, *Memoirs of American Jews, 1775–1865* (3 vols., Philadelphia: Jewish Publication Society of America, 1955), I, 247.
3. Jacob R. Marcus, *Early American Jewry* (2 vols., Philadelphia: Jewish Publication Society of America, 1951), I, 30 ff.
4. *A Dictionary of All Religions and Religious Denominations*, cited in Joseph L. Blau and Salo W. Baron, *The Jews of the United States 1790–1840, A Documentary History* (3 vols., New York, 1963), I, 87.
5. Leo Hershkowitz and Isidore S. Meyer, eds., *Letters of the Franks Family (1733–1748)* (Waltham, Mass.: American Jewish Historical Society, 1968), pp. xv, 66.
6. Blau and Baron, I, 85.
7. Lee M. Friedman, *Jewish Pioneers and Patriots* (Philadelphia: Jewish Publication Society of America, 1955), pp. 148-150.
8. Rudolph Glanz, "Jews in Relation to the Cultural Milieu of the Germans in America up to the Eighteen Eighties," *YIVO Bleter*

(New York, 1947), XXV, reprinted in Glanz, *Studies in Judaica Americana* (New York, Ktav 1970), p. 220.

9. Marcus, *Early American Jewry*, II, 512.

10. *The Emergence of Conservative Judaism* (Philadelphia: Jewish Publication Society of America, 1963), p. 26.

11. *Prayers for Shabboth, Rosh Hashanah, and Kippur* (New York, 1766).

12. Letter of I. W. Carpeles to Rabbi Saul Lowenstamm, cited in Hyman B. Grinstein, *The Rise of the Jewish Community of New York 1654–1860* (Philadelphia: Jewish Publication Society of America, 1945, p. 562.

13. Grinstein, p. 229: "A manuscript copy of a Hebrew address which he wrote for Sampson Simson when the latter graduated from Columbia College . . . [is] grammatically faulty." The original copy is in the Columbiana collection. See also Marcus, *Early American Jewry*, I, 95.

14. David de Sola Pool, *Portraits Etched in Stone* (New York, 1952), pp. 349-351, 357, 359.

15. Marcus, *Early American Jewry*, II, 444. Seixas was formally designated "minister" in 1784 when New York State gave formal status to "ministers."

16. Washington's reply to the Hebrew congregation in Newport, Rhode Island, cited in Blau and Baron, I, 9.

17. David and Tamar de Sola Pool, *An Old Faith in the New World* (New York, 1955), p. 215.

18. Blau and Baron, III, 955.

19. Blau and Baron, II, 554, 559.

2 . BLAZING A TRAIL

1. de Sola Pool, *An Old Faith in the New World*, pp. 275-276.

2. Ibid., p. 275.

3. Edwin Wolf 2nd and Maxwell Whiteman, *The History of the Jews of Philadelphia from Colonial Times to the Age of Jackson* (Philadelphia: Jewish Publication Society of America, 1957), p. 230.

4. Hansen, *The Atlantic Migration*, pp. 90, 97.

5. Mordecai M. Noah, *Discourse Delivered at the Consecration of the Synagogue of K. K. Shearith Israel in the City of New York, on*

Friday, the 10th of Nisan, 5578, Corresponding with the 17th of April, 1818 (New York, 1818), p. 45. A careful study of the records of the census of 1820 was undertaken by Ira Rosenwaike. He concluded that in 1820, "the Jewish population of the United States numbered fewer than three thousand." Rosenwaike, "The Jewish Population of the United States as Estimated from the Census of 1820," *American Jewish Historical Quarterly*, LIII (1963), 148.

6. Isaac Harby, *Discourse before the Reformed Society of Israelites* (Charleston, 1825), published in the *North American Review*, XXIII (July 1826), 67-79.

7. Cited in Blau and Baron, III, 880-884, 887, 889.

8. *The Diary of John Quincy Adams, 1794–1845* (New York, 1929), p. 244.

9. Abraham B. Makover, *Mordecai M. Noah, His Life and Work* (New York: Bloch Publishing Co., 1917), pp. 35-60. See also Isaac Goldberg, *Major Noah: American Jewish Pioneer* (Philadelphia: Jewish Publication Society of America, 1944), pp. 189-215; and Selig Adler and Thomas E. Connolly, *From Ararat to Suburbia: The History of the Jewish Community of Buffalo* (Philadelphia: Jewish Publication Society of America, 1960), pp. 7-10.

10. Lewis F. Allen, "Founding of the City of Ararat on Grand Island by Mordecai Manuel Noah," *Publications of the Buffalo Historical Society*, I (1866), 305-328. Reprinted in *Publications of the American Jewish Historical Society*, VIII (1900), 97-118. In summarizing the Ararat project, Allen writes: "Major Noah, a day or two afterwards, departed from his home in New York; the 'cornerstone' was taken from the audience-chamber of the church and deposited against its rear wall, outside; and the great prospective City of Ararat, with its splendid predictions and promises, vanished, 'and, like an unsubstantial pageant faded—left not a rock behind' [Noah] was known to be eccentric in many things, and this was put down as the climax of his eccentricities."

11. Grinstein, p. 146.

12. Wolf and Whiteman, pp. 225-226. See also Edward Davis, *History of Rodeph Shalom Congregation 1802–1926* (Philadelphia: Press of Edward Stern and Co., 1926), pp. 12-13. The precise date when this congregation assumed an independent existence is uncertain. Wolf and Whiteman cite evidence of the existence of the congregation beginning in 1795. Davis begins the history of the congre-

gation with the formal organization of the Society in 1802 under the name German Hebrew Society Rodeph Shalom.

13. Wolf and Whiteman, pp. 227, 231.

14. *Constitution and By-Laws of the Hebra Hinuch Nearim* (New York: printed by S. H. Jackson, 1825).

15. Grinstein, pp. 43-49. De Sola Pool, *An Old Faith in the New World*, pp. 436-439. Israel Goldstein, *A Century of Judaism in New York* (New York: Congregation B'nai Jeshurun, 1930), p. 51.

16. De Sola Pool, *An Old Faith in the New World*, p. 436.

17. Goldstein, pp. 52, 68.

18. Ibid., p. 56.

19. Ibid., p. 131.

20. De Sola Pool, pp. 276-277.

21. Grinstein, p. 49. Moshe Davis speaks of the "struggle to maintain the all embracing character of the synagogue which ended in failure." See Davis, *The Emergence of Conservative Judaism*, p. 29. The documents of the period reflect no such struggle.

22. Rosenwaike, "The Jewish Population of the United States," pp. 136-144.

23. David Philipson, "The Jewish Pioneers of the Ohio Valley," *Publications of the American Jewish Historical Society*, VIII (1900), 43-52. The name "Kal a Kodish Beneh Israel" is a corrupt transliteration of the Hebrew "Kahal Hakadosh Bnai Israel" (The Holy Congregation of the Children of Israel).

24. Hansen, *The Atlantic Migration*, p. 120.

3. THE RISING TIDE

1. H. G. Reissner, "The German-American Jews (1800–1850)," *Leo Baeck Institute Yearbook*, X, (London, 1965), p. 70.

2. Hansen, *The Atlantic Migration*, p. 140.

3. Mack Walker, *Germany and the Emigration, 1816–1885* (Cambridge, 1964), pp. 43, 47-50, 54-55, 65. Jewish authors frequently cite restrictions on marriage as a primary motive for emigration. They occasionally assume that such restrictions were imposed only on Jews and were therefore manifestations of anti-Semitic persecution. In fact, while marriage restrictions were frequently enforced with special severity against Jews, they were applied to all elements of the "surplus population." Marriage legislation was adopted in Bavaria in

1818 and in 1834, in Wurttemberg in 1828, 1833, and 1852, in Hann-over in 1827, in the Hildesheim district in 1835 and 1840, and in most Thuringian states during the 1830's. The force of all of this legisla-tion was to "prevent the establishment of households without ade-quate economic bases." The same economic dislocation which led to the imposition of marriage restrictions, led to emigration from the same areas. The Kingdom of Prussia which was in the midst of a period of economic expansion, experienced neither marriage restric-tions nor emigration. During the years 1824–1848, Prussia was an area of in-migration and population growth. Not until the late 1840's did migration begin to flow out of Prussia rather than into it. See Walker, pp. 52-56, 162-164.

4. Guido Kisch, "Israel's Herold: The First Jewish Weekly in New York," *Historia Judaica*, II (1940), 80.

5. Louis M. Hacker, *The Triumph of American Capitalism* (New York, 1965), p. 222.

6. Jones, *American Immigration*, pp. 93, 118.

7. Association Tseire Ha-Tson, *Address and Articles of the Asso-ciation* (New York, 1837). The proposed use of Yiddish rather than German in the proceedings indicates a lack of exposure to German language and secular learning.

8. *Rise of the Jewish Community*, p. 122. See also Moshe Ringel, "Further Information Concerning the Colony 'Sholem' on Yageville Hill, Ulster County, New York," *Publications of the American Jew-ish Historical Society*, XXXV (1939), 306-309.

9. From time to time articles appeared in European journals stat-ing that "over there (in America) they devote themselves to handi-crafts and agriculture." These reports lack any specific information such as names and places and are second-hand repetitions of vague hearsay. They must therefore be disregarded as evidence of wishful thinking and romanticization which frequently colored European information about immigrant experience in America. See the report from *Allgemeine Zeitung des Judentums* (1845), cited by Rudolph Glanz, "Source Materials on the History of Jewish Immigration to the United States, 1800–1880," *YIVO Annual of Jewish Social Sci-ence*, VI (1951), 123.

10. Rudolph Glanz, "Notes on Early Jewish Peddling in Amer-ica," *Jewish Social Studies*, VII (1945), reprinted in Glanz, *Studies in Judaica Americana* (New York, 1970), p. 107.

11. Testimony of numerous immigrant experiences is confirmed

ᴜʏ ᴀ report in *Israelitische Annalen* in 1839: "As a result of emigrants' letters, many skilled workers abandon their calling to go peddling in America many hundreds of English miles inland." Cited in Glanz, "Source Materials on Jewish Immigration," p. 91.

12. Joshua Trachtenberg, *Consider the Years: The Story of the Jewihs Community of Easton (1752–1942)* (Easton, Pennsylvania, 1944), p. 125.

13. Stephen Birmingham, *Our Crowd: The Great Jewish Families of New York* (New York, 1967), pp. 52-53.

14. Allan Tarshish, "The Economic Life of the American Jew in the Middle Nineteenth Century," *Essays in American Jewish History* (Cincinnati: American Jewish Archives, 1958), p. 269. See also Eric E. Hirshler, "Jews from Germany in the United States," in his edition of *Jews from Germany in the United States* (New York, 1955), p. 37.

15. Abram Vossen Goodman, "A Jewish Peddler's Diary 1842–1843," *American Jewish Archives*, III (1951), 81-111. As Selma Stern-Taeubler commented, German Jewish immigrants wrote their memoirs "when they were old men, completely rooted in the New World. Filled with the desire to render to themselves and their children an account of their eventful and successful, and often adventurous lives, they were too harassed by the abundance of changing scenes to find time for critical introspection and self-examination, or even to ponder what spiritual or moral forces had at one time shaped them." Selma Stern-Taeubler, "The Motivation of German Jewish Emigration," *Essays in American Jewish History* (Cincinnati: American Jewish Archives, 1959), pp. 247-248.

16. Guido Kisch, "A Voyage to America Ninety Years Ago," *Publications of the American Jewish Historical Society*, XXXV (1939), 65-113.

17. Kisch, "Voyage," p. 113. For an undisclosed reason, Kisch surmises in his introduction that the postscripts were written by Rosenbaum fifty years later. The content of the diary, the related experiences of other immigrants, and the little that is known of Rosenbaum's later life all make this conjecture implausible.

18. Wise, *Reminiscences*, p. 37.

19. Ibid., pp. 37-38.

20. Reissner, p. 79.

21. James G. Heller, *As Yesterday When It Is Past* (Cincinnati, 1942), p. 22.

22. Reissner, p. 64.

23. Raphael Mahler, "The Economic Background of Jewish Emigration from Galicia," *YIVO Annual of Jewish Social Science*, VII 1952), 267.

24. Kisch, "Voyage," p. 158.

25. Stern-Taeubler, p. 247.

26. Glanz, "Source Materials on Jewish Immigration," reprinted in Glanz, *Studies in Judaica Americana*, p. 22.

27. Ibid., p. 20.

28. The earliest reliable source from which a list of congregations may be compiled is the first United States census of religious bodies conducted in 1850. However, as Uriah Z. Engelman has pointed out, "the definition of a church used in the censuses of 1850, 1860, and 1870, must have affected unfavorably the census of churches of religious bodies which had comparatively large number of small congregations, newly organized, as did the Jewish." Engelman, "Jewish Statistics in the United States Census of Religious Bodies, 1850–1936," *Jewish Social Studies*, IX (1947), 10. In 1854 a list of congregations was published in Jacques I. Lyons and Abraham de Sola's *A Jewish Calendar for Fifty Years* (Montreal, 1854). The compilers themselves apologize for the inadequacy of their list; they had to rely on "friends who afforded them items of information" and "gleanings from the Jewish press." "Any irregularity," they explain, "has arisen from the difficulty . . . experienced in obtaining any [information] of a more uniform character" (ibid., p. 148).

Subsequent authors were less than meticulous in checking these sources and in comparing them with records available in individual congregations. For example, Joseph Krauskopf in "Half Century of Judaism in the United States," *American Jews Annual*, IV (Cincinnati, 1888), p. 70-71 omits a number of pre-1840 congregations from his list but includes two congregations in St. Louis: United Hebrew, listed as having been founded in 1838, and Achduth Israel [the Hebrew name means Unity of Israel], listed as having been founded in 1839. The minute books of the United Hebrew Congregation reveal that these two are in fact one and the Achduth Israel is the Hebrew equivalent of United Hebrew. In a work like Moshe Davis' *The*

Emergence of Conservative Judaism, Krauskopf's list is repeated and the error is perpetuated.

Hyman Grinstein's carefully researched list of New York synagogues differs considerably from that published in the Lyons directory of 1854. Grinstein, pp. 472-474.

The greatest discrepancy in dates is found in regard to the establishment of the first Ashkenazi congregation in America, Rodeph Shalom in Philadelphia. Rudolph Glanz sets the date as early as 1780 ("The Immigration of German Jews up to 1880," *YIVO Annual of Jewish Social Science,* II-III, 1947-1948, 82.) Wolf and Whiteman accept 1795 as the date and carefully document their contention. (Edwin Wolf 2nd and Maxwell Whiteman, *The History of the Jews of Philadelphia,* pp. 225-226). Edward Davis cites the exact date of the organization of Rodeph Shalom Synagogue as that given in its charter, namely October 10, 1802. (Davis, *History of Rodeph Shalom Congregation,* p. 13).

These discrepancies illustrate the informality and structural looseness characteristic of early (and in many instances later) synagogue life in America.

29. Lyons and de Sola, pp. 148-173; Engelman, pp. 10-12.

30. *The Occident,* VI (Philadelphia, 1848), 317, 366.

4. THE PATTERN OF CONGREGATIONAL LIFE

1. Lewis Abraham, "Correspondence Between George Washington and Jewish Citizens," *Publications of the American Jewish Historical Society,* III (1895), 87-94.

2. For a detailed description of patterns of authority and organization in various Jewish communities see Salo W. Baron, *The Jewish Community, Its History and Structure to the American Revolution* (3 vols., Philadelphia: Jewish Publication Society of America, 1948.

3. Jacob Katz, *Tradition and Crisis, Jewish Society at the End of the Middle Ages* (New York, 1961). See especially Katz's discussion of the disintegration of traditional society, pp. 245-274.

4. Sydney E. Ahlstrom, *A Religious History of the American People* (New Haven, 1972), pp. 429-490.

5. *An Original History of the Religious Denominations at Present*

Existing in the United States (Philadelphia: J. Y. Humphreys, 1844).

6. Davis, *History of Rodeph Shalom Congregation*, pp. 13-14. In 1810, when twenty-five members of the congregation signed a newly adopted constitution, all but one wrote in "Jewish script" (p. 23).

7. Ibid., p. 35. A resolution adopted on April 18, 1826, reads: "Resolved that all subscribers except Aaron Dropsie who may have been married or who may in the future marry contrary to the Jewish rites, shall not have, nor be entitled to any honors or privileges in our synagogue, and any member who shall from and after this date, marry contrary to the Jewish Law, shall forfeit his membership."

8. Goldstein, *Century of Judaism in New York*, p. 56.

9. Ibid., p. 85. Bnai Jeshurun was one of the few Ashkenazi congregations to address inquiries to Europe. The presence in the leadership of this congregation of a number of English Jews and the existence of a "Chief Rabbi" in England after 1845 explain this practice. The number of inquiries was few and the responses were generally disregarded.

10. David Philipson, *The Oldest Jewish Congregation in the West* (Cincinnati: Press of C. J. Krebhail and Co., 1894), p. 14.

11. Isaac M. Fein, *The Making of an American Jewish Community* (Philadelphia: Jewish Publication Society of America, 1971), pp. 43, 68.

12. *History of Congregation Adath Israel* (Louisville, Kentucky, 1906), pp. 13, 16, 17, 22.

13. *Constitution of United Hebrew Congregation of St. Louis* (1841).

14. By Laws of United Hebrew Congregation of St. Louis (1843).

15. Minutes of United Hebrew Congregation of St. Louis: July 23, 1843; March 5, 1847; October 2, 1848; February 5, 1850.

16. Trachtenberg, *Consider the Years*, pp. 113, 114.

17. Constitution of Congregation Covenant of Peace, Easton, Pennsylvania (1839), in Trachtenberg, pp. 235-236.

18. Ibid. (1842), Trachtenberg, pp. 237-241.

19. Trachtenberg, pp. 145-146.

20. Minutes of Congregation Anshe Chesed of New York (1835–1858), December 3, 5596 (1835).

21. Ibid., March 30, 5596 (1836); April 20, 5596 (1836); August

14, 5596 (1836); December 10, 5596 (1835); March 15, 21, 28, 5601 (1841); November 15, 5601 (1840).

22. Ibid., July 28, 5604 (1844); May 7, 5603 (1843).

23. Ibid., January 28, 5604 (1844).

24. Ibid.

25. Bertram W. Korn, *The Early Jews of New Orleans* (Waltham, Massachusetts: American Jewish Historical Society, 1969), pp. 196-197, 202-204.

26. Ibid., p. 248.

27. Charles Reznikoff and Uriah Z. Engelman, *The Jews of Charleston* (Philadelphia: Jewish Publication Society of America, 1950), pp. 138-139.

28. Ibid., p. 142. See also Joseph Buchler, "The Struggle for Unity —Attempts at Union in American Jewish Life: 1654-1868," *American Jewish Archives*, II (1949), 27.

29. *Reminiscences*, pp. 142-143.

30. Walker, *Germany and the Emigration*, p. 69.

31. Of the six Sephardic congregations organized prior to 1789, five were still in existence. The sixth, in Newport, Rhode Island, ceased functioning in the 1820's. According to the most reliable estimates, thirteen Ashkenazi congregations were founded prior to 1840.

32. Engelman, "Jewish Statistics in the United States Census of Religious Bodies," pp. 5-64. See also *Statistics of the Jews of the United States* (Philadelphia: Union of American Hebrew Congregations, 1880).

5. THE FIRST LEADERS

1. Henry S. Morais, *The Jews of Philadelphia* (Philadelphia: Levy Type Company, 1894), pp. 89-90.

2. Minutes of Congregation Anshe Chesed, December 10, 5596 (1835) (New York, in the library of Temple Emanu-El).

3. *The Occident and American Jewish Advocate*, X (1852), 23, 524.

4. Fein, *Making of an American Jewish Community*, p. 42.

5. Henry Englander, "Isaac Leeser," *Central Conference of American Rabbis Yearbook*, XXVIII (1918), 214-217. Leeser's article was a reply to anti-Semitic allegations that had appeared in the *London Quarterly Review*.

6. Herbert I. Ezekiel and Gaston Lichtenstein, *The History of the Jews of Richmond* (Richmond, Virginia, 1917), p. 55.

7. From 1817 until 1824 the ministry of Mikveh Israel was unfilled. A Mr. E. L. Lazarus of New York, who was elected in 1824, declined the position because the term and the salary were unacceptable. The vacancy was filled at last by "Reverend" Abraham Isaac Keys of Barbados. In 1828, when Keys died and the position once more became vacant, Lazarus was again a candidate, but Leeser was chosen. Morais, pp. 43–46. Leeser was elected for a term of three years at a salary of $800 per year. Although the salary was hardly munificent, it compares most favorably to that paid later by German congregations. When Leo Merzbacher was elected as minister by Congregation Emanu-El of New York in 1845, his annual salary was $200, which was regarded as a "liberal sum." Myer Stern, *The Rise and Progress of Reform Judaism, Embracing a History Made from the Official Records of Temple Emanu-El of New York* (New York, Myer Stern, 1895), p. 19.

8. Maxwell Whiteman, "Isaac Leeser and the Jews of Philadelphia," *Publications of the American Jewish Historical Society*, XLVIII (1959), 213. See also Morais, p. 46.

9. Englander, p. 220.

10. The German work was entitled *Alumei Yosef, Unterricht in der Mosaischen Religion;* it was written by Joseph Johlson and published in Frankfurt in 1819.

11. Isaac Leeser, *Discourses, Argumentative and Devotional on the Subject of the Jewish Religion* (Philadelphia, 5597 |1836|), p. xii.

12. Joseph R. Rosenbloom, "Rebecca Gratz and the Jewish Sunday School Movement in Philadelphia," *Publications of the American Jewish Historical Society*, XLVIII (1958), 71.

13. In 1835 Leeser published a circular entitled *To the Jewish Inhabitants of Philadelphia*. In it he proposed a school "where the children might acquire a correct knowledge of Hebrew, together with a thorough English education." No steps were taken to implement the proposal.

14. Isaac Leeser, *Memorial of the Sunday School for Religious Instruction of Israelites of Philadelphia* (Philadelphia, 1840), quoted in Blau and Baron, *Jews of the United States*, II, 448.

15. Bernard Weinryb cites a school established by German Jewish immigrants in Cleveland in 1844 in which the curriculum included

"Hebrew and German reading and writing, Jewish [Yiddish] writing and reading." "The German Jewish Immigrants to America, A Critical Evaluation," *Jews from Germany in the United States*, ed. Eric E. Hirshler (New York, 1955), p. 115.

16. Letter of Rebecca Gratz to Maria Gist Gratz, April 18, 1830, Library of the American Jewish Historical Society; quoted in Bertram W. Korn, "Isaac Leeser: Centennial Reflections," *American Jewish Archives*, XIX (1967), 132. Rebecca Gratz regarded Leeser's determination to publish as a mark of youthful enthusiasm which "experience will aid in checking." She was also pleased that Leeser was clean shaven. "Fortunately he is a beardless youth. Did he wear the chin of a rabbi, he would be scoffed at by his congregation." We have no reason to doubt that her comment accurately reflects the sentiment of the congregation. It provides additional evidence of the assimilationist bias of a Sephardic congregation which remained traditional in its formal ritual.

17. Leeser, *Discourses*, p. xi.

18. *Persecution of the Jews in the East, containing the Proceedings of a Meeting Held at Mikveh Israel, Philadelphia, on Thursday Evening, the 28th of AB, 5600 Corresponding with the 27th of August, 1840* (Philadelphia, 1840), reprinted in Blau and Baron, III, 934.

19. Jasper Chasseaud to John Forsyth Beyrout, March 24, 1840; MSS RG 59, General Records of the Department of State, National Archives, reprinted in Blau and Baron, III, 924-926. See also Morris U. Schappes, *A Documentary History of the Jews in the United States 1654–1875* (3rd edition, New York, 1971), pp. 202-203.

20. John Forsyth to John Glidden, Washington, August 14, 1840; MSS RG 59, General Records of the Department of State, National Archives, reprinted in Blau and Baron, III, 928-929.

21. Joseph Jacobs, "The Damascus Affair of 1840 and the Jews of America," *Publications of the American Jewish Historical Society*, X (1902), 121.

22. Blau and Baron, III, 930-954. See also Jacobs, pp. 119-125.

23. Montefiore and Cremieux arrived in Alexandria on August 4. On August 28, Mehemet Ali promised to set the prisoners free. They were released on September 6. See Jacobs, p. 124.

24. "Letter to His Excellency Martin Van Buren, President of the United States" (New York, August 24, 1840), reprinted in Jacob

Ezekiel, "Persecution of the Jews in 1840," *Publications of the American Jewish Historical Society*, VIII (1900), 142.

25. The officers of the Philadelphia committee included old Sephardic names like Peixotto; members of the early Ashkenazic family who were affiliated with Mikveh Israel, like Lewis Allen; and more recent German immigrants, like Louis Bomeister, president of Rodeph Sholom. See Blau and Baron, III, 1001, n. 80. See also Davis, *History of Rodeph Sholom Congregation*, p. 57.

26. Rebecca Gratz to Solomon Cohen (Philadelphia, October 4, 1840), MSS, University of North Carolina Library; reprinted, from a photostatic copy in the American Jewish Archives, in Blau and Baron, III, 954-955.

27. *Proceedings of a Public Meeting of the Citizens of Charleston, Held at City Hall on the 28th August, 1840, in Relation to the Persecution of the Jews in the East. Also, the Proceedings of a Meeting of the Israelites of Charleston, Convened at the Hall of the Hebrew Orphan Society on the Following Evening, in Reference to the Same Subject* (Charleston, 1849), quoted in Blau and Baron, III, 950-951.

28. *Proceedings of Meeting Held at Philadelphia*, reprinted in Blau and Baron, III, 936.

29. *The Occident and American Jewish Advocate*, I (1843), 2, 5.

30. *An Original History of the Religious Denominations at Present Existing in the United States*, pp. iii, v.

31. Ibid., p. 368.

32. Marvin Lowenthal, *The Jews of Germany* (Philadelphia: Jewish Publication Society of America, 1939), pp. 245-248. See also David Philipson, *The Reform Movement in Judaism* (Rev. ed., New York, 1931), pp. 128-224, and Michael A. Meyer, *The Origins of the Modern Jew* (Detroit, 1967).

33. Adolph Guttmacher, *A History of the Baltimore Hebrew Congregation* (Baltimore, Lord Baltimore Press, 1905), p. 27.

34. Fein, p. 55.

35. C. A. Rubenstein, *History of Har Sinai Congregation of the City of Baltimore* (Baltimore: Press of Kohn and Pollack, 1918), pp. 3-4.

36. Fein, p. 59.

37. *The Occident*, III (1845), 367.

38. Guttmacher, p. 40. Not until 1860 were the Piyyutim omitted from the ritual at the Baltimore Hebrew Congregation.

39. *The Occident,* II (1844), 599. Rice was no more successful in business than in the rabbinate. His venture in dry goods failed and he became a grocer. In 1851 he organized a small synagogue, which functioned on an informal basis for a number of years. Rice served as leader of this group without compensation. In 1862, under circumstances not entirely clear, he was invited back to his old congregation but died shortly after conducting services for the Day of Atonement.

40. Fein, pp. 56-57.

41. Robert Cross, *The Emergence of Liberal Catholicism* (Cambridge, 1948), p. 24.

42. *The Occident,* IV (1846), 265.

43. Max Lilienthal, "Necrology of Leo Merzbacher," *Die Deborah,* II (1856), 81, cited in Bernhard Cohn, "Leo Merzbacher," *American Jewish Archives,* VI (1954), 22.

44. *Menorah Monthly,* XI (1887), 67. Cited in Cohn, p. 22.

45. This opinion is held by Grinstein, *Rise of the Jewish Community,* pp. 543-544, n. 16. Cohn concurs and concludes: "Contrary to former opinion, it is hardly to be doubted any more that Merzbacher did have proper rabbinic ordination" (p. 24).

46. Minutes of Congregation Anshe Chesed: May 7, 5603 (1843); October 29, 5605 (1843). The dates cited are but two of numerous instances in which references are made to "Mr. Merzbacher."

47. *The History of the Congregation Rodeph Sholom of New York* (New York, 1892), p. 11.

48. Grinstein, p. 90. The history of Rodeph Sholom (1892) states that "Rev. Dr. Merzbacher was the first rabbi of the Congregation." Such reports are unreliable. In view of the absence of any records, we must assume that the account is a specimen of filiopietistic embellishment.

49. Minutes of Congregation Anshe Chesed, May 7, 5603 (1843); June 21, 5603 (1843); November 8, 5604 (1843); November 27, 5604 (1843); December 30, 5604 (1843).

50. Ibid., May 12, 5604 (1844). The chazan whose presence is required is the same man whom the congregation subsequently censured for "being round in parter[?] houses at all times of day and night, playing at cards, billiards, dominoes, etc and very often with persons unfit for him to be associated with."

51. An account written many years later claimed that Merzbacher

had "advocated the uncovering of the hair" by the women of Anshe Chesed and that opposition to the proposal led to Merzbacher's leaving Anshe Chesed with several of his followers to form Emanu-El. Grinstein, p. 347. This suggestion is altogether implausible. The wearing of perukes by women was rapidly abandoned and never became an issue. Moreover, the minutes of both congregations give no evidence of this issue. Myer Stern in his history of Temple Emanuel (1895) declares that the founders of the congregation were not connected with any of the existing New York congregations. Moreover, Merzbacher was not one of the founders of the new congregation. He was "engaged as rabbi and lecturer" after the "verein" had been established. Stern, pp. 13-18.

52. Stern, p. 18.
53. Ibid., p. 30.
54. Cohn, p. 23.
55. Stern, pp. 33, 41.
56. Temple Emanuel Minute Book, March 6, 1852.
57. Cohn, p. 23.
58. Cited in Beryl Levy, *Reform Judaism in America* (New York, 1933), p. 49.
59. Stern, p. 51.
60. *The Occident*, II (1844), 314.

6. RELIGIOUS REFORM

1. Albert H. Friedlander, "Cultural Contributions of the German Jew in America," in *Jews from Germany in the United States*, ed. Eric Hirshler (New York, 1955), p. 153.
2. For a discussion of the characteristics of German immigrants from small towns in the mid-nineteenth century and especially of the fact that Yiddish was their mother tongue see Weinryb, "The German Jewish Immigrants to America," pp. 111-124. Weinryb believes that the German immigrants assimilated more rapidly than the later East European immigrants because "they did not bring with them a highly developed sense of Jewish group life from home, for they had not lived in compact Jewish settlements." Whether or not one accepts this conclusion, the similar typology of the immigrants is striking. As late as 1868 Isaac Mayer Wise felt it necessary to

polemicize against Yiddish in his German language newspaper, *Die Deborah*: "Thinking Israelites must know what a drawback the jargon [Yiddish] was to the German Jew in the old fatherland." *Die Deborah*, XIV (1868–1869), 190.

3. David Einhorn, the German reform leader who arrived in the United States in 1855, was vitriolic in his denunciation of the expediency he found to be the rule in American Jewish life. His journal, *Sinai*, was filled with attacks against reformers like I. M. Wise, as well as so-called traditionalists like Isaac Leeser, for their lack of principles. His attitude is discussed in detail below.

4. For a discussion of the inseparable relationship between emancipation and Jewish religious reform in Germany see Natan Rotenstreich, "The Bruno Bauer Controversy," *Leo Baeck Institute Yearbook*, IV (1959), 3-36. See also H. D. Schmidt, "The Terms of Emancipation 1781–1812," ibid., I (1956), 28-45, for a discussion of the "self reformation" required of German Jews before they were "deemed worthy of admission to society."

5. Reform Judaism in Germany was regularly referred to as a "party" or a "movement." The movement and its institutions were frequently suppressed in the various German states as well as in Austria and Hungary. Often, governmental interference was invited by traditional elements in the Jewish community. See Philipson, *Reform Movement*.

6. For a discussion of social and psychological factors at work, see Stephen Steinberg, "Reform Judaism: The Origin and Evolution of a 'Church Movement,'" *Journal for the Scientific Study of Religion*, IV (1965), 117-129.

7. The founders of Reformed Society of Israelites in Charleston knew of the existence of German reform but apparently did not know any details concerning its experience. There is no record of any direct communication between Charleston Jews and Germany. Reznikoff and Engelman, *The Jews of Charleston*, p. 126. Their leaders of the Charleston Reformed Society of Israelites, especially Isaac Harby, were on very friendly terms with Unitarians in Charleston. The year 1825 was the high tide of Unitarian development and the one in which the American Unitarian Association was formed. See Clifton E. Olmstead, *History of Religion in the United States* (Englewood Cliffs, New Jersey, 1960), p. 297.

8. Wise, *Reminiscences*, pp. 142-143.

9. Reznikoff and Engelman, pp. 138-140.

10. Ibid., p. 296. *The Occident and American Jewish Advocate*, IX (1851), 209.

11. Minutes of Congregation Beth Elohim of Charleston (July 10, 1839), quoted in Reznikoff and Engelman, p. 296.

12. Charleston *Courier* (March 20, 1841), cited by Reznikoff and Engelman, p. 139.

13. Leeser, who was hostile to reform, altered the quotation in charging that Poznanski "evidently denied the coming of the Messiah and the restoration of the Temple and the ancient worship." *The Occident*, IX (1851), 214. Philipson, who was a partisan of reform, also misquoted Poznanski in attempting to find an early expression of reform ideas. See his "The Progress of the Jewish Reform Movement in the United States," *Jewish Quarterly Review*, X (London, 1898), 61.

14. Charleston *Courier* (March 20, 1841), cited by Reznikoff and Engelman, p. 140.

15. Ibid.

16. In ancient times, the Hebrew lunar calendar was set by observation at Jerusalem. The calendar determined the date when festivals were to be observed. When the Jewish diaspora grew, residents of distant places could not always be informed which day was the beginning of a new month and when a festival was to be observed. An extra day was therefore added to each festival to make absolutely certain that the festival would be observed on the proper date. The extra days (except for Rosh Hashanah, which fell on the first day of the month of Tishri) were observed everywhere outside of Palestine and were called "the second day of festivals for the diaspora." Even though the reason for the extra days was eliminated when the calendar was fixed by calculation, the observance continued. Wherever discussions of modifying Jewish worship began, consideration was given to eliminating the extra days and returning to the observance of the festivals as stipulated in the Biblical legislation. For Poznanski's suggestion of this modification see Reznikoff and Engelman, p. 141.

17. Reznikoff and Engelman, pp. 141, 142, 144, 200, 201.

18. Fein, *Making of an American Jewish Community*, p. 56.

19. Ibid., p. 62.

20. Rubenstein, p. 10.

21. *Israelite*, XI (January 15, 1864), cited in Fein, p. 110.

22. Rubenstein, pp. 8-9.

23. Fein, pp. 64-65.

24. Rubenstein, p. 21.

25. Bertram W. Korn, *American Jewry and the Civil War* (Philadelphia: Jewish Publication Society of America, 1951), p. 22.

26. Stern, *Rise and Progress of Reform Judaism*, p. 13.

27. Birmingham, *Our Crowd*, p. 35.

28. *The Occident*, II, 515.

29. Ibid., pp. 14-17.

30. Grinstein, *Rise of the Jewish Community of New York*, p. 355.

31. Stern, p. 16. It is interesting to note that at this time, the cantor received $50 more per annum than Merzbacher. While neither sum can be considered munificent, the cantor's larger salary indicates a continued emphasis on the conduct of ritual as opposed to more intellectual functions. Within a few years, the attitude at Emanuel changed and the rabbi replaced the cantor as the chief religious functionary.

32. Grinstein, pp. 543-544.

33. Minutes of Emanu-El (June 8, 1845).

34. Stern, pp. 22-23.

35. Grinstein, p. 398.

36. Stern, p. 24. By way of contrast, Congregation Anshe Chesed, which was founded in 1828, did not consider whitewashing the walls of the synagogue until 1843.

37. Ibid., p. 28.

38. Minutes of Emanu-El (January 16, 1848).

39. Hirshler, *Jews from Germany in the United States*, p. 61.

40. Stern, p. 31.

41. Ibid., p. 41.

42. Grinstein, "Reforms at Temple Emanuel of New York 1860–1890," *Historia Judaica*, VI (1944), 173.

43. Anshe Chesed Congregation introduced a few modest reforms in the 1850's. However, the congregation remained essentially traditional in its ritual until the late 1860's.

7. EMERGING OPTIONS

1. Goodman, "A Jewish Peddler's Diary," p. 101.

2. Olmstead, *History of Religion in the United States*, p. 329.

3. Ibid., p. 328.

4. *Statistics of the Jews of the United States* (Philadelphia: Union of American Hebrew Congregations, 1880).

5. Adler and Connolly, *From Ararat to Suburbia*, pp. 42, 50.

6. Ibid., pp. 43, 54, 70, 72.

7. B. Felsenthal and Herman Eliassof, *History of Kehillath Anshe Maarabh* (Chicago, 1897), p. 16. See also Grinstein, *Rise of the Jewish Community*, p. 226.

8. Extracts from the unpublished memoirs of Mayer Klein are printed in Hyman L. Meites, *History of the Jews of Chicago* (Chicago, 1924), p. 40.

9. Ibid., pp. 45, 54. See also Felsenthal and Eliassof, p. 19.

10. Felsenthal and Eliassof, p. 24.

11. Ibid., p. 21.

12. Irving I. Katz, *The Beth El Story* (Detroit, 1955), p. 66.

13. Stuart E. Rosenberg, *The Jewish Community in Rochester, 1843–1925* (New York, 1954), p. 26.

14. This was the case in Chicago where the first congregation Kehillat Anshei Maarav, organized in 1846, followed the German minhag. The second congregation, Kehillat Bnai Sholom, followed the Polish minhag. Some accounts date the founding of this congregation in 1849 and others in 1852. See Morris A. Gutstein, *A Priceless Heritage: The Epic Growth of Nineteenth Century Chicago Jewry* (New York: Bloch Publishing Company, 1953), pp. 29-30.

15. In cities such as St. Louis and Cincinnati the first congregations followed the Polish minhag. The second congregations adopted the German minhag. There are no theological differences between the two rites, and textual differences are minor. However, regional differences in pronunciation, in melodies, and in minor procedures during the conduct of the service existed and assumed importance to immigrants seeking to find a home away from home in the synagogue. See Heller, *As Yesterday When It Is Past*, pp. 24-26.

16. Schindler, *Israelites in Boston* (Boston: Press of Berwick and Smith, 1889), chap. II (pages unnumbered).

17. Heller, p. 27.

18. Ibid., pp. 25, 26, 81.

19. *Sinai*, I (1856), 406.

20. For a discussion of reactions to the Damascus Blood Libel see above, chap. V.

21. The text of Leeser's proposal is reproduced as Appendix I in Buchler, "The Struggle for Unity," pp. 39-44.

22. Grinstein, p. 150.

23. For a discussion of the formation of the Hebrew Benevolent Society and its relation to the split between Shearith Israel and Bnai Jeshurun, see above, chap. II.

24. Goldstein, *A Century of Judaism in New York*, p. 69. See also de Sola Pool, *An Old Faith in the New World*, p. 358. De Sola Pool reports that the Society "became affiliated with [Bnai Jeshurun], meeting as a rule in the basement of its synagogue."

25. Grinstein, p. 150.

26. Lyons and de Sola, *A Jewish Calendar for Fifty Years*, pp. 165-167. The purpose of a Hebra Ahavat Nashim is a mystery. No such group exists in the traditional Jewish roster of congregation committees. I can find no record of such a committee having existed elsewhere before or since.

27. *Address of the Jewish Publication Committee to the Israelites of America* (Philadelphia, 1845). Cited in Solomon Grayzel, "The First American Jewish Publication Society," *Jewish Book Annual* (New York 5795 [1944–1945]), p. 42.

28. Isaac Leeser, *The Law of God* (Philadelphia, 5605 [1845]).

29. Grayzel, p. 42.

30. Julius Bien, "A History of the Independent Order Bne B'rith," *Menorah*, I-IV (July 1886–June 1889). See also Bernard Postal, "Bnai Brith: A Century of Service," *American Jewish Yearbook*, XLV (5704 [1943–1944]).

31. Bien, chap. II, pp. 64-66. Bien describes Bnai Brith as a society "based on the teachings of Judaism." He cites a discussion reported to have taken place among the founders in which the fraternal society is portrayed as a restoration of the ideal synagogue which no longer existed: "The Jewish religion has many observances and customs corresponding to the secret societies known to us. The synagogue, for instance, might be compared to a lodge room. It used to be open twice a day; for a Jew desiring to find a friend, he had but to go there and make himself known by certain signs and tokens; he was sure to find assistance. . . . But now since the synagogue is open but once a week . . . it becomes necessary for us to try at least to remedy this evil and show the beauties of our Holy Religion."

32. Preamble to the first constitution, quoted in Postal, pp. 98-99.

33. Bien discusses the issue of alleged anti-Semitism at some length. Apparently there was a difference of opinion among the founders on this issue. While some of these men (including Bien himself) denied its existence, since they were themselves Masons and Odd Fellows, the report of William Renau states: "It was in the year 1843 that . . . several Israelites were rejected in some Masonic and Odd Fellows Lodges; as they believed then for no reason than their being Jews. Hebrew Masons and Odd Fellows felt aggrieved at this action." See Bien, chap. II, pp. 65-68.

34. Ibid., chap. IV, p. 163.

35. Grinstein, p. 205.

36. Ibid., p. 114. The three were Free Sons of Israel (1849), Brith Abraham (1859), and Kesher Shel Barzel (Link of Iron) (1860). None of these ever attained the size or prominence of Bnai Brith, and eventually all of them went out of existence.

37. Address of Henry Jones cited in Bien, chap. XIV, p. 49.

38. Ibid.

39. Grinstein, p. 203.

8. PROSPERITY AND PROVINCIALISM

1. Address of Merzbacher to Zion Lodge No. 2 of Bnai Brith in April 1844, cited in Bien, chap. VIII, p. 68.

2. While details of quarrels are usually omitted in synagogue minutes, reports such as "the president was silenced" and "the meeting broke off without transacting any business" are common. See Fein, *Making of An American Jewish Community*, p. 51. Isaac Wise reports an incident in which "a man rushed breathlessly into the room and with difficulty uttered the words, 'Blows at the congregational meeting'. . . . When I opened the door, the fight had not yet commenced; but the fighters stood ready to begin and messengers had been sent to call the police." *Reminiscences*, p. 89.

3. Wise, p. 165.

4. Minutes of Congregation Rodeph Sholom of Philadelphia (May 25, 1840).

5. Minutes of Congregation Bnai Jeshurun of Cincinnati (February 27, 1848). During the same period some members of the congregation were still "staying up Shebuos Night for reading and

learning according to our wholly Law of Germany." Minutes (June 2, 1848).

6. Minutes of Congregation Knesseth Israel of Philadelphia (October 3, 1852).

7. David Philipson, *Max Lilienthal, American Rabbi: Life and Writings* (New York: Bloch Publishing Co., 1915), pp. 1-45.

8. Lilienthal's rabbinic credentials were established beyond doubt when he was required to produce proof of his ordination at the time he was hired to become rabbi of the Union of German Synagogues in New York. Hyman B. Grinstein, "The Minute Books of Lilienthal's Union of German Synagogues in New York," *Hebrew Union College Annual* (Cincinnati, 1943–1944), p. 329.

9. Philipson, *Max Lilienthal*, pp. 12-45.

10. Ibid., p. 51.

11. Grinstein, "Minute Books," p. 327. The minutes record a decision not to invite Bnai Jeshurun. This entry indicates that the possibility was considered and may have been explored with that congregation.

12. Minutes of Congregation Emanu-El of New York (January 22, 1847).

13. Minutes of Congregation Anshe Chesed of New York (February 13, 1848).

14. Grinstein, "Minute Books," pp. 324-352.

15. *The Occident and American Jewish Advocate*, III (1846), 574-576. The report in the *Occident* was written by James Gutheim, who was a teacher in New York, who later became minister of congregations in Cincinnati and New Orleans, and who ended his career at Emanu-El in New York.

16. He was granted permission to proceed at the meeting of January 4, 1846. See Grinstein, "Minute Books," p. 331.

17. The minutes make an interesting distinction between "sh'elot" (the Hebrew word for questions), which refers to ritual questions to be answered according to the Shulchan Aruch (Jewish Code of Law), and "Fragen" (the German word for questions), which apparently refers to problems of belief and theology. Lilienthal was expected to provide answers for both kinds of questions.

18. The ceremony of halitza whereby the brother of a childless deceased man is released from the obligation of levirate marriage is described in Deuteronomy XXV: 5-10. For further information on

this ceremony see Halizah, *Jewish Encyclopedia*, VI, 170-174. The Minutes of the Congregation Union contain the form for the halitza document proposed by Lilienthal: Grinstein, "Minute Books," p. 351. The Minutes of Congregation Anshe Chesed (September 18, 1846) resolve to have a halitza shoe made providing that "the parnassim of the two other Congregations are willing to pay part of the expense."

19. Philipson, p. 55. He gives the date of the meeting of the Beth Din as October 1846. However, the report in *Occident*, V, 109-111, states that the meeting was held on the 2nd of Iyar, 5607 (April 18, 1847).

20. Grinstein, *Rise of the Jewish Community*, p. 397.

21. Grinstein, "Minute Books," p. 329.

22. One of the detailed provisions recorded is that the Cantor "prays a short psalm" (Der *Chasan* betet einen kurzen Psalm).

23. Minutes of Congregation Anshe Chesed of New York (December 14, 1847).

24. David Philipson and Louis Grossman, eds., *Selected Writings of Isaac M. Wise with a Biography* (Cincinnati: Robert Clarke Co., 1900), p. 2. Wise is usually described as "Bohemian" and the location of his birthplace in the Austrian Empire did affect his education and subsequent experience. However, the proximity of the town to Bavaria and South Germany highlights the fact that the area was part of the same Central European Jewish community from which most of the immigrants came.

25. Wise's *Reminiscences* were originally published in his German language periodical, *Die Deborah*, in 1875, almost thirty years after his arrival in America. The work is not only colored by his later attitudes, but is full of inaccuracies. For example, Wise reports a lengthy battle concerning his right to deliver the opening prayer at a meeting of the New York State legislature, for which there is no corroborating evidence. See Bertram W. Korn, "The First Jewish Prayer in Congress," *Eventful Years and Experiences* (Cincinnati: American Jewish Archives, 1954), p. 117. Wise claims to have had dinner in Washington with Daniel Webster and "Senator" Judah P. Benjamin in 1850. Benjamin did not take office as Senator from Louisiana until 1854 and "as far as we know, Benjamin was nowhere near Washington during the time of Wise's visit." Furthermore, in an article written in 1861 defending the loyalty of the Jews to the

Union, Wise implied that he had never met Benjamin. See Bertram W. Korn, "Judah P. Benjamin as a Jew," *Eventful Years*, pp. 83-86. Wise's account of his visit to Charleston and his confrontation there with Morris Raphall was described by Barnett Elzas as "very much distorted." See Elzas, *The Jews of South Carolina from the Earliest Times to the Present Day* (Philadelphia, 1905), pp. 217-218. Numerous other examples of inaccuracies could be cited. It is clear that Wise's account of events tends to exaggerate his own role and gives full rein to his later prejudices in describing events and individuals. His version, especially of his early years, must be treated with healthy skepticism. Unfortunately, a series of uncritical biographies have accepted Wise's statements (even where they contradict each other) without question, so that his own account has become generally accepted. For a valiant (but unsuccessful) attempt to explain some of the inconsistencies, see the worshipful biography by James G. Heller, *Isaac M. Wise—His Life, Work and Thought* (New York: Union of American Hebrew Congregations, 1965), pp. 701-707.

Wise himself was more earthy than those who would canonize him. He viewed with humor the tendency of immigrants to exaggerate their prior training. Among those he described was one who "claimed to be an optician, sold spectacles, called himself professor, pretended to be able to grind glasses even for half-blind horses . . . until one fine morning he called to mind that he had been a lawyer in Europe. [After 1848] well nigh every immigrant could lay claim to some title, belonged to some prominent family and had been a staff officer, a high official, of noble birth, or at least a physician or professor." Wise, pp. 102-105. If pressed about some of his own claims, Wise might have acknowledged (and justified) a bit of hyperbole.

26. Heller, p. 702.

27. *The Occident*, XI (1854), 158-163.

28. Heller, p. 70.

29. Wise's account of his difficulties in Bohemia cannot be confirmed. He alleges that he had some differences with the rabbinic authorities because of a divorce he granted, and with civil authorities because of his refusal to give a flattering sermon about the emperor on his birthday. See Philipson and Grossman, pp. 11-14.

30. Wise, p. 19.

31. Heller, p. 702.

32. *American Israelite*, XLI (February 14, 1895), cited in Heller, p. 128. Heller, who goes to great lengths to confirm most of Wise's claims, concedes that "this is an exaggeration."

33. Wise, pp. 42-43.

34. Ibid., p. 73. Wise reported that as a result of his efforts "even many peddlers promised to rest on the Sabbath."

35. Letter of Dr. Isaac M. Wise to Rev. Mr. Leeser, Albany (December 1, 1849), MS, New York Public Library, Division of Manuscripts. Cited by Whiteman, "Isaac Leeser," p. 223.

36. Wise, pp. 88-96. According to Wise the trouble began at Passover when the peddlers, who had not been consulted, were home.

37. Ibid., p. 103.

38. Ibid., pp. 63-67. Wise undoubtedly exaggerates his heroism and his success, but it is unlikely that the incident is entirely fictitious.

39. Ibid., pp. 134-139. For a comment on the accuracy of these claims, see above, n. 25.

40. Korn, "The First Jewish Prayer in Congress," *Eventful Years*, p. 116. Wise claimed to be the first Jewish clergyman to deliver such a prayer anywhere in America. He was actually the second.

41. *The Occident*, V, (1848), 110.

42. Philipson and Grossman, p. 53. The congregations that responded were Shaarey Tefillah of New York, Mikveh Israel of Philadelphia, Beth El of Albany, Bnai Jeshurun of Cincinnati, Nefutzoth Jehudah and Shaare Chesed of New Orleans, Beth Shalom of Richmond, Shaare Shomayim of Mobile, and Adath Israel of Louisville.

43. Wise was rebuffed by Emanu-El in New York. Several days after he was invited by Merzbacher to preach a sermon there, the Board "adopted a resolution to the effect that in future no one should be permitted to preach in the temple without their consent." Wise, pp. 101-102. The short-lived Society of Friends of Light consisted of an intellectual group of German Jews who showed no interest in Wise, and he labeled them "an influential element, rich in words but poor in energy," Wise, p. 90.

44. Ibid., p. 155. Wise neglects to mention one circumstance that may have contributed to the conflict. Shortly before the incident occurred, he had applied for the position of minister of Beth Elohim in Charleston. He had gone there, been elected, and then returned

to Albany and changed his mind. The Charleston Congregation passed "strong resolutions of condemnation . . . against Dr. Wise and transmitted . . . them to Albany." See Elzas, pp. 217-218. Wise's account of his visit to Charleston (pp. 141-145) totally misrepresents the circumstances of his visit. It is quite likely that his solicitation of another position created animosity against him in the Albany Congregation.

45. Whiteman, p. 223.

46. Morais, *Jews of Philadelphia*, p. 59.

47. Fein, p. 56.

48. Stern, *Rise and Progress of Reform Judaism*, p. 33.

49. Wise, pp. 45, 51.

50. Goldstein, *Century of Judaism in New York*, p. 112.

51. Grinstein, *Rise of the Jewish Community*, p. 56.

52. Grinstein, "Minute Books," p. 327.

53. Goldstein, *Century of Judaism in New York*, pp. 110-111.

54. Ibid., p. 112.

55. Ibid., p. 113, reports that only the chazan of Shearith Israel and a Reverend Schlesinger, who was a visitor in New York, participated in Raphall's installation. Wise, p. 128, 131, reports that both Lilienthal and Leeser were snubbed by Raphall.

56. Raphall, who was allegedly orthodox, gave permission for the transferral of bodies from the cemetery of Bnai Jeshurun and helped to maintain secrecy about the plan. When the project was discovered, it created a furor in the German-Jewish community. See Grinstein, *Rise of the Jewish Community*, p. 327.

57. In 1850 Raphall and Wise were in Charleston at the same time. Raphall "met with a most enthusiastic reception. The *Courier* spoke of him as a scholar, critic, orator, and artist. All the papers gave extended notices of his lectures and he was praised editorially. Beyond the announcement of his arrival, Wise's visit to Charleston went unnoticed in the local press. See Elzas, pp. 217-218. As indicated above (nn. 25, 44) Wise's account of his Charleston experience is grossly distorted.

58. Korn, "The First Jewish Prayer in Congress," *Eventful Years*, pp. 98-118. Grinstein, *Rise of the Jewish Community*, p. 182.

59. Bertram W. Korn, "Jewish 'Forty Eighters' in America," *American Jewish Archives*, II (1949), 3-20.

9. PROGRESS AND PROSPECTS

1. Cited in Julius Bien, "A History of the International Order of Bne Br'ith," *Menorah*, III (1887), chap. XVII, 250.

2. Bien, *Menorah*, III (1887), chap. XVIII, 325.

3. Oscar Handlin, *The Americans* (Boston, 1963), p. 229.

4. Jones, *American Immigration*, p. 93. See also Hansen, *Atlantic Migration*, p. 280.

5. Walker, *Germany and the Emigration*, pp. 156-157.

6. Matthew A. Berk, in a *History of the Jews up to the Present Time* (3rd edition, Boston, 1844), p. 289, writes: "From the best information it would appear that there are about 50,000 Jews in the United States." Israel Joseph Benjamin, *Three Years in America 1859–1862*, trans. Charles Reznikoff (2 vols., Philadelphia: Jewish Publication Society of America, 1856), I, 80, reports a population of 200,000 in 1860.

7. Bertram W. Korn, "The Know Nothing Movement and the Jews," in *Eventful Years and Experiences*, ed. Korn (Cincinnati: American Jewish Archives, 1954), p. 75.

8. Ibid., p. 62.

9. *The Occident*, XII (1855), 558.

10. Goldstein, *Century of Judaism*, p. 120.

11. Korn, "Know Nothing Movement," p. 22.

12. Minutes of Congregation Bnai Jeshurun of Cincinnati (April 14, 1860).

13. Walker, p. 153. See also Hansen, p. 274.

14. Walker, pp. 161, 173-174.

15. Korn, "Jewish 'Forty Eighters' in America," pp. 1-26.

16. Max J. Kohler, "The German Jewish Migration to America," *Publications of the American Jewish Historical Society*, IX (1901), 102.

17. Trachtenberg, *Consider the Years*, p. 120.

18. See excerpts from *Allgemeine Zeitung des Judentums* and other German Jewish periodicals cited in Rudolph Glanz, "Source Materials on the History of Jewish Immigration to the United States, 1800–1880," *YIVO Annual of Jewish Social Science*, VI (1951), 96-108.

19. The Jewish population of Berlin increased from 6,456 in 1840

to 36,015 in 1871. Other cities showed comparable growth. See Hirshler, *Jews from Germany in the United States*, p. 125.

20. Bien, chap. XXV, in *Menorah*, IV (1888), 514.

21. Ibid., p. 515. No details concerning Mr. American are known; however, he is mentioned in the Lyons-de Sola list of Jewish institutions (1854) as superintendent of the "Hebrew and English School attached to Congregation Rodeph Shalom" of Philadelphia.

22. The United States census of religious bodies lists 37 congregations in 1850, 77 in 1860, and 189 in 1870. The figures, particularly for 1850, are unreliable, because the informal nature of many Jewish congregations. The lack of synagogue property at that time, and the absence of professional clergy meant that many congregations were overlooked. Nevertheless, as comparisons they testify to the continuous growth in the number of institutions and their visibility in the general community. See Engelman, "Jewish Statistics in the United States Census of Religious Bodies," pp. 9-17.

23. (January 28, 5604 [1844]).

24. Ibid. (December 30, 1849, and following).

25. Goldstein, p. 114.

26. Stern, *Rise and Progress of Reform Judaism*, pp. 34-36.

27. *The History of the Congregation Rodeph Sholom of New York* (New York, 1892), p. 12.

28. Heller, *As Yesterday When It Is Past*, p. 39.

29. Minutes of United Hebrew Congregation of St. Louis (July 17, 1859).

30. Minutes of Congregation Achdut Ve-Sholom, Fort Wayne, Indiana (September 26, 27, 1859).

31. *Israelite*, I (1854–1855), 28.

32. In general congregations whose founders included acculturated immigrants or immigrants from England wrote their minutes in English. This was true of Bnai Jeshurun, Anshe Chesed, and Shaarey Tefillah of New York, and Bnai Israel of Cincinnati. In the West, even congregations like Bnai Jeshurun of Cincinnati and United Hebrew Congregation of St. Louis, which consisted almost entirely of recent immigrants, frequently wrote their minutes in English. Rodeph Sholom of Philadelphia, founded in 1802, initially wrote in Yiddish. After 1820 minutes were written in English until about 1840, after which German was used. In the 1850's the language alternated between German and English, apparently depending on the proclivity of the secretary.

33. W. Gunther Plaut, *The Jews in Minnesota* (New York: American Jewish Historical Society, 1959), p. 36.

34. Stern, p. 41.

35. Temple Emanuel Minute Books (April 4, 1856). The English lecturer hired was a well-known humorist of Sephardic Jewish origin named Raphael De-Cordova.

36. Stern, p. 65. Gottheil was a native of Posen, but he served as a rabbi in Manchester, England, for thirteen years prior to coming to America. He was well known as an English orator.

37. Bernhard N. Cohen, "Early German Preaching in America," *Historia Judaica*, XV (1953), 105.

38. Wise, p. 293.

39. Bien, *Menorah*, III (1887) chap. XV, 103-104.

40. Grinstein, *Rise of the Jewish Community*, p. 253.

41. Adler and Connolly, *From Araratto Suburbia*, p. 43.

42. Grinstein, *Rise of the Jewish Community*, p. 253.

43. Goldstein, pp. 116-118.

44. Adler and Connolly, p. 43.

45. Minutes of Congregation Rodeph Sholom of Philadelphia (October 28, 1848; June 12, 1850; October 4, 1854).

46. Bien, *Menorah*, III (1887), chap. XV, 104.

10. TRANSFORMATIONS IN PROCESS

1. Weinryb, "German Jewish Immigrants to America," pp. 123-124.

2. Minutes of United Hebrew Congregation of St. Louis (April 15, 1855; July 17, 1859).

3. Minutes of Congregation Rodeph Sholom of Philadelphia (April 4, 1854). A strictly observant Jew would not shave his beard, in keeping with the commandment in Leviticus 21:5: "They shall not shave off the edges of their beard." Jewish practice also required ritual washing of hands before meals and keeping the head covered, especially during meals, when prayers were recited. The lulob (a palm branch bound together with sprigs of willow and myrtle) is used in celebration of the harvest festival of Tabernacles (Leviticus 23:40). Normally the lulob is prepared before the beginning of the holiday. "Tying up" a lulob on the "first day of the Feast of Tabernacles" would be a transgression. For a goose (or any other fowl)

to be fit to eat, it would have to be slaughtered according to prescribed ritual and examined by the shochet for signs of disease.
Illowy's goose had apparently not been properly inspected before it
was cooked.

4. Minutes of Congregation Anshe Chesed of New York (April
14, 28; May 12, 19; July 14, 1850).

5. Minutes of Congregation Bnai Jeshurun of Cincinnati (June
21, October 9, 1848; April 14, August 14, 1850; October 1, 1851;
August 25, 1852. See also Heller, pp. 69-72; Krauskopf, "Half Century of Judaism in the United States," p. 74.

6. Heller, p. 70.

7. Bernard Felsenthal, *The Beginnings of Chicago Sinai Congregation* (Chicago, 1898), p. 36.

8. *Israelite*, VI (1860), 165. Szold was a graduate of the Rabbinical
Seminary in Breslau, which was founded by Zacharia Frankel in
1854. The seminary was the fountainhead of the so-called historical
school of Jewish religious thought. The Conservative movement
that emerged in America fifty years later considered itself the American expression of this outlook.

9. Minutes of Congregation Bnai Jeshurun of Cincinnati (October
27, November 6, 1853).

10. Wise, p. 242.

11. Minutes of Congregation Bnai Jeshurun of Cincinnati (August
14, 1854).

12. Wise, pp. 281, 344.

13. Benjamin, *Three Years in America*, I, 310.

14. Wise, pp. 269, 270, 331. He was particularly offended that the
German Jewish press virtually ignored him and his paper.

15. *Israelite*, I (1854-1855), 13, 20-22. The quotations that follow
are also from this issue of the *Israelite*.

16. Wise was probably mistaken in this statement. The Jewish
population of Cincinnati had grown rapidly, but it is doubtful that
Cincinnati had surpassed Philadelphia as the second largest Jewish
community. Even so, it was the third largest and by far the largest
inland community.

17. Wise, p. 325.

18. *Israelite*, II (1855-1856), 52, 171; III (1856-1857), 331.

19. Wise, pp. 313-314.

20. Philipson, *Reform Movement in Judaism*, pp. 280-282.

21. Einhorn's inaugural sermon delivered September 29, 1855. Reprinted in Rubenstein, *History of Har Sinai Congregation,* pages unnumbered.

22. Ibid.

23. *Sinai,* I (1856), 27-29. The Board of Emanu-El of New York also repudiated the decisions of the Cleveland Conference even though its rabbi, Leo Merzbacher, was an active participant. However, Emanu-El's statement was less polemical, stating merely: "Resolved: that the Talmud in reference to the adopted platform of the Cleveland Conference is not the legal and obligatory commentary of the Bible." Temple Emanuel Minute Books (December 2, 1855).

24. *Israelite,* II (1855), 157.

25. *Sinai,* VI (1861), 175.

26. *Israelite,* II (1856), 1.

27. *Sinai,* II (1857), 442-443.

28. Correspondence of Einhorn and Reuben Oppenheimer, August 12, 1861, cited in Fein, *Making of an American Jewish Community,* p. 98. Einhorn's "bacon reformers" implies that the members of his congregation were interested in convenience (abrogating dietary restrictions) but not in principles.

29. Minutes of Congregation Knesseth Israel of Philadelphia (September 13, 1861).

30. *Olat Tamid* (New York: M. Thalmessinger and Co., 1858).

31. *Liturgy and Ritual Reform—The Order of Prayer for Divine Service* (New York, 1855).

32. Grinstein, *The Rise of the Jewish Community of New York, 1654–1860,* p. 365.

33. Levy, *Reform Judaism in America,* p. 49.

34. Sol M. Strook, "Switzerland and the American Jew," *Publications of the American Jewish Historical Society,* XI (1903), 8.

35. *Israelite,* IV (1858), 33.

36. Bertram W. Korn, *The American Reaction to the Mortara Case: 1858–59* (Cincinnati: American Jewish Archives, 1957), pp. 3–11.

37. *Israelite,* IV (1858), 157.

38. *Proceedings of the Board of Delegates of American Israelites, November 1859* (New York: Jewish Messenger Printing Office, 1859), p. 6.

39. *Constitution of the Board of Delegates of American Israelites* (New York, 1859).

40. Allan Tarshish, "The Board of Delegates of American Israelites," *Publications of the American Jewish Historical Society*, XLIX (1959), 32.

11. THE SYNTHESIS

1. Grinstein, "Reforms at Temple Emanu-El of New York," p. 173.
2. Benjamin, *Three Years in America*, I, 82.
3. In 1868 Mikveh Israel of Savannah adopted a resolution stating that "the second days of all Festivals and Holy Days being non-essential to true Biblical Judaism as expounded by Moses be dispensed with." In addition, the introduction of an organ and mixed choir was approved, together with a number of omissions in the recitation of the prayers and reading from the Prophets. On May 10, 1870, calling of congregants for recitation of Torah blessings was eliminated except for the Bar Mitzvah. Reform thereafter was continuous, culminating in 1894 when the wearing of hats was made optional. Minutes of Congregation Mikveh Israel of Savannah (February 11, 1868; May 10, 1870; May 27, 1894).
4. Levy, *Reform Judaism in America*, p. 49.
5. Hansen, *Atlantic Migration*, p. 306.
6. Korn, *American Jewry and the Civil War*, pp. 45-120.
7. Between 1860 and 1890, the bulk of the immigrants to the United States were from the British Isles, Germany, and Scandinavia. Within Germany the place of origin of most immigrants changed from Bavaria and Wurttemberg to Prussia and Saxony, which had smaller Jewish populations. Those on the move were primarily wheat growers and agricultural laborers—who were displaced by the importation of wheat from Eastern Europe and overseas. The number of immigrants to the United States from Russia grew from 5,000 in 1880, to 81,000 in 1892, to 258,000 in 1907. Jones, *American Immigration*, pp. 193-202.
8. Reissner, "The German-American Jews 1800–1850," pp. 109-111.
9. Hirshler, ed., *Jews from Germany in the United States*, pp. 59-64.

10. Stow Persons, *Free Religion, An American Faith* (New Haven, 1947), p. 1.

11. Ibid., p. 19.

12. Olmstead, *History of Religion in the United States*, p. 447.

13. Engelman, "Jewish Statistics in the United States Census of Religious Bodies," pp. 15, 30.

14. Minutes of Congregation Emanu-El (August 26, 1868). See also Stern, *Rise and Progress of Reform Judaism*, p. 63.

15. Goldstein, *Century of Judaism*, pp. 145-146.

16. Minutes of Congregation Knesseth Israel of Philadelphia (December 20, 1863).

17. Minutes of Congregation Rodeph Sholom of Philadelphia (July 7, 1867). See also Davis, *History of Rodeph Sholom Congregation*, pp. 87-88.

18. Fiftieth Anniversary booklet of Congregation Bnai Jeshurun of Cincinnati, quoted in Heller, *As Yesterday When It Is Past*, p. 101.

19. Heller, pp. 102, 105, 110.

20. Ibid., pp. 106, 108.

21. Goldstein, pp. 154-155.

22. White shrouds were worn on these solemn days as a mark of purity, simplicity, and equality before God. The shrouds also served as a reminder of man's mortality and his destiny after death, to stand in judgment before the Throne of Glory.

23. Goldstein, p. 162. Bnai Jeshurun is one of the few congregations of the pre-1860 period which did not remain a reform congregation. In the last decade of the nineteenth century, it was well on its way toward reform. One of its rabbis during this period was Stephen Wise, who later became a leading reform rabbi. At the close of the century the congregation was no longer active. It survived only because of the influx of East European immigrants who became the new constituency. When this group assumed control, the congregation reverted to a more traditional pattern and became a leading conservative synagogue.

24. Minutes, (May 22, 29, 1859; April 3, May 1, 1864).

25. In every instance, the removal of hats was the last step following such changes as the introduction of the organ, mixed seating, revision of the liturgy, and elimination of the second day of holidays. In Congregation Beth El of San Antonio, Texas, hats were

removed in 1874 (Minutes, July 5, 1874). In Congregation Bnai El of St. Louis the decision was taken in 1877 (Minutes, September 23, 1877). In Beth Zion of Buffalo removal of hats was made compulsory in 1882 (Minutes, September 19, 1882). The precise time when this step was taken varied in accordance with special circumstances of each congregation. In every case the transition to reform outlook in which the congregation determined what to preserve and what to reject had been accomplished previously. The removal of hats usually marked the repudiation of the last enclaves of resistance to radical change.

26. Minutes of Congregation Bnai Jeshurun of Cincinnati (September 23, 1871; May 20, 1872; August 19, 1874; November 3, 1875).

27. Minutes (October 22, 1865).

28. It was customary among pious Jews not to wear leather shoes on Yom Kippur.

29. Minutes of Hebrew Association, Akron, Ohio (January 20, 27; April 7; October 6, 1867).

30. Cross, *The Church and the City* (Indianapolis, 1967), p. xv.

31. Ahlstrom, *Religious History of the American People*, p. 738.

32. Fein, *Making of an American Jewish Community*, p. 117.

33. Henry Berkowitz, "Notes on the History of the Earliest German Jewish Congregation in America," *Publications of the American Jewish Historical Society*, IX (1901), 127.

35. Benjamin Szold, *Abodath Israel* (Baltimore, 1873), p. 589.

36. *Jewish Messenger*, XXXVIII (1875), November 12, 19, 26; December 3, 10, quoted in Davis, *Emergence of Conservative Judaism*, p. 164.

37. Korn, "The First American Jewish Theological Seminary: Maimonides College, 1867–1873," in *Eventful Years and Experiences*, ed. Korn (Cincinnati: American Jewish Archives, 1954), pp. 163-195.

38. Philipson, *Reform Movement in Judaism*, p. 354.

39. Ibid., p. 378.

40. Levy, *Reform Judaism in America*, p. 61.

41. *American Israelite*, XXVI (1879), 4.

42. Heller, p. 465.

43. *Proceedings of the Pittsburgh Rabbinical Conference* (Cincinnati, 1927).

Bibliography

I. DOCUMENTS RELATED TO COMMUNAL AFFAIRS

Congregational Minutes

Achdut Ve-Sholom, Fort Wayne, 1848–1885.
Adath Israel, Louisville, 1842–1866.
Anshe Chesed, New York City, 1835–1858.
Beth El, San Antonio, 1874–1880.
Beth El-Beth Emeth, Albany, 1843–1882.
Beth Zion, Buffalo, 1866–1885.
Bnai Jeshurun, Cincinnati, 1841–1880.
Bnai Jeshurun, Newark, 1848–1871.
Emanu-El, New York City, 1845–1887.
Har Sinai, Baltimore, 1876–1879.
Hebrew Association, Akron, 1865–1875.
Kahl Montgomery, Montgomery, 1858–1880.
Mikveh Israel, Savannah, 1790–1880.
Oheb Shalom, Baltimore, 1870–1880.
Ohef Sholom, Norfolk, 1867–1880.
Rodeph Shalom, Philadelphia, 1802–1893.
She'erith Israel, San Francisco, 1851–1856 and 1867–1890.
United Hebrew, St. Louis, 1841–1859.

Miscellaneous

Address of the Jewish Publication Committee to the Israelites of America.
    Philadelphia, 1845.
Association Tseire Ha-Tson, *Address and Articles of the Association.*
    New York, 1837.

Constitution of the Board of Delegates of American Israelites. New York, 1859.

Constitution of Congregation Covenant of Peace. Easton, Pennsylvania, 1839.

Constitution and By-Laws of the Hebra Hinuch Nearim. New York: printed by S. H. Jackson, 1825.

Constitution and By-Laws of United Hebrew Congregation of St. Louis. 1841.

Harby, Isaac. *Discourse before the Reformed Society of Israelites*. Charleston, 1825. Published in *North American Review*, XXIII (1826).

Leeser, Isaac. *Memorial of the Sunday School for Religious Instruction of Israelites of Philadelphia*. Philadelphia, 1840.

———. *To the Jewish Inhabitants of Philadelphia*, circular. 1835.

Letter of Rebecca Gratz to Maria Gist Gratz, April 18, 1830. Library, American Jewish Historical Society.

Proceedings of the Board of Delegates of American Israelites, November 1859. New York: Jewish Messenger Printing Office, 1859.

Statistics of the Jews in the United States. Philadelphia: Union of American Hebrew Congregations, 1880.

II.   PRAYER BOOKS

Einhorn, David. *Olat Tamid*. New York, Thalmessinger and Co., 1858.

Liturgy and Ritual Reform—The Order of Prayer for Divine Service (Merzbacher Prayer Book). New York, 1855.

Pinto, Isaac. *Prayers for Shabboth, Rosh Hashanah, and Kippur*. New York, 1766.

Szold, Benjamin. *Abodath Israel*. Baltimore, 1873.

Wise, Isaac Mayer. *Minhag America*. Cincinnati, 1870.

III.   PERIODICALS

The Asmonean. New York, 1849–1857.

Die Deborah. Cincinnati, 1855–1875.

Israelite (after 1874: *American Israelite*). Cincinnati, 1854–(1880).

The Jew (monthly, March 1823–1825). Ed. Solomon H. Jackson, New York.

Jewish Messenger. New York, 1857–(1880).

The Occident and American Jewish Advocate. Philadelphia, 1843–1868.

Sinai. Baltimore and Philadelphia, 1856–1862.

IV. NINETEENTH CENTURY BOOKS

Adams, Hannah. *A Dictionary of All Religions and Religious Denominations.* Boston, 1817.

Adams, John Quincy. *The Diary of John Quincy Adams, 1794–1845.* New York, Longmans, Green and Co., 1929.

Benjamin, Israel Joseph. *Three Years in America, 1859–1862.* Translated by Charles Reznikoff. 2 vols., Philadelphia: Jewish Publication Society of America, 1956.

Berk, Matthew A. *History of the Jews up to the Present Time.* 3rd ed., Boston, 1844.

Johlson, Joseph. *Alumei Yosef, Unterrich in der Mosaischen Religion.* Frankfurt, 1819.

Leeser, Isaac. *Discourses, Argumentative and Devotional on the Subject of the Jewish Religion.* Philadelphia, 5597 (1836).

———. *The Law of God.* Philadelphia, 5605 (1845).

Lyons, Jacques I., and Abraham de Sola. *A Jewish Calendar for Fifty Years.* Montreal, 1854.

Rupp, I. Daniel. *An Original History of the Religious Denominations at Present Existing in the United States.* Philadelphia, J. Y. Humphreys, 1844.

Schindler, Solomon. *Israelites in Boston.* Boston: Press of Berwick and Smith, 1889.

Wise, Isaac M. *Reminiscences.* Ed. and trans. David Philipson. Cincinnati: Leo M. Wise and Co., 1901.

V. DOCUMENTARY COLLECTIONS

Blau, Joseph L., and Salo W. Baron. *The Jews of the United States, 1790–1840: A Documentary History.* 3 vols., New York: Columbia University Press, 1963.

Glanz, Rudolph. "Source Materials on the History of Jewish Immigration to the United States, 1800–1880," *YIVO Annual of Social Science,* VI (1951).

Letters of the Franks Family, 1733–1748. Ed. Leo Hershkowitz and Isidore S. Meyer. Waltham, Massachusetts: American Jewish Historical Society, 1968.

Marcus, Jacob R. *Memoirs of American Jews, 1775–1865.* 3 vols., Philadelphia: Jewish Publication Society of America, 1955.

Schappes, Morris U. *A Documentary History of the Jews in the United States, 1654–1875.* 3rd ed., New York: Schocken Books, 1971.

Selected Writings of Isaac M. Wise with a Biography. Ed. David Philipson and Louis Grossmann. Cincinnati: Robert Clarke Co., 1900.

VI. CONGREGATIONAL HISTORIES

Cohen, Simon. *Shaaray Tefila. A History of Its Hundred Years, 1845–1945.* New York: Greenberg, 1945.

Cohn, Louis F. *The History of Oheb Shalom (1853–1953).* Baltimore: Oheb Shalom Congregation, 1953.

Davis, Edward. *The History of Rodeph Shalom Congregation, Philadelphia, 1802–1926.* Philadelphia: Press of Edward Stern and Co., 1926.

De Sola Pool, David and Tamar. *An Old Faith in the New World.* New York: Columbia University Press, 1955.

Felsenthal, Bernard. *The Beginnings of Chicago Sinai Congregation.* Chicago, 1898.

Felsenthal, Bernard, and Herman Eliassof. *History of Kehillath Anshe Maarabh.* Chicago, 1897.

Goldstein, Israel. *A Century of Judaism in New York.* New York: Congregation B'nai Jeshurun, 1930.

Guttmacher, Adolph. *A History of the Baltimore Hebrew Congregation.* Baltimore: Lord Baltimore Press, 1905.

Heller, James G. *As Yesterday When It Is Past.* Cincinnati: privately published, 1942.

History of Congregation Adath Israel. Louisville, Kentucky: privately printed, 1906.

History of the Congregation Rodeph Sholom of New York. New York: privately printed, 1892.

Growth and Achievement: Temple Israel, 1854–1954. Ed. Arthur Mann. Cambridge: Houghton Mifflin, 1954.

Katz, Irving I. *The Beth El Story.* Detroit: Wayne State University Press, 1955.

Philipson, David. *The Oldest Jewish Congregation in the West.* Cincinnati: Press of C. J. Krebhail and Co., 1894.

Rubenstein, C. A. *History of Har Sinai Congregation of the city of Baltimore.* Baltimore: Press of Kohn and Pollack, 1918.

Stern, Myer. *The Rise and Progress of Reform Judaism, Embracing a History Made from the Official Records of Temple Emanu-El of New York.* New York: Myer Stern, 1895.

Temple Mishkan Tefila: A History, 1858–1958. Newton, Massachusetts: Temple Mishkan Tefila, 1958.

VII.   COMMUNAL HISTORIES

Adler, Selig, and Thomas E. Connolly. *From Ararat to Suburbia: The
    History of the Jewish Community of Buffalo.* Philadelphia:
    Jewish Publication Society of America, 1960.
Breck, Allen D. *A Centennial History of the Jews of Colorado.* Denver,
    Colorado: Hirshfield Press, 1960.
De Sola Pool, David. *Portraits Etched in Stone.* New York: Columbia
    University Press, 1952.
Elzas, Barnett A. *The Jews of South Carolina from the Earliest Times to
    the Present Day.* Philadelphia, 1905.
Ezekiel, Herbert T., and Gaston Lichtenstein. *The History of the Jews
    of Richmond.* Richmond, Virginia: Herbert T. Ezekiel, 1917.
Fein, Isaac M. *The Making of an American Jewish Community.*
    Philadelphia: Jewish Publication Society of America, 1971.
Gartner, Lloyd P., and Louis J. Swichkow. *The History of the Jews of
    Milwaukee.* Philadelphia: Jewish Publication Society of America,
    1963.
Grinstein, Hyman B. *The Rise of the Jewish Community of New York,
    1654–1860.* Philadelphia: Jewish Publication Society of America,
    1945.
Gutstein, Morris A. *A Priceless Heritage: The Epic Growth of
    Nineteenth Century Chicago Jewry.* New York: Bloch
    Publishing Co., 1953.
———. *The Story of the Jews of Newport: 1658–1908.* New York:
    Bloch Publishing Co., 1936.
Korn, Bertram W. *The Early Jews of New Orleans.* Waltham,
    Massachusetts: American Jewish Historical Society, 1969.
Meites, Hyman L. *History of the Jews of Chicago.* Chicago: Jewish
    Historical Society of Illinois, 1924.
Morais, Henry S. *The Jews of Philadelphia.* Philadelphia: Levy Type
    Co., 1894.
Plaut, W. Gunther. *The Jews in Minnesota.* New York: American
    Jewish Historical Society, 1959.
Reznikoff, Charles, and Uriah Z. Engelman. *The Jews of Charleston.*
    Philadelphia: Jewish Publication Society of America, 1950.
Rosenberg, Stuart E. *The Jewish Community in Rochester, 1843–1925.*
    New York: Columbia University Press, 1954.
Sharfman, Dr. I. Harold. *Nothing Left to Commemorate.* Glendale,
    California: Arthur H. Clark Co., 1969.
Trachtenberg, Joshua. *Consider the Years: The Story of the Jewish
    Community of Easton (1752–1942).* Easton, Pennsylvania:
    Centennial Committee of Temple Brith Sholom, 1944.

Vorspan, Max, and Lloyd P. Gartner. *History of the Jews of Los Angeles*. San Marino, California: Huntington Library, 1970.
Wolf, Edwin, 2nd, and Maxwell Whiteman. *The History of the Jews of Philadelphia from Colonial Times to the Age of Jackson*. Philadelphia: Jewish Publication Society of America, 1957.

VIII.   ARTICLES

Abraham, Lewis. "Correspondence Between George Washington and Jewish Citizens. *Publications of the American Jewish Historical Society*, III (1895).
Allen, Lewis F. "Founding of the City of Ararat on Grand Island by Mordecai Manuel Noah." *Publications of the Buffalo Historical Society*, I (1866). Reprinted in *Publications of the American Jewish Historical Society*, VIII (1900).
Berkowitz, Henry. "Notes on the History of the Earliest German Jewish Congregation in America." *Publications of the American Jewish Historical Society*, IX (1901).
Bien, Julius. "A History of the Independent Order Bnē B'rīth." *Menorah*, I-IV (July 1886–June 1889).
Buchler, Joseph. "The Struggle for Unity—Attempts at Union in American Jewish Life: 1654–1868." *American Jewish Archives*, II (1949).
Cohn, Bernhard N. "Early German Preaching in America." *Historia Judaica*, XV (1953).
―――. "Leo Merzbacher." *American Jewish Archives*, VI (1954).
Engelman, Uriah Z. "Jewish Statistics in the United States Census of Religious Bodies, 1850–1936." *Jewish Social Studies*, IX (1947).
Englander, Henry. "Isaac Leeser." *Central Conference of American Rabbis Yearbook*, XXVIII (1918).
Ezekiel, Jacob, "Persecution of the Jews in 1840." *Publications of the American Jewish Historical Society*, VIII (1900).
Friedlander, Albert H. "Cultural Contributions of the German Jew in America." *Jews from Germany in the United States*. Ed. Eric Hirshler. New York: Farrar, Straus and Cudahy, 1955.
Glanz, Rudolph. "The Immigration of German Jews up to 1880." *YIVO Annual of Jewish Social Science*, II-III (1947–1948).
―――. "Jews in Relation to the Cultural Milieu of the Germans in America up to the Eighteen Eighties." *YIVO Bleter* (New York, 1947).

————. "Notes on Early Jewish Peddling in America." *Jewish Social Studies*, VII (1945).

Goodman, Abram Vossen. "A Jewish Peddler's Diary, 1842–1843." *American Jewish Archives*, III (1951).

Grayzel, Solomon. "The First American Jewish Publication Society." *Jewish Book Annual* (New York: 5795 [1944–1945]).

Grinstein, Hyman B. "The Minute Books of Lilienthal's Union of German Synagogues in New York." *Hebrew Union College Annual* (Cincinnati, 1943–1944).

————. "Reforms at Temple Emanuel of New York, 1860–1890." *Historia Judaica*, VI (1944).

Hirshler, Eric E. "Jews from Germany in the United States." In his edition of *Jews from Germany in the United States*. New York: Farrar, Straus and Cudahy, 1955.

Jacobs, Joseph. "The Damascus Affair of 1840 and the Jews of America." *Publications of the American Jewish Historical Society*, X (1902).

Kisch, Guido. "The Founders of 'Wissenschaft des Judentums' and America." *Essays in American Jewish History*. Cincinnati: American Jewish Archives, 1958.

————. "A Voyage to America Ninety Years Ago." *Publications of the American Jewish Historical Society*, XXXV (1939).

————. "Israel's Herold: The First Jewish Weekly in New York." *Historia Judaica*, II (1940).

Kohler, Max J. "The German Jewish Migration to America." *Publications of the American Jewish Historical Society*, IX (1901).

Korn, Bertram W. "The First American Jewish Theological Seminary: Maimonides College, 1867–1873." *Eventful Years and Experiences*, edited by B. W. Korn. Cincinnati: American Jewish Archives, 1954.

————. "The First Jewish Prayer in Congress," in *Eventful Years and Experiences*, edited by Bertram W. Korn. Cincinnati: American Jewish Archives, 1954.

————. "Isaac Leeser: Centennial Reflections." *American Jewish Archives*, XIX (1967).

————. "Jewish 'Forty Eighters' in America." In *Eventful Years and Experiences*, edited by Bertram W. Korn. Cincinnati: American Jewish Archives, 1954.

————. "Judah P. Benjamin as a Jew." In *Eventful Years and Experiences*, edited by Bertram W. Korn. Cincinnati: American Jewish Archives, 1954.

————. "The Know Nothing Movement and the Jews." In *Eventful*

Years and Experiences, edited by Bertram W. Korn. Cincinnati: American Jewish Archives, 1954.

———. "German-Jewish Intellectual Influences in American Jewish Life, 1824–1972." *The B. G. Rudolph Lectures in Judaic Studies* (April, 1972).

Krauskopf, Joseph. "Half Century of Judaism in the United States." *American Jews Annual*, IV (Cincinnati, 1888).

Mahler, Raphael. "The Economic Background of Jewish Emigration from Galicia." *YIVO Annual of Jewish Social Science*, VII (1952).

Neusner, Jacob. "The Role of English Jews in the Development of American Jewish Life, 1775–1850." *YIVO Annual of Jewish Social Science*, XII (1958–1959).

Philipson, David. "The Jewish Pioneers of the Ohio Valley." *Publications of the American Jewish Historical Society*, VIII (1900).

———. "The Progress of the Jewish Reform Movement in the United States." *Jewish Quarterly Review*, X (London, 1898).

Postal, Bernard. "Bnai Brith: A Century of Service." *American Jewish Yearbook*, XLV (5704 [1943–1944]).

Reissner, H. G. "The German-American Jews, 1800–1850." *Leo Baeck Institute Yearbook*, X (London: East and West Library, 1965).

Ringel, Moshe. "Further Information Concerning the Colony 'Sholem' on Yageville Hill, Ulster County, New York." *Publications of the American Jewish Historical Society*, XXXV (1939).

Rosenbloom, Joseph R. "Rebecca Gratz and the Jewish Sunday School Movement in Philadelphia." *Publications of the American Jewish Historical Society*, XLVIII (1958).

Rosenswaike, Ira. "The Jewish Population of the United States as Estimated from the Census of 1820." *American Jewish Historical Quarterly*, LIII (1963).

Schmidt, H. D. "The Terms of Emancipation, 1781–1812." *Leo Baeck Institute Yearbook*, I (1956).

Silberman, Lou H. "American Impact: Judaism in the United States in the Early Nineteenth Century." *The B. G. Rudolph Lectures in Judaic Studies* (1964).

Steinberg, Stephen. "Reform Judaism: The Origin and Evolution of a 'Church Movement.'" *Journal for the Scientific Study of Religion*, IV (1965).

Stern-Täubler, Selma. "The Motivation of German Jewish Emigration." *Essays in American Jewish History*. Cincinnati: American Jewish Archives, 1959.

Strook, Sol M. "Switzerland and the American Jew." *Publications of the American Jewish Historical Society*, XI (1903).

Tarshish, Allan. "The Board of Delegates of American Israelites."
Publications of the American Jewish Historical Society, XLIX
(1959).
———. "The Economic Life of the American Jew in the Middle
Nineteenth Century." *Essays in American Jewish History*.
Cincinnati: American Jewish Archives, 1958.
Voorsanger, Jacob. "A Few Chapters from the History of Jews on the
Pacific Coast from 1849 to 1860." *American Jews Annual*, V
(New York, 1889).
Weinryb, Bernard D. "The German Jewish Immigrants to America, A
Critical Evaluation." *Jews from Germany in the United States*.
Edited by Eric E. Hirshler. New York: Farrar, Straus and
Cudahy, 1955.
Whiteman, Maxwell. "Isaac Leeser and the Jews of Philadelphia."
Publications of the American Jewish Historical Society, XLVIII
(1959).

IX.   BOOKS

Ahlstrom, Sydney E. *A Religious History of the American People*.
New Haven: Yale University Press, 1972.
Baron, Salo W. *The Jewish Community, Its History and Structure to the
American Revolution*. Philadelphia: Jewish Publication Society
of America, 1948.
Birmingham, Stephen. *Our Crowd: The Great Jewish Families of New
York*. New York: Harper and Row, 1967.
Blau, Joseph L. *Modern Varieties of Judaism*. New York: Columbia
University Press, 1966.
Commager, Henry S., ed. *Immigration and American History*.
Minneapolis: University of Minnesota Press, 1961.
Cross, Robert, ed. *The Church and the City*. Indianapolis:
Bobbs-Merrill Co., 1967.
———. *The Emergence of Liberal Catholicism in America*. Cambridge,
Massachusetts: Harvard University Press, 1948.
Davis, Moshe. *The Emergence of Conservative Judaism*. Philadelphia:
Jewish Publication Society of America, 1965.
Eliassof, Herman. *German-American Jews*. Chicago: German American
Historical Society of Illinois, 1915.
Felsenthal, Emma. *Bernhard Felsenthal, Teacher in Israel*. New York:
Oxford University Press, 1924.
Friedman, Lee M. *Jewish Pioneers and Patriots*. Philadelphia: Jewish
Publication Society of America, 1955.

———. *Pilgrims in a New Land*. Philadelphia: Jewish Publication
Society of America, 1948.

Glanz, Rudolph. *Studies in Judaica Americana*. New York: KTAV,
1970.

Goldberg, Isaac. *Major Noah: American Jewish Pioneer*. Philadelphia:
Jewish Publication Society of America, 1944.

Gordon, Milton M. *Assimilation in American Life*. New York: Oxford
University Press, 1964.

Gottheil, Richard J. *The Life of Gustave Gottheil*. Williamsport,
Pennsylvania: Bayard Press, 1936.

Hacker, Louis M. *The Triumph of American Capitalism*. New York:
McGraw-Hill Paperback Edition, 1965.

Handlin, Oscar. *Adventure in Freedom—Three Hundred Years of
Jewish Life in America*. New York: McGraw-Hill Book Co., 1954.

———. *The Americans*. Boston: Little, Brown and Co., 1963.

Handy, Robert T. *The Social Gospel in America*. New York, Oxford
University Press, 1966.

Hansen, Marcus. *The Atlantic Migration, 1607–1860*. Cambridge,
Massachusetts: Harvard University Press, 1945.

Heller, James G. *Isaac M. Wise—His Life, Work and Thought*. New
York: Union of American Hebrew Congregations, 1965.

Higham, John. *Strangers in the Land*. New York: Atheneum, 1963.

Hirshler, Eric E., ed. *Jews from Germany in the United States*. New
York: Farrar, Straus and Cudahy, 1955.

Hopkins, Charles. *The Rise of Social Gospel in American Protestantism,
1865–1915*. New Haven: Yale University Press, 1940.

Jones, Maldwyn Allen. *American Immigration*. Chicago: University of
Chicago Press, 1960.

Katz, Jacob. *Tradition and Crisis, Jewish Society at the End of the
Middle Ages*. New York: Free Press, 1961.

Knox, Israel. *Rabbi in America: The Story of Isaac M. Wise*. Boston:
Little, Brown and Co., 1957.

Korn, Bertram W., ed. *Eventful Years and Experiences*. Cincinnati:
American Jewish Archives, 1954.

———. *American Jewry and the Civil War*. Philadelphia: Jewish
Publication Society of America, 1951.

———. *The American Reaction to the Mortara Case: 1858–59*.
Cincinnati: American Jewish Archives, 1957.

Levy, Beryl. *Reform Judaism in America*. New York: Bloch Publishing
Co., 1933.

Lowenthal, Marvin. *The Jews of Germany*. Philadelphia: Jewish
Publication Society of America, 1939.

Mahler, Raphael. *A History of Modern Jewry, 1780–1815.* New York: Schocken Books, 1971.

Makover, Abraham. *Mordecai M. Noah, His Life and Work.* New York: Bloch Publishing Co., 1917.

Marcus, Jacob R. *The Colonial American Jew, 1492–1776.* 3 volumes. Detroit: Wayne State University Press, 1970.

———. *Early American Jewry.* 2 volumes. Philadelphia: Jewish Publication Society of America, 1951.

Masserman, Paul, and Max Baker. *The Jews Come to America.* New York: Bloch Publishing Co., 1932.

May, B. Max. *Isaac Mayer Wise.* New York: G. P. Putnam's Sons, 1916.

Meyer, Michael A. *The Origins of the Modern Jew.* Detroit: Wayne State University Press, 1967.

O'Connor, Richard. *The German Americans.* Boston: Little, Brown and Co., 1968.

Olmstead, Clifton E. *History of Religion in the United States.* Englewood Cliffs, New Jersey: Prentice-Hall, 1960.

Persons, Stow. *Free Religion, An American Faith.* New Haven: Yale University Press, 1947.

Philipson, David. *The Reform Movement in Judaism.* Revised edition. New York: Macmillan Co., 1931.

———. *Max Lilienthal, American Rabbi: Life and Writings.* New York: Bloch Publishing Co., 1915.

Sachar, Howard M. *The Course of Modern Jewish History.* New York: Dell Publishing Co., 1958.

Simonhoff, Harry. *Jewish Participants in the Civil War.* New York, Arco, 1965.

Sklare, Marshall. *Conservative Judaism.* Glencoe: Free Press, 1955.

Smith, Timothy. *Revivalism and Social Reform.* New York: Harper Torchbooks, 1965.

Sontag, Frederick, and John K. Roth. *The American Religious Experience.* New York: Harper and Row, 1972.

Walker, Mack, *Germany and the Emigration, 1816–1885.* Cambridge, Massachusetts: Harvard University Press, 1964.

Warner, W. Lloyd, and Leo Srole. *The Social Systems of American Ethnic Groups.* New Haven: Yale University Press, 1965.

Wilansky, Dena. *Sinai to Cincinnati.* New York: Renaissance Book Co., 1937.

Wolf, Simon. *The American Jew as Patriot, Soldier and Citizen.* New York: Brentano, 1895.

Index

UNIVERSITY PRESS OF NEW ENGLAND publishes books under its own imprint and is the publisher for Brandeis University Press, Brown University Press, Clark University Press, University of Connecticut, Dartmouth College, Middlebury College Press, University of New Hampshire, University of Rhode Island, Tufts University, University of Vermont, and Wesleyan University Press.

Library of Congress Cataloguing-in-Publication Data

Jick, Leon A.
   The Americanization of the Synagogue, 1820–1870 / Leon A. Jick.
— 1st pbk. ed.
      p.   cm.
   Includes bibliographical references (p.   ) and index.
   ISBN 0–87451–573–4 (pbk.)
      1. Judaism—United States—History—19th century. 2. Jews—
United States—History—19th century. I. Title.
BM205.J52 1992
296'.0973'09034—dc20   91–50817
∞